AFTER

EMPIRE

AFTER

EMPIRE

SCOTT, NAIPAUL, RUSHDIE

MICHAEL GORRA

THE UNIVERSITY OF CHICAGO PRESS

CHICAGO & LONDON

Michael Gorra is associate professor of English at Smith College. He is also the author of *The English Novel at Mid-Century.*

The University of Chicago Press, Chicago 60637
The University of Chicago Press, Ltd., London
© 1997 by The University of Chicago
All rights reserved. Published 1997
Printed in the United States of America
06 05 04 03 02 01 00 99 98 97   1 2 3 4 5
ISBN: 0-226-30474-4 (cloth)
ISBN: 0-226-30475-2 (paper)

Gorra, Michael Edward.
    After Empire : Scott, Naipaul, Rushdie / Michael Gorra.
        p.   cm.
    Includes bibliographical references (p.) and index.
        ISBN 0-226-30474-4 (cloth : alk. paper). — ISBN 0-226-30475-2
    (paper : alk. paper)
        1. English fiction—20th century—History and criticism.
    2. Scott, Paul, 1920–   Raj quartet.   3. Naipaul, V. S. (Vidiadhar
    Surajprasad), 1932–   —Knowledge—India.   4. National
    characteristics, British, in literature.   5. Indic fiction
    (English)—History and criticism.   6. Anglo-Indian fiction—
    History and criticism.   7. Rushdie, Salman.   Midnight's children.
    8. Decolonization in literature.   9. Imperialism in literature.
    10. India—In literature.   I. Title.
    PR888.I6G67   1997
    823′.91409358—dc20   96-23769
                                                                    CIP

For my mother

CONTENTS

ACKNOWLEDGMENTS

My first thanks go to the National Endowment for the Humanities for awarding me a Fellowship for College Teachers that allowed me to begin work on this book during the academic year 1989–90. Smith College has been a beneficent employer, and I must thank the office of the Dean of the Faculty for awarding me both a Jean Picker Fellowship that gave me course release in 1991 to continue the project and a Faculty Exchange Fellowship that let me lecture on this material at the University of Hamburg in 1993. I have learned a great deal from my students at Smith, and especially from many conversations about V. S. Naipaul with Bridget Laffler.

Elizabeth von Klemperer was the first to suggest I might teach postcolonial literature, Eden Ross Lipson the first to suggest I should write about it. Kwame Anthony Appiah and Houston A. Baker Jr. offered some necessary encouragement at an early stage in my work, while Alan Thomas, my editor at the University of Chicago Press, has made it possible to bring that work to a happy conclusion. My students Lori Kauffman and Melanie Benson provided valuable help with the book's documentation. Jeff Hunter, Chris Benfey, Ronald Macdonald, and Thomas J. Ferraro read portions of the manuscript. Brigitte Buettner's careful reading gave this book whatever precision its argument may have; but that is the least of what I owe her.

A portion of my introduction appeared, in somewhat different form, in "Imperialism to Postcolonialism: Rudyard Kipling to Salman Rushdie," in *The Columbia History of the British Novel*, ed. John Richetti (New York: Columbia University Press, 1994). Portions of chapter 1 appeared in *Identities*, edited by Kwame Anthony Appiah and Henry Louis Gates Jr. (Chicago: University of Chicago Press, 1995), 434–38. Copyright 1995 The University of Chicago. All rights reserved. The appendix was first published in the *Threepenny Review*, Summer 1989. I am grateful for permission to reprint these pieces.

After Empire

Rudyard Kipling's first great story, "The Man Who Would Be King" (1888), describes how two soldiers, Peachy Carnehan and Daniel Dravot, try to carve out a private kingdom in a region of the Hindu Kush called Kafiristan. It's a real place, a part of Afghanistan that's now named Nuristan, but not much was known about it when Kipling wrote; in the words of the story's nameless narrator, "no Englishman ha[d] been through" it.[1] That was a half-truth. A British expedition to the area had turned back after a few days in 1885, and the first ethnographic survey was done in 1889–90— dates that effectively bracket the tale. What the British did know was that the people were neither Hindus nor Muslims, and it was believed that, like many hill tribes, they claimed descent from Alexander the Great. The two men disregard the narrator's warning that they'll be "cut to pieces" (38) in the Afghan hills, and indeed with twenty smuggled Martini rifles, the conquest of Kafiristan goes smoothly. They pick out "twenty good men and shows [sic] them how to click off a rifle, and form fours, and advance in line" (49), and the two Englishmen are soon spoken of as gods, the sons of Alexander. But as a late Victorian story of imperial conquest, "The Man Who Would Be King" is also inevitably about the dynamics of racial difference that underlie that conquest. The Kafiristanis, Peachy says, are "fair men . . . with yellow hair" (47). And Dravot declares: "These men aren't niggers. They're English. . . . They're the lost tribes, or something like that, and they've grown to be English" (56).

Lost white tribes at the heart of the unknown figured heavily in the mythology of empire, for they marked the land as the white man's after all;[2] in fact, the people of Kafiristan resemble those of North India. But in saying that the people have "grown" to be English, Dravot has in mind the way they take to military drill as much as their fair skin, thereby suggesting that "Englishness" may be an acquired characteristic, a matter of culture, not color. And that suggestion is underlined by one of their most "English" characteristics: they know the rudiments of Masonic ritual. What confirms Carnehan's and Dravot's new status as gods, in fact, is their superior mastery of the "Craft" (52). Kipling himself had been initiated into a multiracial lodge in Lahore, and Freemasonry stood for him as a prime example of the place he imagined in "The Ballad of East and West," where "two strong men stand face to face" in a way that cancels the difference between "East . . . West . . . Border . . . Breed . . . [and] Birth."[3] The Kafiristanis do, however, remain Asian, even if they are also Masons and Englishmen—"other" and yet not, in a way that begs the question of the basis of British rule. Does that rule depend on the superior discipline of British culture? But the story shows how culture can be acquired. Does it depend on the color of their skin? Not in Kafiristan—which makes one think that, whatever Kipling's intentions, it might in India indeed depend on color. Or does that rule perhaps rest on those twenty Martini rifles?

Kipling sets Carnehan's and Dravot's adventures against a frame tale of life in a stable British India, and yet their eventual disaster implicitly challenges that stability. If they are gods, one remembers that Indian servants in other stories call their masters "Heaven-born." For Kafiristan serves as a trope for an issue Kipling could never squarely face—the Anglicization of India, Thomas Babington Macaulay's plan to create, through education, "a class of persons, Indian in blood and colour, but English in taste, in opinions, in morals, and in intellect."[4] Kipling's belief in both an essential India and an essential England made him always contemptuous of such cultural hybrids; a good example is Wali Dad in "On the City Wall," a young Muslim "suffering acutely from education of the English variety."[5] And he was equally suspicious of sexual desire across racial lines, a situation that in his work always ends unhappily. For that desire threatens to erase the barriers that the Raj insisted on maintaining. The juxtaposition of dark skin and light underlines the difference between the races while suggesting either that the difference doesn't matter—that they are "sisters under the skin"[6]—or that it is, indeed, a positive attraction. So the crisis comes when Dravot decides he wants a wife. But the woman he is offered bites his cheek, and the spout of blood both confirms the two men's kinship with the Kafiristanis and proves that they are indeed men, not gods. Dravot is killed outright; Carnehan is first crucified and then taken down so he can limp home and tell the story.

This book looks at three novelists whose work depends on the questions raised by Dravot's words about growing "to be English," on the perpetually drawn and perpetually blurred boundaries of identity that British imperialism has left behind it. And that includes the national identity of the English themselves. My chapter on Paul Scott's retrospective account of the Raj turns on his portrait of Hari Kumar—a seeming oxymoron, "an English boy with a dark brown skin."[7] Homi Bhabha has written that to be Anglicized is "*emphatically* not to be English";[8] and certainly Hari's fate depends on the fact that the Raj believes in that distinction. But Scott's seminal presentation of the imperial endgame suggests that Hari isn't the only one whose Englishness has been acquired. For Scott shows how Britain made India function as "a part of England's idea about herself," the Orientalized proving ground for British identity, a place in which to demonstrate, even as the empire disintegrates, that "we are English and have demonstrably English ideas."[9] Those words, like Hari's very existence, undercut the belief on which the Raj depends: the belief in an absolute distinction between England and India, in a racialized model of cultural identity and authenticity.

I follow my chapter on Scott with ones on V. S. Naipaul and Salman Rushdie, examining the way those novelists present both the longing for and a critique of such beliefs. To the Trinidadian Naipaul, the great novelist of the Indian diaspora, the idea of an authentic and irreducible identity provides a dream of a "pure

time,"[10] of fulfillment in the "landscapes hymned by [one's] ancestors." Yet he also suggests the ways in which history has perpetually
undermined that dream of wholeness, leaving behind a "deep disorder," a legacy of cultural violation and dependency.[11] The fully autonomous identity for which his characters yearn remains impossible; and the mimicry of other peoples and other values becomes
inevitable. Rushdie's work stands as a later moment in both the
literature and the historical process of decolonization; he takes what
Bhabha describes as that "separation from origins and essences" as
his starting point.[12] In attempting to define an independent India's
"national longing for form,"[13] he uses what he terms a "historically
validated eclecticism" to mount an attack on "the confining myth
of authenticity" itself—an attack located in the very ground of his
work's language.[14] The most important writer that Anglophone
South Asia has yet produced, Rushdie remakes English into a new
Indian language called "Angrezi," in a move that at once destabilizes the imperial idea of a standard English to which one must
conform and challenges the nativist assumption that there's only
one "good, right way" to be Indian.[15] To the Rushdie chapter I
have appended an essay on *The Satanic Verses;* written immediately
after the Ayatollah Khomeini issued his *fatwa* against the novel in
February 1989, this essay was published later that year in *The Threepenny Review* and is reprinted without change.

    The "postcolonial" as an object of study has sprung up so
quickly that it has often seemed to create itself in the very act of
being described. Yet even so, one can already isolate stages in the
development of a critical literature on postcolonial fiction. The first
books on what we then called "Commonwealth" literature often
opposed British novels to works from India or Africa—E. M. Forster with R. K. Narayan, Joyce Cary with Chinua Achebe.[16] A later
phase in that scholarship discards such a "Manichaean aesthetics"
in favor of examining a work in terms of its cultural specificity, its
local and indigenous origins. In such accounts the postcolonial
writer often becomes a figure of resistance or perhaps, as is frequently the case in studies of Naipaul, one co-opted by metropolitan values and tastes.[17] A corollary to that work can be found in what
Edward Said calls, in *Culture and Imperialism,* the "contrapuntal"

reading of English texts, nineteenth-century fiction in particular,
brushing them against the grain to reveal their ideological absences,
their naturalization of historical processes.[18] Such approaches have,
however, tended to settle for a Manichaeanism of their own, a too-
easy reliance on binary distinctions between the center and the margin, the canonical and the noncanonical, relying on the tired vocabulary they would nevertheless destabilize. To me a more interesting
development is that suggested by Sara Suleri's *The Rhetoric of English India*, whose powerfully ambiguous title evokes a discourse
whose "idiom of . . . colonial trauma" is shaped and shared by writers from England and South Asia alike.[19] My own emphasis on a
body of concerns held in common by writers from different countries is clearly indebted to hers; in particular, I use her argument
that " 'books about India' [are] . . . more accurately books about
the representation of India" to clarify Scott's relation to his predecessors, Kipling and Forster.[20]

    What that body of criticism has found hard to provide is a
generally agreed upon definition for its foundational term. In an
English department the word *postcolonial* is of course most commonly employed to denote a body of non-British, non-American
novels, poems, and plays that can, however problematically, be
grouped together on a common syllabus. Yet as soon as one attempts to define it by something other than negatives—not this,
not that—the word threatens "to break down," for as Aijaz Ahmad
has written, "It designates far too many things, all at once."[21] The
difficulty lies in the ambiguous meaning of its prefix. The word
can, as Linda Hutcheon has written, be taken quite simply to mean
"resistance and opposition, the anticolonial." But because that prefix maintains its Latin sense it may also be used to signify " 'after,'
'because of' and even unavoidably 'inclusive of' the colonial."[22] The
assumption behind Hutcheon's first definition is that a literature
that comes after colonialism will by definition be opposed to it. Yet
that is precisely what some recent theory has begun to question.
Ella Shohat, for example, has argued that although the word "suggests a distance from colonialism," the nature of that distance remains unclear.[23] The term is to her curiously "passive . . . [it] posits
no clear domination, and calls for no clear opposition,"[24] and there-

fore risks what Anne McClintock describes as "a premature celebration of the pastness of colonialism." Organized around what
McClintock calls a "binary axis of time rather than power," de-
pending on the sense of linear progression contained in the prefix
post, the word can serve to obscure the "continuities and discontinuities" of past and present power.[25] In emphasizing the passing away
of empire's formal political structures, it ignores the continued in-
equities of relations between the metropolitan West and the decolonizing world; a facile use of the word can be so universalizing as
to obliterate the differences between a country like Nigeria and a
white settler colony like Canada.

   Yet even though such qualifications remain important, we
could not have gained that "distance from colonialism" without
first being opposed to it, and so the term is often—most often—
used in a way that does indeed equate *post* with *anti*. The temporal
definition should not be entirely discarded. It remains useful in
drawing distinctions between periods: Naipaul is a postcolonial
writer, even though his work is a consequence of colonialist assumptions about the ineradicable differences between peoples.
Nevertheless, a postcolonial literature, a postcolonial politics, is one
that rests on and requires a foundation of anticolonialism even if
it cannot, at the end of the century, be limited to that. I do not
share Shohat's view of the term's passivity; still I would agree with
her that such a periodization does indeed imply a distance—a historical distance not only from colonialism but also from the first
articulation of an anticolonialist politics. The postcolonial acknowledges the continuing power of neocolonialism and the need to op-
pose it. But the postcolonial also assumes that though the argument
against imperialism as a political structure may need to be repeated,
it no longer needs to be made as such, that a space has been cleared
into which something new may come, and that its concern lies as
much with what comes after empire as with the anticolonial struggle itself.

   It is in this sense that Paul Scott can figure as a postcolonial
novelist—in his concern with what empire has left behind, in the
way he pursues its consequences into the realm of culture. That

emphasis joins his work to Naipaul's attempt to come to terms with the "deep disorder" produced by the "great upheaval[s]"[26] of both imperialism and its passing; while Rushdie's sport with language and identity depends on a world in which those cultural consequences—migrancy, mimicry—have themselves become creative forces. Yet though these writers may share a set of questions, their individual strengths and emphases have prompted me to examine each of them from a somewhat different angle. The chapter on Scott is largely historical and thematic, and to the degree that it treats his work as an argument about the nature of British imperialism it is less concerned than my other chapters with questions of style and form. My essay on Naipaul is an exploration of, an attempt to think within, a difficult writer's sensibility and shows how his work elides the home for which his characters search with the Jamesian house of fiction, with the writer's own quest for canonicity. With Rushdie, my analysis is primarily formal, an account of the way the language of the most innovative contemporary fiction both foregrounds and contests the role of ideology in the world it attempts to define.

Those separate chapters are, however, joined by an argument grounded not only in the shared concerns of these novelists but also in my very linking of their names. The fetishization of the nation, by those on either end of the political spectrum, has meant that British writers like Scott are still too often considered either in isolation from or in some sense inevitably opposed to those whose origins lie in the countries of England's former empire. Clearly national origin and identity matter, in ways that the words of Kipling's Dravot suggest; yet clearly, as those words also suggest, they are never absolute. Naipaul and Rushdie provide a case in point. Each stands as the embodiment of what Gilles Deleuze and Felix Guatarri have called a "minor literature . . . that which a minority constructs within a major language." Their work is a consequence of the "deterritorialization" of the English language itself that accompanied the spread of British power.[27] Indeed Rushdie's case runs parallel to that of Deleuze and Guatarri's example, Franz Kafka. For in using English, as the Czech Kafka did German, Rush-

die marks his own privileged position and separates himself from
the mass of his homeland's people even as his Indian origins, like
Kafka's Judaism, makes him a minority within that language itself.
But Naipaul and Rushdie have also both chosen to write
within—or upon—the territory of the literature to which their
work is the "minor" counterpart. Each holds British citizenship and
has spent his adult life in England; and certainly the experience of
living and working there has been crucial, for each has an abiding
concern with the issues of mimicry and authenticity and assimilation that face a self caught on a cultural border. On the one hand,
their emigration underlines their minor status. On the other, it
gives their work an immediate relation to the language's major literature and makes their work fundamentally different from the books
of those postcolonial writers—Nadine Gordimer, Wole Soyinka—
who have built their careers at home. Yoking them with Scott, the
last great chronicler of British India, serves of course to illustrate
that new cliché, the way the empire now writes back. But more
important, it suggests that if Britain today is a postimperial nation,
it is also, albeit in a special sense, a postcolonial one, a country
whose recent history of immigration ensures that the conflicts of
postcolonial identity are now enacted on the site of the imperial
power itself.

And linking their names does something still more. It underlines the fact that much of the most important fiction published in
London has not, for a very long time, been "English"—not English, that is, in a sense that Kipling would have recognized. His
Kafiristanis may not be British, but empire did make its rulers into
the people we recognize as such. Indeed, to pursue Said's argument,
imperialism made English literature itself into what it was. And the
end of empire, in Scott's words, also brought an end to the English
"as they were."[28] So when I speak of redefining "Englishness," as
I will in the remainder of this preface and, at greater length, in my
conclusion, I am also, if implicitly, speaking of redefining English
as a field of study. For just as modernism in Britain is inconceivable
without the presence of a Pole, a couple of Americans, and the Irish,
so the novel in England has continued to rely on the work of writers
born elsewhere—not only Naipaul and Rushdie but younger novel-

ists like Timothy Mo, Kazuo Ishiguro, and Caryl Phillips as well. Insofar as literature has customarily been seen in relation to national origin, such figures pose the kind of cultural conundrum that Scott explored through his invention of the Indian Englishman Hari Kumar: a conundrum that in an age of liquid borders seems increasingly the norm. The "case" of Naipaul and Rushdie would therefore seem to suggest that national identity provides no more useful a way to think of literature in the late twentieth century than it did in the Latin Middle Ages.[29] Yet in another sense their situation points toward the need to reconfigure British national identity itself. Of course there have always been writers in exile, writers living abroad for one reason or another, writers working in something other than their native tongue. What separates Naipaul and Rushdie from such superficially similar cases as Samuel Beckett or Vladimir Nabokov, and what makes Scott's Kumar such a resonant figure, is the fact that they haven't come alone but were instead part of the large immigrant populations that entered postwar Britain from South Asia and the Caribbean.

What is a nation? In Benedict Anderson's now classic formulation, it is above all an imagined community, one whose members are conscious of their links to people they don't know but with whom they feel they have something in common. And for Anderson that community finds its origin in language—or rather in the way that the development of printing assembled the "varied idiolects" spoken in "pre-print Europe" into languages, whose "new fixity" created the illusion not just of their permanence but of their antiquity.[30] Printing made it possible to think that both a language and the people who spoke it had always existed as a coherent whole, presenting an intimation of immortality that allowed one to believe, as George Orwell put it, that a nation "is continuous, it stretches into the future and the past, there is something in it that persists, as in a living creature."[31] Yet seeing the nation as an organism inevitably leads to a concern with the seed or the primitive tissue from which the community has grown. Languages remain "historical formations," as Ernest Renan wrote in 1882, "which tell us very little about the blood of those who speak them."[32] Nevertheless those who claim descent from that oxymoron, the original speakers of a modern language, have also always claimed a purity of identity from which others remain excluded. "The language in which we are speaking," thinks James Joyce's Stephen Dedalus as he talks to the English dean of his college, "is his before it is mine."[33] Those words point to the uncertainties, the pain, and—with *Ulysses* in our minds—the possibilities of a world marked, as Bhabha puts it, by its separation from origins and essences. Populations long settled in the same place do of course tend toward a relative homogeneity in both language and physiognomy. But few polities of any time have corresponded to the ideal purity of the nineteenth-century European nation-state, in which the state is also the "homeland" of a single "people," in which language is equated with ethnicity, and in which both are seen in relation to their territorial origins. People travel, learn new languages, and flee their rulers; they do not, or cannot, always choose to be particular about the parentage of their sexual partners. "To make politics depend upon ethnographic analysis," in Renan's words, "is to surrender to a chimera."[34]

In 1701 Daniel Defoe, angry at the mistreatment of the Dutch immigrants who had come to Britain with William III, reminded his island nation that the "True-Born Englishman" was but a "heterogeneous thing . . . / In eager rapes, and furious lust begot / Betwixt a Painted Briton and a Scot"—someone whose "well-extracted blood" also contained corpuscles of Roman, Irish, Welsh, Saxon, Danish, and Dutch, in addition to several transfusions from the French.[35] But a nation's citizens do, as Renan admits, have many things in common. They have had to forget many of the same things, and indeed "historical error, is a crucial factor in the creation of the nation." For such errors allow one to forget "the deeds of violence" that have shaped the nation and so, over time, to create the unifying fiction of a common ancestry.[36] Because a nation is also a narrative.[37] It's made up of people who believe they share a common story, when in fact the possession of that story is in itself what makes them a people. Recent scholarship on the concept of national identity has stressed the degree to which that identity is formed by contact with the world outside, formed in opposition to some Other. In particular, Linda Colley's *Britons*

(1992) has charted the ways in which, despite the tension between England and its Celtic fringe, a commonly held British identity emerged in the eighteenth century as an expression of Protestant patriotism against Catholic France—an identity confirmed, for the Scots especially, by a subsequent history of imperial service.[38] "Britishness" became inseparable from the official nationalism of empire; one holds a British passport, not an English one. Yet within that political identity a more narrowly defined English one has always exercised hegemony, in a way that often makes the terms interchangeable. Peachy Carnehan's name is Irish; nevertheless he speaks of "us English."

The imagined community of the British Empire took a particularly powerful form: a community scattered around the world, whose members were conscious both that they were doing similar sorts of work and that they had all emanated from a few islands off the coast of France. For Forster's characters, as Naipaul writes, "their Englishness is like an extra quality which challenges, and is challenged by, all that is alien."[39] That had always been true for the English abroad; wogs begin at Calais, as the old saying has it. In 1765 Robert Clive described his officers in Calcutta as "Englishmen, not assassins," as if the two were mutually exclusive;[40] it is, perhaps, an early example of what Forster would call the "Public School attitude."[41] And two centuries later Scott would write that in India the English stopped "being unconsciously English and become consciously English," in a way that inevitably makes identity seem exaggerated, a cartoon of itself.[42] But of course that exaggeration also throve in the land the Raj called "home." To Adam Smith the word *nation* defined a territory, not a people.[43] For Dickens's Mr. Podsnap, however, a pride in being English is inseparable from his contempt for foreigners, and by Forster's time, as Naipaul has argued, that identity had come to represent something more, a code of behavior and a canon of taste shared not even by the French or the Germans and still less by the subject peoples of Africa and Asia.[44]

One can of course learn such codes, as indeed Kipling's story suggests. But can one grow to be English? Certainly the Electors of Hanover did, and so did people with names like Rossetti and

Rothschild, though the Rothschilds, being Jewish as well as German, had an ambiguous position for generations. They were once merely Anglicized—and that, as Bhabha writes, is "*emphatically* not to be English*.*" You become an American by becoming a citizen—an Italian-American, a Korean-American—but is naturalization enough to be, to become, English? To what degree does national identity depend on what we may call "ethnicity"? The English might hyphenate their last names, but a hyphenated identity seems something else again, in ways I'll describe in my chapter on Scott. The French allowed their subject peoples to become French, provided they were willing to play what Naipaul calls "the French colonial monkey-game": to surrender their parents' culture and acknowledge their ancestors the Gauls.[45] Yet for the British that was never enough. Ancestry—the blood that spurts from Dravot's cheek—mattered more than learning to be English "in opinions, in morals, and in intellect," and so Anglicization finally stands, in Bhabha's words, as a reminder that one is "*almost the same but not quite . . . almost the same but not white.*"[46]

The "Englishness" of Kipling's Kafiristanis is of course a moot point. But what about that of the United Kingdom's "not white" population? I do not presume to define the terms of a black British identity. But I can, perhaps, suggest the nature of the ground against which those terms are now being defined. There were approximately ten thousand blacks in England in the eighteenth century, most of them household servants or slaves, and by 1919 the black community in Liverpool alone numbered five thousand.[47] Most Indians in Britain at the time of the Great War were either students or doctors, with a sprinkling of Sikh peddlers. Even in 1949 the South Asian population amounted to no more than eight thousand. Historians date the start of postwar immigration to 1948, when the SS *Empire Windrush* brought nearly five hundred Jamaicans to England, but the numbers of emigrants remained small until 1954, when entry from the Caribbean into the United States was sharply restricted. Eleven thousand West Indians arrived in Britain that year, and immigration topped out at sixty-six thousand in 1961, shortly before the British government began to impose strict controls of its own. South Asian immigrants had begun to arrive in the

mid-fifties as well—seventy-five hundred in 1955—in response to
a demand for cheap industrial labor. Their numbers in any given
year have never approached those of the West Indies at its peak
but they have been far more sustained over time, including, in 1972,
twenty-seven thousand Uganda Asians thrown out by Idi Amin. In
1988 South Asian immigration stood at twelve thousand; that from
the West Indies was at just over one thousand. "Not-whites" now
make up approximately 5 percent, or 2.7 million, of the total British
population, with South Asians outnumbering Afro-Caribbeans by
about 3 : 1.

Those immigrants, and their children, live in a country in
which, as Paul Gilroy has memorably put it, "There ain't no black
in the Union Jack"—indeed, a country in which the Union Jack's
imperial past makes it available, an English version of the stars and
bars, to the white supremacist National Front.[48] Britain's first seri-
ous postwar race riots occurred in London's Notting Hill in 1958;
the riots of 1981 and 1985 punctuated the decade of Prime Minister
Margaret Thatcher's rule. Immigration was severely restricted in
1962, 1965, and again in 1968; the National Front was formed in
1966 and grew steadily throughout the 1970s until Thatcher began
to woo its voters by adopting its rhetoric. The Nationality Act of
1971 abandoned an earlier distinction between "aliens" and citizens
of Commonwealth nations; a successor bill in 1981 denied citizenship to the British-born children of parents of "uncertain status."[49]
The most memorable statement of anti-immigrant feeling, however, remains Enoch Powell's 1968 self-fulfilling prophecy that the
presence of nonwhites would make rivers of blood flow down England's streets. "The West Indian or Asian," Powell argued, "does
not, by being born in England, become an Englishman. In law he
becomes a United Kingdom citizen by birth; in fact he is a West
Indian or an Asian still."[50]

So Hanif Kureishi could write, in the first sentence of his
1990 *The Buddha of Suburbia*, "My name is Karim Amir, and I am
an Englishman born and bred, almost."[51] "Almost" because although his mother is white, his father comes from Pakistan, because
the narrative of Englishness hasn't yet been reimagined to include
him. He doesn't have the same relation to the English past as do

the whites with whom he goes to school—a past in which people who look like them have defined themselves by conquering people who look like him. For how long, and on what terms, does that "almost" obtain? In 1983 Thatcher's party seemed to reverse itself with a campaign poster that read, "Labour says he's black, Tories say he's British." But that's a case of "Nos ancêtres les Gaulois," as the French schoolbooks used to say, in which assuming a new identity requires the repudiation of an old one. Why not both? Is it possible—and yet how can it not be?—to be both English and nonwhite? Or as Rushdie puts it in *The Satanic Verses*, "How does newness come into the world?"[52]

The Situation: Paul Scott
and *The Raj Quartet*

I

"Imagine, then"—these are the words with which Paul Scott opens *The Jewel in the Crown* (1966), the first volume of *The Raj Quartet*. Imagine, then, a "flat landscape, dark for the moment, but even so conveying to a girl running in the still deeper shadow cast by the wall of the Bibighar Gardens an idea of immensity, of distance" (J, 3).[1] Who is she? Is she running toward something or from it? But perhaps such questions are, for the moment, irrelevant; she is not "the girl" but "a girl." The definite article would make her someone in particular and, in doing so, would imply an action, a narrative unfolding over time. The indefinite article generalizes her and makes this not a narrative but a visual composition, a spatial arrangement frozen in time. And so the picture of her forever running, and not yet having run, stays with us for the four hundred pages it takes to reach the incident from which that image comes, when she will at last stop, stumble, fall, and crawl on "her hands and knees the rest of the way to safety and into the history of a troubled period" (J, 69). For of course she will become "the girl," the Manners girl, the girl in the Bibighar Gardens affair.

The whole of *The Jewel in the Crown* is an attempt to explain its opening command, to tell its readers how that girl has come to be running in the shadow of that wall. But the image isn't self-contained, and the novel's first sentence strides on past it, comparing that idea of immensity, of distance, to that which "years before

Miss Crane had been conscious of standing where a lane ended and cultivation began: a different landscape but also in the alluvial plane between the mountains of the north and the plateau of the south" (J, 3). We pause, uncertain. Are Miss Crane and "a girl" the same person? No—and yet that momentary confusion collapses our consciousness of those different immensities into one, the distance between them erased. So during our reading it is "as if time were telescoped and space dovetailed" (J, 125), the images pulled out of their moments—the present in which she runs and the past in which she stood—and fused together in a cinematic tableau. As a child, Scott made films for a hobby, not motion pictures but elaborate series of hand-drawn still images presented in sequence; he came from a family of commercial artists and was himself a skilled draftsman. And in an essay, he wrote that for him the inspiration for a novel always came in the form of an image—"a girl in the dark, running, exhausted" (W, 82). This was "the first . . . [image] in the story to be told" (S, 6), a deliberately ambiguous phrase that makes one think he isn't telling a story so much as telling an image. For Scott, the work of writing involved "bombarding" the image with "knowledge, experience, imagination" (W, 84) until he had a story that could explain it: who she is, why she runs, where she is going. But that's not the only image he has to tell. Any reader of *The Raj Quartet* remembers the way Scott organizes the work around a series of such tableaux, images so rich in significance that to explain them goes a long way toward explaining the work in its entirety. So I'll begin with the image that seems to serve as a prelude to the *Quartet* as a whole: not the girl running but the "sight of old Miss Crane sitting in the pouring rain by the roadside holding the hand of a dead Indian" (J, 59–60).

The dead man is a Mr. Chaudhuri, the teacher at the Protestant mission school in the town of Dibrapur; Miss Crane is his supervisor. And an explanation of how he has been killed can begin with the lithograph that Miss Crane has hung on the wall of her study: a "semi-historical, semi-allegorical picture entitled *The Jewel in Her Crown*," a picture of Queen Victoria "surrounded by representative figures of her Indian Empire" (J, 19) and being offered the large gemstone that stands for India itself.[2] Miss Crane has for years carried the picture from post to post, and over the decades it has "acquired a faint power to move her with the sense of time past, of glory departed, even although she knew there had never been glory there to begin with" (J, 22). But though she doesn't believe in imperial glory, she does believe in an imperial mission, in an ideal of service whose "duties and obligations" are undertaken "not for self-aggrandizement, but in self-denial . . . in order to rid the world of the very evils the picture took no account of: poverty, disease, misery" (J, 23). She feels uneasy about that duty, however, and wonders whether it can ever be adequately discharged. For always she is conscious of what she calls "this little matter of the colour of the skin" (J, 63). Always, when she talks to an Indian, she hears in her voice "the note of authority, the special note of *us* talking to *them*" (J, 49), a perpetual reminder that the rulers are different from the ruled.

It is August 9, 1942. The British have imprisoned the leaders of the All-India Congress in response to their ratification of the Mahatma Gandhi's Quit India Resolution. Disturbances are expected. Miss Crane has that day paid her weekly visit to Mr. Chaudhuri's school, but she resists his plea to stay another night in Dibrapur, "where everyone is your friend." She has friends as well, she replies, at her home in the district capital of Mayapore, and what is more, she adds, "I also have responsibilities" (J, 51). But she does allow him to ride with her as protection against rioters and looters. On the way they learn that the telephone lines have been cut and a police inspector has been abducted. Even then she refuses to turn back, but she does accede to Mr. Chaudhuri's plea that "if we see a crowd of people on the road, you put your foot hard on the accelerator" (J, 55). Blow your horn and put your foot down, he says. "Close your eyes if you must but keep going!" Yet when they do encounter a line of "rioters . . . spread out across the road" (J, 56), Miss Crane can't keep her promise. She cannot bring herself to plow through them because she cannot accept that he, an Indian, knows more about how to act in an emergency than she does. Instead she stops, trusting the Heaven's command of the Raj to see them safely home. And so she watches as the rioters harm not her but him, dragging Mr. Chaudhuri from the car for the crime of accompanying an Englishwoman. "Go!" he screams, as they begin to beat him, "or do you only take orders from white men? Do you only keep promises you make to your own kind?" And now she does drive on—but stops again, a few hundred yards on, to watch the sticks fall about his back and head, until he lies dead on the road with a "couple of them . . . going through his pockets" (J, 58).

There is only one thing Miss Crane can do. She was unable to reciprocate the trust that, while living, he placed in her, but now she limps back to his body, sits down in the mud beside him, and takes his hand. " 'It's taken me a long time,' " she says, "meaning not only Mr. Chaudhuri, 'I'm sorry it was too late' ", (J, 59). The British can no longer protect those whom it is their self-appointed mission to protect. Miss Crane cannot protect her subordinate because her very presence is what makes him vulnerable in the first place. The imperial mission cancels itself out, dies of its own contradictions. For the Raj cannot now pretend that it rules India for India's sake. Not only can the British no longer preserve the order that they take as a justification for their rule; they are themselves responsible for its destruction.

II

"This is the story of a rape" (J, 3), Scott writes in the third paragraph of *The Jewel in the Crown*, a story whose implications he explores throughout the three succeeding volumes of his grand tetralogy about the end of British rule in India: *The Day of the Scorpion* (1968), *The Towers of Silence* (1971), and *A Division of the Spoils* (1975.) Yet *The Raj Quartet* appears even in its first book to provide not a single story but a collection of them, whose unifying principle seems far from clear; if, for example, the author did not announce its subject, we wouldn't know for some hundred pages and more that the novel will concentrate on that running girl, Daphne Manners, and not on Miss Crane. *The Jewel in the Crown* is composed of seven sections that provide a series of approaches—"through different eyes, through different histories, from different vantage points of time" (W, 89)—to that original image, to Daphne's rape in the Bibighar Gardens during the riots over the Quit India Resolution. Part of the book is written in the third person, and part takes the form of a series of first-person monologues, responses to questions asked by an unnamed "stranger" on a visit to Mayapore in the 1960s (J, 112). Still other sections are cast as documents, as the personal testimony of journals, memoirs, and letters. And Scott maintains that complex structure throughout the *Quartet's* later volumes. For not one of the "sieves" (J, 341) through which he suggests we order experience is in itself adequate to what he terms "the moral continuum of human affairs" (J, 3), and so he persistently juxtaposes one character's experience with another's, using both multiple first-person narrators and an ever-shifting free indirect discourse to return again and again to certain crucial scenes.

Most of *The Towers of Silence*, for example, revisits the incidents described in *The Day of the Scorpion*, not to undercut that earlier version but to reenvision it from the point of view of previously marginal characters. In *A Division of the Spoils*, the civil servant Nigel Rowan remembers his first meeting with Sarah Layton, the central figure of the *Quartet's* last three books. Traveling at the end of the second volume from Calcutta to her home in the hill station of Pankot, she had joined Rowan and the White Russian Count Bronowsky for supper in a nawab's private railway car. To Rowan the incident had not then seemed important. Five hundred pages and a year later it does, and now we learn what the men talked about before she arrived and after she left. No plot summary could do full justice to the complexity of the *Quartet's* narrative procedures, to its intricate layering of one character's point of view upon another's, its Faulknerian sense of the way in which the past is never really past, or its awareness of the fictiveness of historical interpretation. Scott's ambition is perhaps best understood, in the terms that Joseph Conrad proposed for his own work in the Preface to *The Nigger of the Narcissus*, as an attempt "to render the highest kind of justice to the visible universe, by bringing to light the truth, manifold and one, underlying its every aspect. . . . My task . . . is, before all, to make you *see!*"[3] The task is to make us see that truth, not only by freezing an image into a tableau but by demonstrating the intimate involvement of that image, that moment, with other moments, so that as the self-ordained Sister Ludmilla says, "At once past, present and future are contained in your cupped palm" (J, 125). Daphne's rape cannot be understood as a self-contained event but must be seen in relation to "the events that led up to it and followed it and of the place in which it happened. There are the action, the people, and the place; all of which are interrelated but in their totality incommunicable in isolation from the moral continuum of human affairs" (J, 3).

"Not the intense moment / Isolated, with no before and after," as T. S. Eliot wrote in "East Coker," Scott's favorite poem, "But a lifetime burning in every moment."[4] To Scott a "historical event has no definite beginning, no satisfactory end" (J, 125), and so he disrupts chronology to counterpoint one moment on that continuum with another, insisting that we see it as inseparable from its causes and consequences. For as he quotes from Ralph Waldo Emerson, "Man is explicable by nothing less than all his history" (T, 67).[5] To understand anything about the rape, one must understand everything.

When, for example, did the Bibighar Gardens affair begin? For Sister Ludmilla it started on the night she found the Indian Englishman Hari Kumar "on the waste ground near the river, lying as if dead" (J, 126) though in fact only dead drunk. But perhaps it had another beginning; Scott won't reveal the reason for Kumar's drunkenness for another 150 pages. Sister Ludmilla has him carried to her charity hospital, the Sanctuary, where in the morning he has a crucial confrontation with Ronald Merrick, the district superintendent of police. Merrick has come looking for an escaped prisoner but instead finds Kumar, "buttoning up his shirt" (J, 134) by the pump; a man who answers the policeman's "Englishman's Urdu" by saying "I'm afraid I don't speak Indian" in an English better accented than Merrick's own. After that, Sister Ludmilla says, Bibighar "could not be stopped because of what Mr. Merrick was and what young Kumar was" (J, 135), though the full implications of her statement won't be played out until the end of *A Division of the Spoils*. So much about these characters becomes clear only as Scott takes us further into the "before and after" as to make it impossible for us fully to understand, on a first reading, just why Bibighar starts here. Nevertheless we cannot see this "intense moment isolated," for Scott has already told us that both Kumar and Merrick will become Daphne's friends, even if in terms of their moment-by-moment experience neither of them has met her yet. And we know too that Hari will be one of those arrested for her rape. Scott's disruption of chronology, that is, tells us enough to ensure that we see this tableau at the pump with an intensity it doesn't yet have for its participants. We know they will be important to each other before they do, and so in our reading it is indeed as if past, present, and future have collapsed into one. We read of Merrick's first meeting with Kumar with a sense that the characters have begun to struggle against a fate that the novel has already told us they won't be able to escape—as if Bibighar already has and has not yet happened and is still happening.

In the Bibighar Gardens affair "there was no trial in the judicial sense" (J, 3), but there was a trial in another sense and not only of those accused of rape. Later in this chapter I'll use Sara Suleri's analysis of rape in colonial discourse as a way to read that affair. But the incident at Bibighar involves more than the rape. Its "case" opens out into "the spectacle of two nations in violent opposition," and to understand it, one must also comprehend the whole of what Scott ironically calls the "imperial embrace" of Anglo-Indian history (J, 3). What seems most useful, then, is to start with Suleri's observation that "books about India" are inevitably books about "the representation of India"[6] and to locate the *Quartet*'s account of that embrace within the history of what she calls "the rhetoric of English India."[7] Scott builds the work around the relation between two names: Bibighar and Chillianwallah. Bibighar means "house of women," and in *The Jewel in the Crown* the name belongs to the villa that an eighteenth-century prince built for his courtesans in Mayapore. Another house of that name is, however, inseparable from the British consciousness of their history in India. It was at the Bibighar in the city of Cawnpore that two hundred British women and children were first imprisoned and then killed during what English historiography has called the "Mutiny" of 1857, when the soldiers of the East India Company's army rose up against their British officers. And the Chillianwallah Bagh, the cul-de-sac in Mayapore where Hari Kumar lives with his Aunt Shalini, echoes the name of the Jallianwallah Bagh in the Punjabi city of Amritsar, where in 1919 General Reginald Dyer ordered his Gurkha soldiers to open fire on a peaceful demonstration. His troops had blocked the only exit.

The memory of 1857—that "epic of the race" as the popular Victorian novelist Flora Annie Steele mistakenly called it—provided the primary myth the British told themselves about their time in India.[8] Jallianwallah made Gandhi declare that "cooperation in any shape or form with this satanic government is sinful."[9] Yet if the Amritsar massacre became one of the energizing moments in the movement for Indian independence, it proved important for the British as well. Bibighar made the English fear that they might be betrayed and destroyed, but Jallianwallah created the fear that they might themselves betray the trust on which they told themselves their empire was founded. As Hari is in a sense betrayed, trapped in Chillianwallah as those protesters were in Amritsar; trapped too by that other echo of Jallianwallah, Chillingborough, the name of his English public school. In England the outcry over Amritsar forced General Dyer's early retirement; but a fund was also raised to reward him. Yet perhaps, as Christopher Hitchens has suggested, the servants of the Raj subscribed so heavily to that fund as a way to drown the suspicion that their whole presence in India was wrong.[10] "Ah, well," says Sir Ahmed Akbar Ali Kasim in *The Day of the Scorpion*, "they were Indians who actually died at Amritsar, but the Jallianwallah Bagh was also the scene of a suicide." For the English who matter most, Sir Ahmed suggests, are not those in India, not the viceroys and generals, but the anonymous public "tucked away in England." And now that public knows "where Jallianwallah Bagh is . . . [and] do not like what they know."

For Sir Ahmed, India has become "part and parcel of the Englishmen's own continual state of social and political evolvement" (S, 63). In the first quarter of the nineteenth century, the East India Company's James Mill saw India as a palimpsest on which to inscribe the utilitarian culture that could not be created in Britain itself.[11] To E. M. Forster in *A Passage to India* (1924), it was a place where "the Public School attitude . . . flourish[ed] more vigorously than it can yet hope to do in England."[12] So for over a century, as the young historian Guy Perron writes in *A Division of the Spoils:*

> India has formed part of England's idea about herself and for the same period India has been forced into a position of being a reflection of that idea. Up to say 1900 the part India played in our idea about ourselves was the part played by anything we possessed which we believed it was right to possess. . . . Since 1900, certainly since 1918, the reverse has obtained. The part played since then by India in the English idea of Englishness has been that of something we feel it does us no credit to have. Our idea about ourselves will now not accommodate any idea about India except the idea of returning it to the Indians in order to prove that we are English and have demonstrably English ideas. . . . But on either side of that arbitrary date (1900) India itself, as itself, that is to say India as not part of our idea of ourselves, has played no part whatsoever in the lives of Englishmen in general (no part that we are conscious of). (D, 105)

For Forster, as Edward Said has written, India is a land destined "to bear its foreignness as a mark of its permanent estrangement from the West."[13] Yet if the dominant trope of colonial discourse is the attempt to find a language that will allow one to know and to describe the Other, the alien, the strange, then Perron's words suggest the difficulty that even such a powerful English critic of the Raj as Scott has in writing about "India itself, as itself." Scott's self-consciousness about his own representation of India anticipates much recent work in cultural studies: no one has written more suggestively about the ways in which the subcontinent became the proving ground for British identity, turning India itself into the missing or repressed term in a rhetoric that purported to be about it.

Scott has nevertheless been criticized, most notably by Salman Rushdie, for concentrating on the British in India rather than on "India itself." Rushdie argues that this amounts to a form of imaginative recolonization in which "Indians . . . remain, for the most part, bit-players in their own history."[14] Even with Jallianwallah, one might say, Scott's attention is drawn as much to the English "suicide" as to the Indian dead. Yet Rushdie misses the degree to which the *Quartet* itself mounts a critique of its own Orientalism. For Scott, India's function as a part of the British "idea about ourselves" precluded any attempt to come to terms with India "as itself." What he presents instead is an analysis of the ways in which the British used the subcontinent's "foreignness" as the ground on which—against which—to define their own self-portrait. He liked to say that the cotton mills of Lancashire were as much a monument to the British Empire as any statue of Queen Victoria; and in *A Division of the Spoils* he suggested that the possession of India was inscribed on the face of every insular Englishman. But those English faces belong "to streets of terraced houses that ended in one-man shops," and they are not conscious of the way in which that possession has "helped nourish [their] flesh, warm [their] blood" (D, 103). The paradox—one with enormous costs for "India itself"—is that they will nevertheless decide its fate.

But Scott's sense of those costs extends as well to the damage the empire inflicted on the British themselves.[15] He has, in both the *Quartet* and its coda, *Staying On* (1977), an acute sense of the dislocation that the servants of the Raj feel after the end of empire, of the way in which, as Perron writes, such people "may now see nothing at all when looking in [the] mirror" of English life, not even themselves (D, 105). Yet though that acknowledgment of individual confusion and pain can hardly be taken as a nostalgia for imperial rule, the *Quartet* is nevertheless marked by a nostalgia of a particular kind: not in its deliberately and ironically clichéd evocations of the swank and the swagger of the Raj, but instead in the seriousness with which Scott takes the belief, memorably voiced by Marlow in *Heart of Darkness*, that empire can be redeemed by some "idea at the back of it."[16] His work is marked by a persistent search for what he just as persistently does not find, for an idea, a belief, that will give a purpose to the centuries of injustice and waste, all the while recognizing that after the partition of India and Pakistan the British have not even the shopworn excuse of the subcontinent's unification. It is the nostalgia of what Richard Rorty calls the "liberal ironist" for a sense of purpose he knows cannot be found and which he would have to discount even if it could; and that is precisely what gives such dialectical force to his interpretation of the end of British rule.[17]

For to Scott, India provided the "mausoleum" for "the last two great senses of public duty we [British] had as a people." The first was "the sense of duty that was part and parcel of having an empire"—the duty, once having taken possession of India, to govern it responsibly and well. The second was "the sense of duty so many of us felt that to get rid of it was the liberal human thing to do" (W, 69). In literary terms the one corresponds to Rudyard Kipling and the other to E. M. Forster. Yet the dichotomy between them no longer seems so clear, and Scott's own achievement lay in synthesizing the work of his two great predecessors to show how those duties came inevitably into conflict. Kipling and Forster do stand on either side of the "arbitrary date" on which one duty superseded another, and they have a correspondingly fundamental disagreement about the morality of the Raj's existence. Kipling subdues the subcontinent to description, establishing a close connection between its imaginative and its literal possession; perhaps the best example is the eponymous Kim's training in cartography, that essential tool of military intelligence. Forster's India, in contrast, seems knowable only in its unknowability; and for him that is in itself a reason why Britain ought not to keep it. But for readers after the end of empire, those positions—India as un/knowable— begin to seem two sides of a single coin, and the rhetoric through which they present the Raj is in many ways the same. For both Kipling and Forster see the Raj as lying outside history; both of them accept what Francis G. Hutchins calls "the illusion of permanence" on which it depended.[18]

V. S. Naipaul has written, "There exists no great English novel in which the growth of national or imperial consciousness is chronicled."[19] Perhaps Macaulay came the closest, not of course in a novel but in his essays on Clive and Hastings—essays that chart the stages through which the English in India began to change from merchants to plunderers to administrators. And Edmund Burke, in his impeachment of Hastings, did approach a sense of the conflict between those "two great senses of public duty."[20] But the novel itself barely touched on the rise of empire, relegating it instead to the outer borders of the genre's concerns. Empire is the place in which fortunes are made and to which social misfits are consigned, and although that very marginality provides in itself a window onto the Victorian mind, the empire per se was not, before Kipling, a subject for major fiction.[21] Even Macaulay can offer only fragments. He doesn't take the story down to his own day, when the evangelical reformers of whom he was one attempted, in what they saw as compensation for the criminality of India's conquest, not "to get rid" of the empire but to give it the benefit of a planned and rational central government. "It is," Hutchins wrote, "one of the many ironies of the British connection with India, that those who first argued for the justness of England's retention of an Indian empire were opposed to its acquisition."[22]

In the 1840s both Wellington and Gladstone had criticized the invasion of Sind, and *Punch* had reported the conquest with a one-word Latin pun— "Peccavi." But the events of 1857 effectively ended such opposition and ambivalence; they were paradoxically taken to prove how badly India needed England's firm guiding hand.[23] The East India Company was abolished, and the subcontinent came under the direct rule of the Crown. The mechanisms of the Raj soon came to seem so naturalized as to obscure the ironies of their origin, and by 1885, when Kipling published *Plain Tales from the Hills*, Britain had lost its last doubts about the justice of its rule. Kipling's work is one of the few imaginative records we have of the Raj at its height, and it exists only, as Orwell wrote, because Kipling was "just coarse enough to be able to exist and keep his mouth shut in clubs and regimental messes," just coarse enough to be acceptable to the people he wrote about and to accept their point of view in turn.[24] Both "The Man Who Would Be King" and "Recessional" suggest that he remained troubled by conquest in itself—conquest untempered by an "idea." But when he criticizes British rule it is almost always from the point of view of someone—a deputy commissioner, a private soldier—whose on-the-spot knowledge challenges the ignorance of his superiors, someone who questions not the fact of the Raj but specific instances of the way in which its power is used.

Kipling's richest tale is, of course, *Kim* (1901). Kimball O'Hara is a soldier's orphan, born in India, "a poor white of the very poorest,"[25] whose tongue is more comfortable in Urdu than in English, a bazaar child who throughout the novel shucks one identity for another, appearing in rapid succession as the companion of an Afghan horse trader, a "Hindu urchin,"[26] a spy in government training, and the disciple of a Buddhist priest. He is still a boy when the novel ends, and its readers have often wondered about him as a man—wondered if, as an adult in the growing struggle for Indian independence, he would be forced to choose between the Raj and the people with whom he lives, if he would feel what Scott identifies as the conflict between those two great duties. But within the novel itself that choice simply doesn't exist. Kim may be able to change identities, but Kipling never raises the question of a political conflict between those identities. For the novel as a whole is deliberately cut loose from history. It presents the events of 1857 as a time out of legend and ignores the enormous exacerbation of racial tension that followed. And though the novel is nominally set in the 1880s, when in his newspaper articles Kipling often satirized the fledgling Indian National Congress, *Kim* does not even glance at either Congress or the issues it addressed, presenting instead an image of an eternal India that corresponds to the illusion of permanence that surrounded British rule. Like all idylls, *Kim* depends on a rigorous exclusion, and indeed what one most remembers from it are its pictures of an India that does not change: the mountains, the great road cutting across the Gangetic plain, the bewildering variety of people.

But Kipling does, in Orwell's words, have one thing that Forster lacks: "A sense of responsibility. . . . The ruling power is always faced with the question, 'In such and such circumstances, what would you *do?*' whereas the opposition is not obliged to . . . make any real decisions."[27] Forster writes as a member of a liberal elite, in revolt against the established pieties of Edwardian society, an elite that sees imperialism as a moral outrage. Yet that in itself

makes *A Passage to India* a more problematic text than its traditional
reputation as the great anti-imperialist novel would suggest. "It's
beginning at the wrong end, isn't it," says the English schoolmaster
Cyril Fielding to the Indian Muslim Dr. Aziz during a discussion
of political reform. "I know, but institutions and governments
don't."[28] Forster insists on seeing British imperialism not in political or historical terms but as a problem in individual human relations. Aziz can't forget that he is the ruled and Fielding the ruler.
Their friendship grows increasingly tense, and finally each retreats
into his own people, the one into a nascent sense of Indian nationalism and the other into an English marriage. For as Aziz says at the
end of the novel, India will have to drive the last Englishman into
the sea before they can be friends once more, and indeed in the
novel's closing image their whole world—"the horses . . . rocks . . .
the temples, the tank, the jail, the palace, the birds . . . the sky"—
weighs in against that friendship, so that imperialism comes to seem
a force of nature, driving them apart.[29]

Because politics stands for him as an intrusion into private
life, because his opposition to the Raj emerges in emotional terms
rather than political ones, Forster's readers can easily draw the conclusion that imperialism's greatest evil lies in keeping these two
men apart. His ironic portrait of British India is a powerful one,
and the novel will remain the canonical statement of the liberal
opposition to imperialism. Yet although there's never any doubt
about his hatred of the Raj, Forster's account of it now seems limited—limited above all by the fact that his India, like Kipling's,
remains essentially abstracted from history. He began the book
after his first visit to the subcontinent in 1912–13; his writing was
interrupted by the Great War, and he resumed his work only after
a second visit in 1921. His characters' manners are those of the
prewar years, but the novel's long gestation led him, as P. N. Furbank has written, to make its setting "neither precisely pre-war nor
precisely post-war, and deliberately free from direct political reference."[30] Both Forster's satire and the sharpness of his opposition
got their edge from the fact that he could not imagine the empire
ending anytime soon. Yet the time the novel took to write also
created its own illusion of permanence. Cutting out any trace of

contemporary reference made Forster's Raj seem incapable of change, and in consequence *A Passage to India* appears to float in time, unconnected to any sense of a continuously unfolding—indeed a rapidly changing—present, its characters' lives seemingly unaffected by Amritsar, Congress, Gandhi, legislative reform, or the growth of communal tensions.

So Forster's India is in a sense as eternal as Kipling's. Both of them take the empire and the sort of people who run it as immutable facts. Neither writer spent much time thinking about what made the Raj the way it was or about what its consequences were; neither had the sense of historical development and change necessary to chronicle what Naipaul calls "the growth of national or imperial consciousness." Because they could not see the Raj in all the complexity of its history, they simply chose the side that the imperatives of their historical moments demanded, the one standing firmly for and the other firmly against imperialism; and each therefore emphasizes just one of those "two great senses of public duty," one-half of the subject they share between them. And perhaps anything more would have been impossible. The tension between those duties was always, if latently, there. Yet insofar as the Raj's illusion of permanence kept any plans for a transfer of power several steps behind Indian demands for independence, that illusion both exacerbated the conflict and made it impossible to perceive. The great English novel about imperialism could not be written until after the empire was gone, and not merely for reasons of "plot," not merely because one needed to know the end of the story. For the synthesis in the dialectic that Kipling and Forster began also required a conceptual change, the change that in my introduction I took as defining the "postcolonial." It had to wait for a writer whose own historical position allowed him to assume that the Raj was a dead letter, who had neither to attack nor to defend it, and who could therefore show how those two great duties came fatally into conflict.

Scott's characters know that they are living within history, know that the British are coming "to the end of themselves as they were" (S, 3). Their rule may be artificially prolonged by the war against the Japanese, but Gandhi and Nehru have a

quarter century of work behind them, there have already been
provincial ministries headed by Indians, and the most sympathetic
of Scott's English characters understand that their long day has
waned. These Englishmen have begun to wonder about how the
empire has shaped both themselves and their nation: about the
way it gave them a scope for action quite at odds with the tight
little island to which they must return, about what it has created
and what it will leave behind. And they have begun to think as
well about the imperial endgame, to search for ways in which
to balance those two duties, to pull out and yet maintain order.
In an essay called "After Marabar," Scott argued that until
midcentury not only India but England too had been locked in
a conflict between "Turtonism and Fieldingism" (W, 163). Turton
is the district collector in Forster's novel, the schoolmaster
Fielding's emblematic conservative counterpart, and their names
point to a confrontation between the status quo of class and
country on the one hand and reform on the other. It was, Scott
wrote, the last time one could feel "the fire of absolute convictions
about the right direction to take" (W, 164). Yet in retrospect
he came to believe that such a conviction had been simplistic.
"Getting rid of India," Perron writes, "will cause us at home
no qualm of conscience because it will be like getting rid of
what is no longer reflected in our mirror of ourselves" (D, 105).
To the Fieldings at home, "Indian independence was something
that would automatically happen when the confrontation with
Turtonism in general was brought to a successful conclusion"—
after the election of the Labour government in 1945 changed
the face in the mirror (W, 164). But it didn't. For the attempt
to display what Perron describes as the "demonstrably English"
idea that it was Britain's duty to shuck its empire led to a hastily
prepared abdication of power shaped by "the indifference and
ignorance of the English at home" (D, 222). It was an abdication
in which "India itself, as itself" played no part whatsoever—no
part except that of victim in the enormous balls-up of the
demission of power, the communal massacres and continuing
legacies of Partition.

III

"They say," Scott wrote, that "two hundred thousand of them died by each others' hands" (W, 70). But he underestimates, and really the dead can never be calculated with any accuracy. The most reliable figure is around half a million, a slaughter prepared by the British but one from which they were themselves exempt and extraneous. Perron writes in *A Division of the Spoils* that he once asked his Aunt Charlotte—the book's embodiment of a liberal and cultivated English prosperity—who should bear the blame. "She said, 'But that is obvious. The people who attacked and killed each other.' " Her own conscience is easy, unburdened by any sense of responsibility. And yet Perron says that in fact both he and his aunt had voted for those deaths, in voting for a Labour government that viewed India "as an economic and administrative burden whose quick offloading was essential" (D, 222). For Scott, "the partition of India lay in the logic of *British* history," and the seeds of its communal massacres were planted not just by the Raj but by British liberalism as well.[31] The triumph of Fieldingism over Turtonism ensured the "victory of liberal humanism over dying paternal imperialism" (W, 69). But in doing so it also *and simultaneously* made India into the site for "the death and interment" (W, 70) of that same liberal humanism: the place in which those "absolute convictions" about the right thing to do came up against the inadequacy of liberalism's own good intentions, inadequacy in the form of Partition's countless dead.

Scott demands that we see history in moral terms—that we allow our consciences to pass judgment on the human costs of impersonal historical forces rather than merely shrugging our shoulders over their inevitability. "It seems to have become fashionable," he wrote in a review of Penderel Moon's *Divide and Quit* (1961), to regard those dead "as a gratifying alternative to the millions who might have died in the civil war that might have raged if we had resisted Pakistan or hung onto India a bit longer." But for him those bodies remained "a measure of our failure"; and one notes his double reliance on the conditional "might have." Not that the

British should not have quit India but that they should not have quit so quickly, not if Partition was the price of withdrawal. Yet though he insists that we cannot use an inexorable history as an excuse for injustice, Scott knows too that by 1947 nothing else could have happened. The illusion of permanence made it impossible to see what Scott describes as the "difference between principle and responsibility" until the conflict between them was full-blown.[32] Partition resulted less from the failure of a particular moment—the removal of Lord Wavell as viceroy, the breakdown of the Cripps Mission—than from the failure of an entire history. Communal tension provided the Raj with an excuse for delay—"comforting proof that the subject people were not yet ready for self-rule"[33]—and so the British in India "did more to assist division than . . . to encourage unity."[34] Those who demanded Indian independence "were unfortunately mostly to be found in England and from that distance the danger looked minimal."[35]

R. J. Moore has argued that Scott overstates the degree of ignorance on the part of the Labour Cabinet, if not on that of the electorate and Parliament at large. And Moore also suggests that Scott's emphasis on the English responsibility for the Partition massacres makes his explanation of Partition itself too radically Anglocentric. It is in effect a denial of agency to the independence movements and, in terms of English politics, a denial of the degree to which the moral force of those movements shaped the public opinion on which Labour relied. That does indeed lay him open to Rushdie's charges; and Scott himself has admitted that "one can hardly expect the generality of Indians"—still less of Pakistanis—to agree with his conclusions.[36] Nevertheless Moore's study of Scott's sources finds much to praise in his analysis of the "relation between the mechanics of empire and the tragedy of Partition."[37] Without any formal training, Scott made himself into what his biographer Hilary Spurling describes as a "formidably knowledgeable Imperial historian."[38] And indeed the *Quartet* found some of its first great admirers among professional students of empire, most notably Max Beloff, whose 1976 *Encounter* review argued that Scott's work offered an interpretive richness unmatched by any nonfictional account.[39] The list of historians from whom Scott learned—or whose work he anticipated—would be a long one. Let me merely note his portrayal of the princely state of Mirat, whose nawab remains always deferential to the British military power that tacitly maintains his rule—a portrait that could serve as a textbook example of John Gallagher's and Ronald Robinson's influential argument about the empire's reliance on the collaboration of local elites.[40]

Scott had a Balzacian delight in describing the rules that allowed the Raj to function as a social machine: the way etiquette turns into protocol in a world in which everyone has some kind of official status; the wheels and gears that run a club or a regimental mess; the confident assertions of colonial architecture, which can be disguised by planting roses and underlined by ripping them out. But his main concern is with the work that fills his characters' days. He took his colonial administrators seriously. Although the last defenders of the empire saw his depiction of its "brutality, complacency, self-righteousness and rigidity" as "anti-British," Spurling suggests that his portrayal of his characters' absorption in their jobs also offended many liberal critics who thought that Forster had had the last word and dismissed the Raj and its servants as either evil or absurd.[41] Scott believed that Forster had paid too little attention to the *work* of running an empire; his own characters are, in contrast, fascinated by it. His early novels *Johnny Sahib* (1952) and *The Mark of the Warrior* (1958) had concentrated on military logistics and training. The *Quartet* expands to include schools and hospitals as well as nearly all aspects of military life—from recruitment to intelligence to the charity work of the officers' wives—along with the administration of a district, a judicial inquiry, newspaper publishing, and above all the minutiae of political strategy. Scott learned a great deal about Partition from Moon's *Divide and Quit*. But he got even more from its account of the moment-by-moment choices Moon faced in 1947 as revenue minister in the princely state of Bawahalpur, choices echoed in the way Scott's characters find historical necessity developing from the contingencies of particular decisions.

Yet Scott's fascination with work as a subject was perhaps but the correlative of the dedication and sacrifice he brought to his own, and it makes one ask, simply, "Why India?" The subcontinent

in the last days of the Raj was, he said, "the metaphor I have pres-
ently chosen to illustrate my view of life"—yet why *this* metaphor?
As he worked on *The Jewel in the Crown* he suggested that Turtonism's defeat had made it hard "to write in a major way about Britain
today" (W, 44). It was a sentiment echoed by Anthony Burgess,
who in 1966 complained that England no longer offered "the subject matter of an expansive vision."[42] Graham Greene, Burgess later
noted, had had to set his novels abroad in order to find a "suitable
stage for the enactment of spiritual drama."[43] And Kennedy Fraser
has argued that India let Scott "get at truths about the British which
he could never have seen so clearly" in dealing with Britain itself.[44]
Writing about the end of the Raj allowed Scott to define both Britain's relegation to the historical margin of the late twentieth century and the concomitant emergence of those lands that were once
its margin, the cultures that produced Rushdie and Naipaul. Yet
that is a consequence, not a cause, and for Spurling, Scott's fascination with "the subcontinent was the first but by no means the last
. . . of the puzzles he set for a biographer."[45] He did see a great
deal of India as a young officer during World War II, but that
hardly seems a sufficient explanation, and neither do the historical
reasons I've just sketched. They simply explain why a major novel
could be written about the end of the Raj, not why Paul Scott might
write it. His concern with the way liberal humanism defeats itself
in the process of its own fulfillment comes a bit closer—and yet in
reading the *Quartet*, I have often had a sense of a puzzle I couldn't
solve, of a missing fragment that, if only I could find it, would make
the work seem all of a piece.

It is, to put it crudely, a question of the necessary connection
between a writer's subject and his sensibility. At times it simply
seemed that Scott had too many gifts: not only a historian's grand
vision, a Tolstoyan awareness of the world's indifference to individual human life, but also a sense of the deep unhappiness of private
experience, of the barriers that silence and pride can create even,
or especially, between people who love one another. Both gifts were
superb. But what was the connection between them: between his
meticulous chronicle of the workings of empire, on the one hand,
and his account, on the other, of the way Sarah Layton, learns in

The Day of the Scorpion to use sexual passion to free herself from the world of her parents? Perhaps this is an unfair question. It's not something one asks of writers who don't have a grand subject, of those whose work seems more entirely private or, conversely, of those whose political novels seem merely public in their implications. But with Scott we ask it just the same and are indeed compelled to do so by the *Quartet*'s frequent appeal to Emerson's essay on history, which posits a hidden identity between biography and history, between "the hours of our life and the centuries of time" (T, 68).

I have always suspected that the answer to these questions lay in the police officer Ronald Merrick, the only figure to play a significant role in all four volumes and the only major character whose point of view Scott never allows himself to enter. Coming from a lower-middle-class background rather like Scott's own, Merrick sees India as a chance to rise. To Sarah's sister Susan, "he isn't one of us" (S, 347), and yet their father, Colonel Layton, discounts that objection. India, he says, has "always been an opportunity for quite ordinary English people . . . to live and work like . . . a ruling class that few of us could really claim to belong to" (D, 370). And to Sarah, Merrick is indeed "one of us"—we catch the allusion to Conrad's Jim. For her Merrick is "our dark side, the arcane side. You reveal something that is sad about us, as if out here we had built a mansion without doors and windows, with no way in and no way out. All India lies on our doorstep and cannot enter to warm us or be warmed. We live in holes and crevices of the crumbling stone, no longer sheltered by the carapace of our history which is leaving us behind. And one day we shall lie exposed, in our tender skins. You, as well as us" (S, 398).

Merrick reveals the truths that the Raj can only rarely risk whispering to itself, even in the privacy of that "mansion without doors and windows." For Sarah that silence is a way to "hide our prejudices and continue to live with them" (S, 217). But Merrick finds silence impossible. Skin color "does matter" (J, 402), he tells Daphne Manners in *The Jewel in the Crown*. And later he tells Sarah much the same thing, adding: "I've said it all very badly. And I've broken one of the sacred rules. . . . One isn't supposed to talk about this kind of thing" (S, 217). But he hasn't said it badly, only baldly. He breaks the code because although he believes in the white man's right to rule, he doesn't accept the fictions with which the Raj cloaks the racism on which it depends: "Devotion. Sacrifice. Self-denial. A cause, an obligation. A code of conduct. . . . The whole impossible nonsensical dream" (S, 397). Merrick knows he doesn't have the same "background" as the imperial servants with whom he lives, and he knows, therefore, that both his privileges and theirs depend not on those enabling fictions of duty and devotion but, in Hutchins's words, "squarely on his membership in a dominant national group" (112).[46]

Yet as an intelligence officer in the Burma campaign, Merrick gets badly wounded in a display of the traditional heroism for which he expresses his contempt, and in *A Division of the Spoils*, Perron argues that Merrick has indeed bought all that "Kiplingesque double-talk" (D, 209). The character remains elusive, marked by the terrible ambiguities, the layers of love and hate, of delusion and desire, that characterize England's "imperial embrace." Francine Weinbaum has suggested that the *Quartet*'s overall vision is that of "thwarted union."[47] But what sort of union? The phrase gives me pause; it is too romantic, too Forsterian, though it does, admittedly, fit the part of Scott that wishes he could find in the Raj some redemptive "idea." Yet it also, and more importantly, fits not only the unhappiness of nearly all Scott's characters but also England's inability to achieve a real understanding of the land it ruled; the phrase is even appropriate for many Indians' attitude toward a culture they admired.[48] And perhaps it suggests something else. For in evoking that "mansion without doors and windows, with no way in and no way out," Sarah unwittingly points to more than the hidden truths of imperialism. She points as well toward the closet within which Merrick has buried his own homosexuality, the closet that will finally open in *A Division of the Spoils*.

Scott was drawn throughout his career to marginal figures, test cases for the operations of the societies he described: to Eurasians trying to pass for white in his early novels; in the *Quartet* to the Indian Englishman Hari Kumar or to the superfluous, discarded missionary Barbie Batchelor. The great achievement of Spurling's biography lies in her discovery of the roots of Scott's interest in the relation between marginality and power, in her providing the missing piece that makes it possible to see what was closeted in the *Quartet* all along. Her research confirmed that as a young man, Scott had himself had a homosexual period: he had been introduced to the world of art through an affair with an older man and had taken *The Picture of Dorian Gray* as the bright book of his own life. Soon after he joined the army in 1940, he got caught and was threatened with exposure. The details remain unclear; but in his fiction there appears again and again an account of what Spurling describes as "the punitive connection between an obsessive authoritarian officer and the youth he selects as his victim."[49] Yet exposure never came; and as if in relief Scott soon after married. Let me turn now to the central events of *The Jewel in the Crown:* to Daphne and Merrick and, in particular, to Merrick's own great victim, Hari Kumar.

IV

"His sharpest memories were of piles of leaves, wet and chill to the touch, as if in early morning after a late October frost. To Hari, England was sweet cold and crisp clean pungent scent." It was the only world he knew as a child, an English world of "park and pastureland," of leaded windows and "benevolent wisteria" (J, 227). But Hari's story starts with his father, Duleep, himself the son of a rich landlord in what is now Uttar Pradesh. Duleep believes in the "intellectual supcriority of the English" (J, 216) and yet remains deeply troubled by the way the "callowest white-skinned boy" can keep any Indian waiting on the veranda of his "sacred" little subdivisional officer's bungalow (J, 202). And Duleep has suffered as well the pain of finding that, in the core of his being, and for all his admiration of English ways, he still remains an Indian. Not because of that wait on the veranda; his humiliation is far more private than that. On the night of his arranged marriage—a marriage against which he fought—he suffered the shame of falling in love with his wife, of finding that he had become a "husband and householder," whose thoughts were all for the future of his "as yet non-existent family" (J, 216). Nevertheless he begs his father to let him study law in England; he leaves his wife behind, goes, studies, and comes back a failure. Yet both the ambition and the shame persist, and when his wife dies in childbirth he decides to go again to England and to take with him his infant son.

Duleep gives the child the name "Hari" because it works in English as well as Hindi; he Anglicizes his last name to "Coomer" and starts an improbably successful career in finance. And when Hari reaches the proper age, Duleep sends the boy to Chillingborough, a public school with a tradition of imperial service, intending that Hari will go on to university, sit the exams for the Indian Civil Service, and take his rightful place in that bungalow. Such an education will let Hari learn what Duleep himself has not discovered—the "secret of the Englishness of the English . . . [a] magical combination of knowledge, manner, and race" (J, 215, 203). It is a secret that for him lies above all in the "infinite" subtleties of the English language, a language Duleep knows he can never fully master. But his son can.

> There came a time when he was able to say . . . "It is not only that if *you* answer the phone a stranger on the other end would think he was speaking to an English boy of the upper classes. It is that you *are* that boy in your mind and behaviour. Conversely when I was your age, it was not only that I spoke English with an even stronger *babu* accent than I speak it now, but that everything I said, because everything I thought, was in conscious mimicry of the people who rule us. We did not necessarily admit this, but that is what was always in their minds when they listened to us. It amused them mostly. Sometimes it irritated them. It still does."
> (J, 205–6)

But there is no mimicry with Hari, for whom England has grown to be "home" and English his "own language" (J, 229). The father of his schoolfriend Colin Lindsey thinks that if "you close your eyes and listen, you can't tell the difference" between Hari and his own fair-skinned son. "And they seem to talk on exactly the same wavelength as well" (J, 227).

Yet when his father's bankruptcy and suicide leave him broke and alone before he has finished his schooling, Hari has nowhere to turn but to the Indian family he does not know. An uncle pays his passage "home," and he settles with his father's sister Shalini in Mayapore's Chillianwallah Bagh. At first he hopes that he'll be allowed to continue preparing for his exams, but his orthodox Hindu family has no use for that kind of education, and instead he's put to work as a clerk in his uncle's warehouse. He tries halfheartedly to learn Hindi, dreaming all the while of that other home; and the pages in which Scott describes the culture shock of Hari's "repugnance for everything the alien country offered" are among the most painfully affecting he ever wrote. Each bath—"a tap, a bucket, a copper scoop . . . a slimy runnel for taking the dirty water out"—seems to drain him "layer by layer of his Englishness, draining him too of . . . hope" (J, 228). Hari has always seen his own Englishness as a matter of class, of education, of a shared code of behavior that is not bound by and supersedes color; and so indeed it had seemed—in England. But in India, as the civil servant V. R. Gopal says in *The Day of the Scorpion*, he is "an English boy with a dark brown skin. The combination is hopeless" (S, 269).

Or perhaps it is impossible, at least conceptually so, at least for the English in India. Nirad C. Chaudhuri dedicated his *Autobiography of an Unknown Indian* (1951) to the memory of the Raj, "which conferred subjecthood on us but withheld citizenship; to which every one of us yet threw out the challenge: 'Civis Britannicus Sum.' "[50] For the Romans, citizenship had, in Hutchins's words, "been a legal status whose possession entitled any provincial, whatever his nationality, to certain privileges." But under the British, "regardless of promises contained in proclamations by the Queen," citizenship remained "firmly based on national exclusiveness."[51] Duleep believes that "for an *Indian* Indian there simply isn't any future in an *Anglo*-Indian world" (J, 215). Hence his decision to raise Hari as one of Macaulay's brown-skinned Englishmen: "Indian in blood and colour, but English in taste, in opinions, in morals, and in intellect."[52] Yet Duleep uses the word "Anglo-Indian" in a way that has never had any currency. Under the Raj, the term carried an interesting confusion of meanings. An Anglo-Indian could be an Englishman who had spent his career in India, and the phrase was most often used to describe such people in their English retirement to Cheltenham or Tunbridge Wells. But it could also be used for someone of mixed blood, like the Eurasians on whom John Masters concentrates in *Bhowani Junction* (1954) and who played as well a major role in Scott's own early work; people whom Scott saw as a colonial equivalent of the "tragic mulattoes" of African-American fiction. What the term could not mean—what British society has not even now permitted it to mean—is a British citizen of Indian ancestry. Duleep himself is merely Anglicized; he even asks people to call him David because Duleep is "such a mouthful" (J, 202).

But to be Anglicized, as Homi Bhabha has written, "is *emphatically* not to be English."[53] It is instead a reminder that one is "*almost the same but not quite . . . almost the same but not white.*"[54] Duleep knows that he has made himself into what Rushdie calls a *chamcha* and Naipaul a "mimic man"[55]—not simply one whose life is modeled in "conscious imitation of the people who rule" him but one who has in consequence become a mimic of a man, wholly dependent on English norms and so without standards or substance of his own, an imitation of what a man should be. Usually the Raj found such colonial mimicry profoundly reassuring; as Duleep says, "It amused them mostly." The mimic man wears the clothes of the man he mimics, he has the same manners and speaks the same language, but they are made different by that "little matter of the colour of the skin," a difference that stands, in effect if not intention, as what Bhabha calls a "disavowal" of the identity that the mimicry seeks to establish.[56] Duleep's *babu* accent only confirms what the Raj has already learned from his skin; and so the Other remains both recognizably and manageably other.

Yet Bhabha argues that such mimicry can also stand as a form of "menace."[57] For sometimes it becomes parodic. "What looks like Westernization," as the sociologist Ashis Nandy has written, "is often only a means of domesticating the West, sometimes by reducing it to the level of the comic and trivial," the level of cricket-club vocabulary and a taste for P. G. Wodehouse.[58] So it is with Sir Nello Chatterjee in *The Jewel in the Crown*, an expert mimic who imitates Daphne's uncle, the governor of a province—to the governor's delight and his aides' consternation. For Bhabha, as indeed for Rushdie, that type of mimicry festishizes the colonial culture in order to master it, performs an act of cultural appropriation that both reverses the geographic appropriation of colonialism and produces in turn a fear of counterdomination. Yet what about Hari? "Menace" is of course the furthest thing from his mind, and he cannot mimic his own Englishness in the way that Nandy describes; perhaps it would be better for him if he could. Instead he presents what Bhabha describes as a "classificatory confusion."[59] To the British in India his "so-called English ways" (J, 157) make him the worst kind of educated Indian, and one is tempted to say that's because he's not really an Indian at all—he only looks like one.[60]

When Merrick has him arrested at the Sanctuary, Hari's voice still, after three years in the Chillianwallah Bagh, has its clipped, public school note of command. It's not that he "does" it so perfectly but that, as Duleep says, he really is that boy in his mind; he sees himself as English, not Anglicized. The color of his skin disavows the voice; but then the voice disavows the skin. Which does one believe? For the Raj, either option seems unsettling. If Hari is indeed a mimic man, then the British must ask if perfect mimicry is mimicry at all. For mimicry is reassuring only when one can see its flaws and its exaggerations and thereby can tell the copy from the original; and perhaps the Raj sees in Hari a sign that its own day is over. And what if he is not a mimic? What if one believes the voice or, rather, finds no necessary contradiction between the voice and the face? That is even more dangerous, for it forces the white English to confront the nature and the basis of their own cultural identity.

Of course they resolve their dilemma; for there remains that "little matter of the colour of the skin." On his voyage out Hari finds that "once past Suez the English people who had spoken to him freely enough from Southampton onwards" begin to ignore him (J, 247). Yet in India he still at first feels that "he would only have to speak . . . to be recognized, to be admitted," and he still believes that his color doesn't matter as much as the common culture expressed by and through the "sahib inflections" of his voice (J, 240). But like Ralph Ellison's unnamed hero, he gradually realizes that he has "become invisible to white people" (J, 242). Or perhaps he is not invisible, not precisely. Mayapore is divided by a river, with the Indian city on one side and the British cantonment on the other. One day an errand takes him to the English side—"well-spaced bungalows . . . mid-morning hush"—and he decides to buy a bar of Pears' soap at a shop in whose window "there were brand goods so familiar, so Anglo-Saxon, he felt like shouting for joy. Or in despair. He could not tell which" (J, 237, 239). Because aside from his language, a taste for such things is all that seems to remain of his own "inner sense of being English" (S, 275); the Englishness of the brand names becomes a substitute for the place itself. But the shop assistants ignore him and wait instead on the memsahibs, whose taste is identical to his own. When he finally gets a clerk's attention he is asked who the soap is for, as if he's a servant, and is addressed in a Hindi he does not understand. In the end he does not buy the soap; it's sold only by the dozen, and he can't afford it.

He catches the eye of another customer, an Englishwoman. "Slowly she turned away with a smile he could only attach two words to: bitter, contemptuous" (J, 241). The Raj sees Hari all right: not as English but as someone trying to pass himself off as English. They can treat him as English in England, but in India it is easier to turn away, to reject him, than it is to face the challenge he presents. For to listen to Hari—to listen even with one's eyes open—is to suspect that one's own Englishness may be nothing more than an acquired characteristic, socially constructed and not essential. They say he's not English. What they mean is that he's not white. For under the Raj, whiteness remains the sine qua non of Englishness. Nothing can make up for its absence; and nothing can quite cancel it out, not even the crass vulgarity of a man who asks Hari if he is "straight down from the tree" (J, 246). But few members of the Raj are honest enough to admit to the racism on which their power depends. They insist instead on the inseparability of culture and color; their own identities are intrinsic, but Hari's is acquired.

For the "man of color" whom Frantz Fanon describes in *Black Skins, White Masks*, salvation lies in finding some way to turn white, most often through sex with a white woman.[61] But Hari doesn't think in racial terms. He doesn't want to be white; he wants to remain English and doesn't see that under the Raj the two amount to the same thing. The mistake lies in his identification of Englishness with the public school code, a code that, like the rules of cricket—which Hari plays superbly—can in fact be learned. Yet it's a code that the white English themselves have had to learn, a code that in India they observe through a set of elaborate rituals designed, like Hari's own pursuit of Pears' soap, "to prove to themselves they [are] still English." For in India, as he soon learns, "the English stop being unconsciously English and become consciously English" (S, 245). And in doing so, they paradoxically reveal the degree to which their own identities are fully as constructed as his own—and constructed in particularly narrow and rigid ways. "English people are not mass-produced," says the Hindu scholar Pandit Baba in *The Day of the Scorpion*. "They do not come off a factory line all looking, speaking, thinking, acting the same" (S, 108). But the empire makes them so, makes them a part of a "robot," of an administrative machine so powerful it can kill any emotion that conflicts "with what the robot was geared to feel" (J, 443). Forster's character Hamidullah says that he gives "any Englishman two years," but after that, in their dealings with Indians, "they all become exactly the same," their friendly edges worn off until they fit a standard of *pukka* uniformity.[62] "A sahib has got to act like a sahib," Orwell wrote in "Shooting an Elephant." A sahib must show the "natives" that he has the qualities the English are supposed to have, that he is masterful, confident, unmarked by doubt. "He wears a mask, and his face grows to fit it."[63] Orwell finds that he has to shoot his elephant, whether he wants to or not. It's what the "natives" expect an Englishman to do, and it's therefore what he must do to maintain his distinction from them, the distinction on which his power rests.

Forster writes that the members of the Raj enjoyed amateur theatricals in which they could "dress up as the middle-class English people they actually were," playing a role, performing themselves, performing their own Englishness.[64] Such moments suggest that the English "character" itself is, in Naipaul's words, but "a creation of fantasy"—a fantasy defined in opposition to the Other that Hari inevitably represents.[65] But the Other cannot be—cannot be allowed to be—the same as the self. Nandy argues that although an Indian can be Anglicized and yet remain within Indian society, an Englishman could not let himself become Indianized. "Going native" threatens the solidarity on which the robot of Englishness depends, and so someone like Hari cannot be admitted to exist: an Indianized—an Indian—Englishman. Without the money or the official standing that would allow him to pass as an Anglicized Indian on the British side of the river, "Hari's Englishness [means] nothing" (J, 375). Yet even though he comes to accept his own invisibility, it's harder to accept its corollary: "That his father had succeeded in making him nothing, nothing in the black town, nothing in the cantonment," nothing in a world where one must be Indian or English but cannot be both, where skin color is indeed basic (J, 242). "I had been unconsciously English too," he tells Nigel Rowan during a prison interview in *The Day of the Scorpion.* "But in India I could never become consciously English. Only consciously Indian. Conscious of being something I'd no idea how to be" (S, 245). He is the "loose end" of empire, caught in the empty space between the cultures of which he stands doubly dispossessed (J, 457)—the worst kind of educated Indian, not only for the English but for Indian nationalists as well.

We may argue that Hari could not possibly have been so naive, that even in an England that hadn't yet experienced the mass immigration of the postwar period, his father's money and an accent like that of a "managing director" would not have shielded him so completely from British racism (J, 244). We may argue as well that after pointing out the "classificatory confusion" that Hari represents, Scott does little to show how one might be both English and yet Indian too, that he poses the question of Hari's identity in terms that are too starkly absolute. Yet Scott does so deliberately, forcing the issue, forcing one to recognize that with Hari, the question is that of the nature of Englishness itself and not that of Anglicization or of some sort of cultural blend. *The Jewel in the Crown* stands as the first anti-essentialist account of national identity in modern British literature. By the time of its publication in 1966, England had already experienced the Notting Hill Riots, and Samuel Selvon and George Lamming had published novels about West Indian immigrants in London. Naipaul's *The Mimic Men* came out in 1967, and Enoch Powell's infamous "river of blood" speech followed in the next year.[66] But the questions Scott poses were not yet matters of public discussion and debate. England had what it thought of as an immigrant "problem." It did not yet fully realize that what it really had was a generation of native-born, nonwhite British citizens. In 1966, Kennedy Fraser has suggested, it was not yet possible "to write a truthful novel about racism in an English setting."[67] Yet Hari Kumar, in India, allowed Scott to undertake a prescient analysis of the relations between culture and identity, an analysis that pointed ahead to some of the central issues that face British society today and to the emergence in the 1980s of a generation of nonwhite British artists.

Most of what Scott tells us about Hari comes in a section of *The Jewel in the Crown* called "Young Kumar"; it ends with Sister Ludmilla's discovery of him lying drunk one night in a ditch. For several days he had seen soldiers wearing the badge of the regiment in which his schoolfriend Colin Lindsey is now a captain. On that day he had seen Colin himself and had not been recognized. And in the morning there follows the event that Scott had described from Sister Ludmilla's point of view 150 pages before: Hari's first meeting with and arrest by Ronald Merrick. Hari is released before midday, but by that time the news has filtered through Mayapore and reached Lili Chatterjee, the widow of Sir Nello, who used to mimic the colonial governor. Lady Chatterjee lives on the "English" side of the river and plays bridge with the deputy commissioner; her house is one of the few places in Mayapore where the two races can amicably meet. After hearing Hari's story, she decides to take an interest in him; she invites him to a cocktail party and introduces him to her English houseguest, the governor's niece, Daphne Manners.

Lady Chatterjee is one of the people visited by Scott's unnamed "stranger" in the 1960s while researching the Quit India riots; most of the *The Jewel in the Crown*'s second section, "The MacGregor House," takes the form of a monologue in her voice, in her "funny old tongue that is only properly at home in English" (J, 72). She gives the stranger two letters that Daphne wrote in 1942 to her aunt, Lady Manners, letters that we read without initially knowing why Scott has shown them to us; for we realize only gradually that Daphne was—that she will become—the running girl in the novel's opening image, the girl in the Bibighar Gardens affair. An awkward girl, large-boned and rather plain, she is clumsy enough to be always afraid of breaking things, embarrassed by the eyeglasses she needs to wear but often doesn't. With her parents dead, she has come out to join Lady Manners in India, and at first she finds things difficult. At her aunt's house in Rawalpindi she snatches a blouse away from the tailor because she "couldn't bear to see him holding it up, examining it, *touching it with his black fingers.*" In Mayapore she soon breaks her resolution not to go to the English-only club, for she craves the sense of comfort that she can find only in conversation with the people she meets there, "even if you disagreed with everything [they] said" (J, 105). She is in many ways an ordinary young woman of her class and period, and she knows that without her aunt, without Lili, without the kind of "open house" (J, 459) the two older women have always tried to keep, she would soon become just a "typical . . . roughshod-riding English mem" (J, 366)—ordinary except in her belief that her "longing for security and peace is wrong" (J, 106).

In those early letters we are told only that she has developed what Merrick describes as an "association with young Kumar" (J, 104). We have to wait until the end of *The Jewel in the Crown* to read the journal in which Daphne describes that "association" and the way it led to the Bibighar Gardens; Lili has held the journal back until she was sure of the stranger's sincerity. Hari and Daphne's first meeting, at Lili's cocktail party, is awkward, edgy, but she is nevertheless attracted by the hopelessness of this "English boy with a dark brown skin." And though he'll always remain afraid that he's being patronized, Hari is drawn to her as well: both to her Englishness and to her acceptance of his own. Yet if a river divides Mayapore into English and Indian sides, the relations between the races are defined by an invisible river as well, one that Sister Ludmilla says cannot be crossed by simply walking over a bridge. To cross it, you need instead to "enter the flood and let yourself be taken with it, lead where it may. This is a courage Miss Manners had . . . jump, jump in, and let the shock wake us up" (J, 142). Those words echo the famous passage in *Lord Jim* that describes life in terms of the "destructive element" to which we must "submit," in which we must learn to move and to live; and Conrad's passage provides a motif for the *Quartet* as a whole.[68] But Daphne herself switches the metaphor from water to land, evoking the "uncertain" ground that lies between the "enclosed little circles" of one race or another. The "important thing," she says, "is to keep [that] ground occupied" (J, 365).

In retrospect Daphne will realize that her friendship with Hari was impossible to maintain. They "could be enemies, or strangers . . . or lovers," she writes, but not friends, for under the Raj "such a friendship was put to the test too often to survive," as indeed was that of Fielding and Aziz in *A Passage to India* (J, 410). But she keeps the ground occupied for as long as she can; she plunges into the destructive element, pursuing Hari even when he wants to turn away. For Hari is now acutely conscious of that "little matter of the colour of the skin" in a way that makes him far more prickly than he'd be if he were not also English; and Daphne will come to understand the self-satisfaction of her own attitude toward "the personal and social barrier I thought my love had helped me to surmount" (J, 422). They quarrel and part, and when they see each other again it is on the dark rainy summer evening that ends the first day's riots. They meet, by chance, in the deserted Bibighar Gardens, in an open-air pavilion to which they've come in the past; it is one of the few places in Mayapore where they can be comfortably alone together. At first they argue, and then, as Daphne writes in her journal, "we were kissing . . . and then we were both

lost. . . . Entering me he made me cry out. And then it was us."
And as they lie there afterward they are attacked. Five or six men,
villagers who had come to Mayapore for the riots, "black shapes
in white cotton clothing; stinking, ragged clothing," were watching
from the shadows (J, 417). They bind Hari, they cover Daphne's
head with her sou'wester, and then, one by one, they rape her.

Rushdie argues that "if rape must be used as the metaphor
of the Indo-British connection, then surely, in the interests of accuracy, it should be the rape of an Indian woman by one or more
Englishmen of whatever class."[69] But his complaint ignores the way
in which Scott fuses two separate conventions for depicting sexual
relations between different races. The first is the rape of a white
woman, a convention—or rather a conventional fear—that was historically held to justify almost any kind of repression. It figures in
most of the Mutiny narratives, in stories of the American South,
and of course in *A Passage to India* as well.[70] But Scott also uses, and
reverses, the convention of the interracial love affair. In the literature of the Raj this had always been described in terms of the relation between a white man and an Indian woman; the best example
is Kipling's "Without Benefit of Clergy." Yet there is inevitably an
element of coercion in such relations—in Kipling's story, money
changes hands—a demonstration of mastery that replicates in min-
iature the structure of the Raj. But what about a white woman and
an Indian man? That, Daphne writes, remained "taboo," a violation
of the Raj's fundamental law (J, 421). For as Fanon suggests:
"When a white woman accepts a black man there is automatically
a romantic aspect. It is a giving, not a seizing." It is a sexual union
that challenges rather than confirms the power of the empire itself.[71]

Daphne's rapists are never caught. But Merrick has Hari and
some other young men from Mayapore arrested. What Scott does
in joining that "giving" to the rape is to suggest that the Indian
man in such a relation might indeed be charged with rape, that the
costs of imagining a willing violation of that taboo were too high
for the Raj to accept. But the effects of that unwritten law go far
beyond this individual case: as Daphne writes, its operations also
ensure that for an English woman in India, "ninety-nine percent

of the men she sees are not men at all, but creatures of an inferior species whose colour is their main distinguishing mark." And the country has in consequence been unsexed, transformed into a "nation of eunuchs" in which the relations between Indian and English men are mediated through the sexual unavailability of white women. Daphne's desire for Hari is therefore a kind of attempt to restore India's masculinity, a symbolic undoing of colonialism's damage. Yet Daphne suggests that the refusal to see Indian men as sexual beings also means that English women have had to unsex themselves. "Our faces reflect the sourness" (J, 411). Like the sahib's mask that Orwell describes, the Raj's code of behavior has become its own psychic prison, and so in making love with Hari, Daphne not only restores the gender of Indian men but also regains her own.

Yet Daphne's argument is but a piece of Scott's complex analysis of the sexual dynamics of imperialism. For Hari is also someone whom Merrick has "chosen . . . chosen . . . as a victim, having stood and watched him washing at the pump," chosen in a way that sexualizes that victimhood (J, 150). Early in *The Jewel in the Crown*, Merrick had pursued his quarry through a form of triangulated desire. After noting Daphne's interest in Hari, he turns his attention toward her and even asks her to marry him, so that he becomes the rival of both the English woman and the Indian man, the force that will come between and destroy them.[72] But the fullest account of that victimization comes during the judicial inquiry into Hari's detention in *The Day of the Scorpion*. There Hari describes how after being arrested on the night of the rape, he was stripped and, with his arms pinioned behind him, displayed for Merrick's gaze—"he just sat and smiled at me" (S, 280–81). Then Merrick beats him bloody in order to demonstrate what he calls "the situation": a ritualized performance of the contempt of the strong for the weak, the contempt on which imperialism depends (S, 281). During a pause in the beating, Hari says, Merrick "had his hand between my legs"; and later the policeman wipes blood across Hari's genitals (S, 291).

Any full account of the interrelation of race and gender has to consider the constantly shifting, the firmly drawn and yet perpet-

ually blurred lines of difference that characterize the boundaries
not only of racial identity but of sexual identity as well. Merrick's
actions are above all an expression of sexual contempt for a man
who, because he has been conquered, is no longer a man. Yet that
paradoxically makes him available as an object of desire, at one with
an India whom the conqueror conventionally sees in feminine
terms, a woman to be grasped in an "imperial embrace," both raped
and yet told she's loved. But are those terms indeed feminine? Suleri has noted the "homoerotic cast" of the colonial gaze, one that
sees India less as an inscrutable "Eastern bride" than as an "effeminate groom." The "sexual ambivalence" behind that image of "gen-
dered weakness"[73] does perhaps explain the peculiar combination
of fascination and horror with which the British saw their possession and explains too—in something more than biographical
terms—the reason why for Forster "the most urgent cross-cultural
invitations occur between male and male."[74] It's surely too easy to
read the famous ending of *A Passage to India* as a simple allegory for
the frustration of homosexual desire: the half-kiss, the affectionate
embrace, of Fielding and the "daintily put together" Aziz, who
know that despite their own wishes they cannot yet be friends.[75]
But it is also too easy to deny its importance or, rather, its centrality.
For in taking the form of a fascination with a racial Other who is
somehow also the same, that homoeroticism is inevitably linked to
the central trope of all colonial encounters—the attempt to find
the words with which to know and to describe the seemingly alien
and strange.[76]

We see that language in Kipling, most obviously in "The
Ballad of East and West," where "two strong men stand face to
face," recognizing each other's manliness in an acknowledgment
that discounts the cultural difference between them; an acknowledgment that nevertheless requires Kamal, the border thief, to submit his son to English rule.[77] Yet that recognition of manliness also
depends on the absence of women; and in this it resembles the com-
panionship between white and nonwhite men that Leslie Fiedler
long ago argued was characteristic of classic American literature—
Huck and Jim, Ishmael and Queequeg.[78] It is an ideal of comradeship in a world without women and hence without the possibility

of miscegenation. Two strong men can stand face to face precisely because there is neither the chance nor the danger of racial mixing, because the binary distinction between them will remain clear even as it is in some sense erased. Such relations take place on what Eve Kosofsky Sedgwick calls the continuum of male "homosocial" relations: a continuum that in Anglo-American society is "radically disrupted" by a homophobia that insists on distinguishing "sexual" from "non-sexual" bonds between men.[79] Yet the very force of that disruption suggests that the borders of identity are in fact never absolute. So too does the existence of Hari Kumar.

In *The Day of the Scorpion* Merrick tells Sarah Layton that the intersection of racial and sexual dominance makes it possible for a white man to have an Indian woman but not for a white woman to take an Indian man. Race does matter, he insists. Then he apologizes: "One isn't supposed to talk about this kind of thing" (S, 217). But Suleri suggests that in Forster, the visibility of the racial body becomes "synonymous with the invisibility of sexual preference," and Merrick could easily be talking about something more.[80] For his statement that "one isn't supposed to talk" about race, in a society where at times it seems that people do little else, has the effect of equating race with sexual preference; both of them stand as closeted truths, something everyone knows about but about which they've agreed they dare not speak, whose existence they cannot afford to acknowledge. And in remembering this conversation, Sarah will later come to her understanding of Merrick as the Raj's "dark side," the side that has in India built a "mansion without doors and windows." Both Merrick and Hari have transgressive identities. The homosexual and the Indian Englishman are both "almost the same but not quite" what they appear on the surface to be, are somehow between the categories into which people are conventionally supposed to fall. They are rivals. But they are also doubles, drawn together by the consonance between their transgressions, by what Sister Ludmilla sees as the darkness in each of them, "a different darkness, but still a darkness" (J, 150). Or as Hari himself describes it, with an understatement that is perhaps the only part of his Englishness left after two years in prison, "We came to have a special personal association" (S, 257).

We learn the details of that relationship in two places: first, through the deposition of a character named Vidyasagar in *The Jewel in the Crown*, one of those men arrested with Hari; and second, from Hari's own point of view, in answer to Nigel Rowan's questions during that inquiry in *The Day of the Scorpion*. Hari is brought before Merrick, a situation that Merrick had long anticipated. But their "being face to face" (S, 281) is a world away from Kipling, for Hari's hands are first held and then manacled behind his back in a literal enactment of the "situation" between them. And then Merrick tells him, as Hari in turn reports to Rowan, that it wasn't enough

> to say he was English and I was Indian, that he was a ruler and I was one of the ruled. We had to find out what that meant. He said people talked of an ideal relationship between his kind and my kind. They called it comradeship. But they never said anything about the contempt on his side and the fear on mine that was basic, and came before any comradely feeling. . . . He said the true corruption of the English is their pretence that they have no contempt for us, and our real degradation is our pretence of equality. He said if we could understand the truth there might be a chance for us. There might be some sense then in talking about his kind's obligation to my kind. (S, 298)

Comradeship is but a myth that masks contempt. Yet Merrick says that even those English people who know that's what they feel will pretend that they don't, will try instead to fit themselves into "the great liberal Christian display," if only through praise for the soldiers and servants whose "bravery and loyalty" is a mark of their inferior status. But at bottom, Merrick argues, even the white liberals "who pretended to admire Indian intellectuals" are as contemptuous of that "black reflection of their own white ideals" as the "arrogant upper-class reactionary" is of "the fellow who blacks his boots" (S, 299).

That shrewd and wicked clarity makes Merrick's analysis of imperialism as damning as anything in the literature of resistance;

or it would if he didn't use it to justify his own power. But Merrick isn't content to talk; and there follows the second and more "persuasive" (S, 286) part of Hari's "degradation" (S, 298). Merrick has the still-naked Hari bent over and strapped to a trestle so that his position is like that which boys assume when they are caned at English public schools, bending over and grabbing their ankles. And Merrick beats him until Hari comes close to losing consciousness. "It's difficult to breathe in that position," Hari says. "It's all you think about in the end" (S, 289). It is as if Merrick has briefly become the head prefect of the Raj or, perhaps, of the sort of school that Hari went to but that Merrick didn't. And indeed the public schools were forcing grounds for both authoritarian rule and certain models of homosexual behavior: places in which young boys were first subjugated by those in their late teens, were often beaten and sexually exploited, and then grew to exercise those privileges themselves; places in which there was tacit approval for a homoerotic sadism that went under the name of building "character." For Hari's position exposes him to something other than Merrick's cane, and Scott suggests that this enactment of the "situation" is also a symbolic anal rape.

In *The Day of the Scorpion* Hari tells us that the prison doctor examined both his "anal passage" and the welts across his rear (S, 289). But the crucial evidence is in Vidyasagar's deposition, which records Merrick's surprise that none of the young men he's arrested have blood on their underwear or genitals—"She wasn't a virgin, was she?" (J, 355). She didn't bleed—but Hari does. Immediately after noting the absence of Daphne's blood, Vidyasagar reports that Hari has blood on his buttocks. That blood does indeed come from his beating, but the coincidence of its presence with the absence of Daphne's blood nevertheless suggests we should see this interrogation as if it were the rape of a virgin.[81] It is an act of colonial buggery, in which Merrick's contempt for the Indian male forces Hari into the passive, the subordinate, position. It doesn't unsex him in the way that Daphne describes so much as it leaves him ineffectual, no more than a boy—not a woman but like one, for by the standards of many traditional societies with open homoerotic traditions it is manly to be the "doer," shaming to be the "done." Merrick's action underlines Hari's conquered state, a physical humiliation whose pain must make him literally aware of that "little matter of the colour of the skin," reminding him that he is indeed an Indian. But it also signals the policeman's class-bound resentment and rejection of the sort of Englishman that Hari's education has made him; or as Merrick himself says, "What price Chillingborough now?" (S, 304). And it is moreover a way in which he can deny his own homosexuality by stripping it of the connotations it has in England, through a punishing assertion of mastery and power that allies his sexuality with the soldier-citizens of ancient Greece or the Pathan tribes of the Afghan hills.[82]

Suleri has argued that a metaphor that sees colonialism in terms of rape is now sterile, a "subterfuge to avoid the strikingly symbolic homoeroticism of Anglo-Indian narrative."[83] But Scott's use of that metaphor seems far less tired than the heterosexual versions she has in mind and far more complicated and historically resonant than Rushdie's criticism of it would allow as well. For although Scott suggests that the Raj depends on the sexual contempt it feels for a defeated nation, that nation, however passive and "effeminate," here remains masculine. It therefore retains the power, as in 1857, to become the "doer" in return and so must be perpetually and continuously subdued. What Merrick wants, Hari says, is "a confession of my dependence on him, my inferiority to him" (S, 298); he wants, in effect, to be reassured that Britain remains the dominant partner. After the beating, Merrick bathes Hari's wounds and then, in a brutal yet oddly moving travesty of a pietà, holds Hari's "head up by the hair" and tips some water into his mouth. "He told me I must say thank you, because he knew that if I were honest I'd admit I was grateful for the water. . . . After a bit I heard myself say it" (S, 300–301). But that drink makes Hari understand how much Merrick needs him. The torturer depends on his victim and not vice versa; he needs his victim's cooperation in easing the pain that he has himself inflicted. "The situation," Hari realizes, "only existed on Merrick's terms if we both took part in it" (S, 303). And so he decides to detach himself from it, to refuse to answer Merrick's questions. "They have the power of description," says a tiger-headed character in Rushdie's *The Satanic Verses*, "and we succumb to the pictures they construct."[84] What Hari does is to begin to take back the power of description—to refuse to see himself in the terms that the master proposes. It marks an end to his colonial complicity in his own degradation, a moment in which he begins the process of decolonizing his own mind.

He will not be entirely successful; will remain always a loose end of both the empire and Scott's narrative. But the scene over the trestle has another complication. During a part of his interrogation, as Hari reports, Merrick said: "Aren't you enjoying it? Surely a randy fellow like you can do better than this?" And Hari adds that Merrick had "his hand between my legs at the time" (S, 290–91). Scott doesn't describe Merrick's physical position when he does this, but since he's been beating Hari, it seems likely that they're no longer face to face, that Merrick is instead reaching around from behind Hari, their bodies close—not simply as if he were raping Hari but as if they had become one, doubles, as if he were grasping himself. When Merrick later daubs Hari's genitals with Hari's own blood, the action seems both to mark him for Merrick's own and to imply that Hari has done this to himself. And in a peculiarly symbolic way perhaps he has. For he is buggered above all by his own Englishness, the Englishness that has made Merrick choose him; and if the two men are indeed doubles, then in buggering India, the British have also buggered themselves. Maybe that is why the sahib's upper lip seems so stiff, why his teeth are so tightly clenched.

In her *Epistemology of the Closet* Sedgwick suggests that her subject has both an affinity to and provides a metaphor for "wider mappings of secrecy and disclosure," that it takes the form of a sexual disinformation that parallels the undercover work of secret agents.[85] Both the closeted homosexual and the spy must try to "pass," in a way that makes each a type of mimic man; and of course the Raj too required the wearing of masks, required that one hide the truth about the self and its motivations behind a rigid code of behavior. Sedgwick asks us to imagine a closeted legal official charged with crafting a homophobic decision, one who hides his own marginality in order to identify himself with power and yet who also uses his special knowledge as a tool of enforcement. So it is with Merrick, who has so deeply repressed his own homosexuality that it can emerge only as a sadism sanctioned by his official position, not only with Hari but also with a Corporal Pinker in *A Division of the Spoils*. Merrick has Pinker seduced by an Indian boy precisely so that he can blackmail the corporal, exchanging silence for access to a set of confidential files. But secrecy is never absolute. The *Quartet*'s other homosexual characters sniff out what the policeman has hidden, and Count Bronowsky even provides an account of Merrick's particular pathology, marked by a "connexion between the homosexuality, the sado-masochism, the sense of social inferiority and the grinding defensive belief in his racial superiority" (D, 571). And Merrick himself tears open the door of other secrets. He may enjoy the privileges of being white in India. Nevertheless his knowledge of his own marginality both separates him from and reveals the lie behind the official beliefs of his race; in this, he is a match for that other villainous homosexual policeman, Balzac's great character Vautrin.

Merrick's actions with Hari go no further than I've described, but late in the novel the policeman will start to dress in Pathan clothing for a series of liaisons with Indian boys. It is as if he can step from the closet only by first becoming the racial Other; and insofar as his whiteness makes him a sahib, this seems to replicate the familiar pattern in which upper-class English homosexuals most easily found satisfaction with working-class men and boys. But those boys are the bait for a trap—part of a plan, in which Hari plays no part, to punish Merrick for his role in the Bibighar Gardens affair, a plan that will lead to his death. The closet crumbles, until he lies quite literally "exposed," strangled and hacked to death in his bedroom, no longer sheltered in that "mansion without doors or windows" in which one tries to hide the truth and to hide from it too; whether that truth be one of private desire or of the very foundations of British rule.

V

Yet what exactly is that truth? For Merrick the ideals of imperial service and comradeship are but the fictions with which the Raj cloaks a "situation" of contempt on the one hand and degradation on the other, a mask that hides a fundamental belief in white superiority. But that too is a mask, a justification for the more basic truth that, as Marlow says in *Heart of Darkness*, a colonial "administration [is] merely a squeeze . . . robbery with violence, aggravated murder on a great scale."[86] And perhaps there is even a closet within that closet, a truth that imperialism dare not breathe, not if it hopes to maintain its belief in itself. Within that deeper closet we find what Marlow realizes in watching the villagers dance on the shore as he journeys up that great river: the suspicion he entertains—however reluctantly admitted, however racist its formulation—"of their not being inhuman."[87] They are the same as you, as me, only different; but that above all is what we can't admit, not if the robbery is to proceed in good conscience. Nothing attests to that essential kinship more than the facts of sexual desire—and perhaps, for a male writer, a desire not for a feminine Other but for an Other who is also the same. But administration must go on; desire must be denied. Merrick scorns the official truth of empire, the idea of comradeship. Yet it is perhaps closer to that final closeted truth than one would have expected. Only it is vitiated by the several layers of falsehood that lie interposed between, like someone pretending to be gay in order to hide the fact that he really is.

Merrick's relation to Hari can be seen in terms of what Sedgwick calls the "paranoid Gothic," in which a male character is "persecuted by . . . transparent to and often under the compulsion of another male."[88] Her examples include such classics of the Gothic as *Frankenstein* and *Caleb Williams*, and she sees in that persecution the "rejection by recasting" of homoerotic desire.[89] Accepting that desire as desire would for Merrick have required "discarding every belief he had" (D, 571); rejecting it allows him to transform it into a conviction of Hari's guilt, a conviction that gives him the license to pursue an Indian man. Yet Merrick also describes himself as a kind of victim, in a way that confirms his status as Hari's double, as having been singled out, haunted, by those he has condemned. They stick to him, he says, even though he feels his conscience is clear. Reminders of Bibighar follow him as he moves from job to job around India: chalk marks appear on his doorstep;

stones are thrown; a woman in a widow's white sari falls at his feet
on a railway platform, begging for mercy. The persecutor is persecuted in turn. At the end he even seems to welcome being caught
in his own lies, in a trap almost identical to the one he had earlier
baited for Corporal Pinker.

It is as if he has turned "the situation" on himself. And perhaps one can say that what Merrick does with Hari is to transform
a situation he knows from another context into a means of imperial
control. For the fear and contempt of which he speaks characterize the closet as much as they do the Raj—the fear of exposure and
the contempt not only of the straight for the homosexual but of
the closeted homosexual for himself as well. That is the sadness
Merrick finally reveals—not his sexuality but its repression. And
that makes it tempting to read the *Quartet*'s paranoid Gothic in
terms of Scott's own biography. I have already quoted Spurling's
judgment that as a young man, Scott had suffered from "the punitive connection between an obsessive authoritarian officer and the
youth he selects as his victim." Scott had his own version of Pinker's
experience, and that victimization by his own double scared him
into the closet and led him to sever all ties with his earlier self. He
was Hari, the victim of another man's desire. But he was Merrick
too, the man who rejected his own desire, who turned in horror
from a part of himself. His mind became a closet whose foundations
were laid on seventy cigarettes and a bottle a day, a mansion without
doors and windows, a structure that was in the end less a form of
sexual denial than of emotional isolation. A daughter's suicide attempts, his wife's increasing misery—nothing brought him out. It
was a world of silence, work, and gin, punctuated only by blackouts
and rage. One night he slashed the throat of his own portrait, in
an imitation of his beloved *Dorian Gray*, imposing on it—on himself—a fate not all that different from the policeman's own.

It's no surprise, then, that in writing *The Raj Quartet*, Scott
could not bring himself to face the challenge of opening the door on
Merrick's consciousness. Within the work itself these issues seem so
elliptically posed as to leave many crucial questions unanswered. If
the Raj was the metaphor Scott chose to illustrate his view of life,
then what about the metaphors he chose to illustrate his view of

the Raj? It's clear that the Forsterian rhetoric of friendship, union, and frustration on which Scott drew owes something to his sexuality; it is clear too that he saw the Raj and the closet as parallel structures. But how far would Scott be willing to extend that metaphor? Would he share the opinion of those recent critics who have seen homoerotic desire as fundamental both to imperialism and to any understanding of it?[90] Or is it for him merely contingent, a matter of particular characters and issues, of what he calls the interpretative "sieve" he has chosen to use? Scott's reticence ensures that such issues remain, not implicit so much as unassessed, a question left to ponder at the end of what stands as the greatest work of fiction the British produced about their empire.

I come back to the most thwarted of all the *Quartet*'s unions, that of Daphne and Hari. Daphne writes in her journal that though she looks for "similes" to explain or clarify their predicament, she cannot find any that seem adequate. "It is itself; an Indian carrying an English girl he has made love to and been forced to watch being assaulted—carrying her back to where she would be safe. It is its own simile." But it is not a simile, an image, that can be seen in isolation, this moment in which Hari begins to carry Daphne toward what will be safety for her but not for him. For as with the sight of Miss Crane holding Mr. Chaudhuri's dead hand, in order to understand that image one must first know all the forces of history and human character that have conspired to produce it, all the "events that led up to it and followed it and . . . the place in which it happened." To comprehend it fully is to understand the impossibility of the Raj's seeing that image for what it is, not "unless you blanch Hari's skin" (J, 421). There are no similes; nevertheless, that image echoes throughout the great house of *The Raj Quartet*. It echoes in the horseback ride that Sarah Layton and Ahmed Kasim take over a broken landscape in *The Day of the Scorpion*, a ride that recalls both Fielding and Aziz's gallop at the end of *A Passage to India* and Daphne's sense of the necessity of occupying that treacherous "ground between." It echoes in Merrick's warning Sarah about Ahmed as he had warned Daphne about Hari; and in the friendship that nonetheless grows between them in the two years between the end of war and the start of Independence, loving one another without the need to become lovers. And that image echoes too in the way that after Sarah and Guy Perron have made love for the first time in *A Division of the Spoils,* a trick of the light makes his hand seem brown; he had just read Rowan's transcript of the prison interview with Hari. And there is another echo, not of Daphne but of Miss Crane. For the novel ends with the Partition massacres and a second dead Indian in the road. A knock on the door of a railway compartment; Ahmed answers and steps out into the corridor. "Be ready to re-lock the door," he says, and then another face appears in the doorway and apologizes to the compartment full of English people for having disturbed them (D, 582). "We just let him go" (D, 607), Sarah says; they stood by, passive, and let the murder happen.

And now I see that I've said little about such echoes, drawing on the last three volumes of the *Quartet* only to define Scott's sense of history and to carry Hari's story forward, but for no more. I have said nothing about Scott's mastery of spoken Indian English; or about the retired missionary Barbie Batchelor, the main figure in *The Towers of Silence;* or about the way Scott presents the political maneuvers of the days just before Independence by describing a series of newspaper cartoons; or about the hospital in Calcutta or the Bombay high-rise or the red sandstone fort at Premanagar. I have mentioned none of that—and instead I return to the girl running in the shadows of the Bibighar Garden.

I always cry: because she doesn't pity herself, and so in reading her journal, I have to do it for her; because she has the self-knowledge to see how close she's come to being a memsahib and the honesty to recognize that color is indeed basic, basic to her love for Hari; because of the questions that always underlie "the moral continuum of human affairs." What if Hari had never seen Colin Lindsey and so hadn't gotten drunk and gone to the Sanctuary and gotten arrested? What if Hari and Daphne hadn't had their quarrel? What if the Indian National Congress hadn't passed the Quit India Resolution, what if the British hadn't then locked up the Congress leaders, what if the riots hadn't happened? Scott's sense of contingency always makes his readers ask "What if history were different?"—different not only for Daphne and Hari but also for India,

England, and the Pakistan that didn't yet exist. But it's not. We know, from the first page of the journal with which Scott concludes *The Jewel in the Crown*, that Daphne is going to die in childbirth; somehow she knows this too, and nothing can be done to save her. Her daughter will be named Parvati and will grow up with Lili Chatterjee in Mayapore. And Hari? In 1947 he earns his living by giving English lessons in the provincial capital. Nothing more was ever heard of him.

2

V. S. Naipaul: In His Father's House

I

At first the tramp seems whole. Standing on the quay, ready to board the "dingy little Greek steamer" (F, 7) for the two-day voyage to Alexandria, he doesn't even "look like a tramp,"[1] resembling instead, with his rucksack and polka-dotted neckerchief, a "romantic wanderer of an earlier generation." But as he approaches, one sees that his clothes are "in ruin," his trousers stained, his jacket held together by safety pins—one sees that he is a tramp. And old, with a "worn face and wet blue eyes" (F, 8), a face "worked over by distress" (F, 11). Once on board, he talks continuously, his speech "full of dates, places and numbers" (F, 9): the visit to Canada in 1923, to New Zealand in 1934. But he isn't "looking for conversation," only for "the camouflage and protection of company . . . [he] knew he was odd" (F, 10). When he opens a magazine, he doesn't read but instead shreds its pages, his "nervous jigging hands" (F, 13) covering the floor around him with litter.

"The Tramp at Piraeus" forms the prologue to V. S. Naipaul's 1971 collection *In a Free State*, a travel sketch whose nameless narrator can be taken as a critical portrait of the author himself. The steamer is "overcrowded, like a refugee ship . . . there wasn't enough room for everybody." And many of the passengers have indeed been refugees: the "humped figures in Mediterranean black" who fill the lower deck, Egyptian Greeks expelled after Suez and now allowed back for a brief visit only. For the British "invaders" have left (F, 7). Egypt now is free. And the Greeks, as Naipaul writes in a phrase whose layered ironies echo throughout the book, have become the "casualties of that freedom" (F, 8). On the upper decks, where the tramp is unaccountably lodged, the passengers group themselves by nationality. The Arabs and the Germans sit together in the "non-American" (F, 12) part of the smoking room; the Lebanese businessmen talk money. The tramp is—or was— English, but what, he asks, is "nationality these days? I myself, I think of myself as a citizen of the world" (F, 9). Yet that's precisely why his shipmates make him the victim of a cruel practical joke— because he is without the protection of a group. And the narrator? Though he writes in English, he says that before the tramp appeared, "we had no English people on board" (F, 8); his own nationality, alone of all the passengers, remains unstated. When the others begin to torment the tramp, he does nothing: "I feared to be involved with him" (F, 12). But why?

Naipaul follows this prologue with a story called "One Out of Many," the first-person narrative of Santosh, an Indian immigrant in the United States, who one day encounters a group of Hare Krishnas chanting in a park. At first he's excited by their "praise of Lord Krishna," by this reminder of home. Then he notices their "half-caste appearance" and turns away, full of the "distaste" that he says "we feel when we are faced with something that should be kin but turns out not to be," something that is instead "degraded . . . deformed . . . like a leper, who from a distance looks whole" (F, 30). Yet by the end of the story, after having "decided to be free," he sees himself in precisely this way—no longer the "brother" (F, 57) of the people around him, no longer at home, as he had been when he slept on the streets of Bombay. Does the narrator of "The Tramp at Piraeus" fear something like that? Would intervening establish some kind of identity between the tramp's tattered life and the narrator's own? For they have both chosen to live without a home, to live in a free state—free not in political terms but in the sense that comes from chemistry: those odd and uncommon atoms that aren't bound in molecules; those elements that usually form part of a compound yet that may for some reason be found by themselves, in isolation.

But the characters of *In a Free State* are far from the only ones in Naipaul's work who have had their wholeness broken by the absence of a home. Bharati Mukherjee has suggested that his "writing is about unhousing and remaining unhoused," about people who are at once free and yet also "cut off from a supporting world."[2] Her observation is to some degree belied by Naipaul's account, in *The Enigma of Arrival* (1987), of his life in a Wiltshire cottage—of how he came to feel at home at last in the deep country of Stonehenge and Salisbury, of how he made a place for himself in both England and its literature. Yet even that great, peculiar, autumnal book depends on an earlier unhousing, on the decision to leave the Trinidad of which he writes with such affection in his most recent autobiographical work, *A Way in the World* (1994);[3] and so Mukherjee's statement stands, an account of the way in which the relation between home and homelessness provides the central metaphor of all Naipaul's work. *The Mimic Men*'s (1967) narrator, Ralph Singh, makes a fortune in real estate but still views his own life as a "shipwreck" (MM, 7) connected to his estrangement from the "landscapes hymned by [his] ancestors" (MM, 32): his family's transplantation, like Naipaul's own, from Hindu India to the sugar plantations of the Caribbean. Salim in *A Bend in the River* (1979) never sees his apartment as home, never even removes the stacks of bad paintings the previous owner has left behind her; he keeps it as he found it, however inconvenient, as a permanent reminder that he has not made himself a place in the world and has therefore, as the novel's first sentence puts it, allowed himself "to become nothing" (R, 3). Yet the homelessness of such characters is primarily a psychic and not a physical condition. For the title figure of *A House for Mr. Biswas* (1961), Naipaul's richest evocation of "unhousing," that shattering absence of home can be taken more literally.

It is an absence that grows not from the tramp's crippling excess of freedom but from what seems at first its opposite, from a dependency that Mohun Biswas cannot escape. Halfway through that long novel he is made into the overseer of a sugar estate called Green Vale. The land belongs to his wife's family, the Tulsis, for whom he's worked since his marriage; they've already given up try-

ing to make him into a shopkeeper and frankly see the new job as
a way to keep a quarrelsome son-in-law out of the house. He moves
into the barracks with the cane cutters, who distrust him; it's a part
of Trinidad in which murder seems routine, and he soon starts to
sleep with a cutlass by his bed. In that world of failure, isolation,
and fear, Mr. Biswas finds that "his mind had become quite separate
from the rest of himself" (B, 266), and he begins to imagine that
a black cloud is funneling its way into his head. One morning he
says to his dog: "You are an animal and think that because I have
a head and hands and look as I did yesterday I am a man. I am
deceiving you. I am not whole" (B, 268). Not to be whole is not
to be a man. It is to be less than fully adult. And indeed manhood in
that sense remains something that Mr. Biswas has failed to achieve.

He has failed, that is, in his *dharma*, his duty, as a Hindu
man; for according to the doctrine of *ashrama*, of life's division into
four stages, after his student days he should have established himself
as a householder. Instead he has accepted a place in his wife's childhood home. For Mr. Biswas—and the novel calls him that even as
a baby, an acknowledgment, at once absurd and profoundly moving,
of the dignity his world denies him—Mr. Biswas is an orphan. His
father's early death has forced him to rely on relatives, and though
in consequence he's learned to read and to write (unlike his older
brothers, already "broken" into estate work), it has also cost him
"the only house to which he had some right" (B, 40) and made all
subsequent dwellings seem a "temporary arrangement" (B, 48) at
best. He does try to build his own house, both at Green Vale and
later at a country plantation called Shorthills. But in each case the
land is owned by the Tulsis; his attempts merely serve to underline
his dependence on them, and it's not surprising that both efforts
fail. Only near the end of his life can he finally stand on his own,
and on his deathbed, in the house that he has, after a lifetime of
trying, acquired at last, Mr. Biswas reflects on the indignity of the
fate he's narrowly missed, on how "terrible it would have been . . .
to have lived without even attempting to lay claim to one's portion
of the earth; to have lived and died as one had been born, unneces-
sary and unaccommodated" (B, 13–14). His words echo those of
Lear on the heath, the mad king's cry that "unaccommodated man"

is but a "poor, bare, forked creature."[4] And indeed the climax of
Mr. Biswas's stay at Green Vale has some of *Lear*'s grandeur: the
wretched father muttering on the bed in his half-built house while
his son, Anand, screams beside him, caught in a world of thunder
and lashing rain and a lightning that "lit up the room and the world
outside, and when [it] went out the room was part of the black void"
(B, 292).

At Green Vale Mr. Biswas meets the future from which he
always flinched, the sense of "blankness" into which he has seemed
always to be falling. It is a fear that the self will be so shredded and
torn as to fade into nonentity, a fear in which the fate of the self
becomes inseparable from that of the house, the home, which
should ideally shelter it; for to create the one is to achieve the other.
But that fear had earlier taken a more precise form, in the "sense
of utter desolation" summed up by a particular memory:

> Once, years before, he was conducting one of Ajodha's mo-
> torbuses that ran its erratic course to remote and unsus-
> pected villages. It was late afternoon and they were racing
> back along the ill-made country road. Their lights were
> weak and they were racing the sun. The sun fell; and in the
> short dusk they passed a lonely hut set in a clearing far back
> from the road. Smoke came from under the ragged thatched
> eaves: the evening meal was being prepared. And, in the
> gloom, a boy was leaning against the hut, his hands behind
> him, staring at the road. He wore a vest and nothing more.
> The vest glowed white. In an instant the bus went by, noisy
> in the dark, through bush and level sugar-cane fields. Mr.
> Biswas could not remember where the hut stood, but the
> picture remained: a boy leaning against an earth house that
> had no reason for being there, under the dark falling sky, a
> boy who didn't know where the road, and that bus, went.
> (B, 190)

"The vest glowed white." In reading, one flashes past that sentence
in an instant, like the bus, but in one's mind the four lonely words
remain—ghostly, limpid, and bleak. For the commas of this

prose—"And, in the gloom, a boy . . ."—slow its pace, etching one's mind with its details; and with its last word, isolated by a comma of its own, the paragraph fades into the distance, evanescent but unforgettable. It is an image that stands for Mr. Biswas as an emblem of colonial futility: the hut on the edge of the "bush," cut off, with no awareness of or connection to a larger world outside—lost, forgotten, with "no reason for being there."

No reason? Or rather reasons too many, reasons too bitter for the mind to accept. Naipaul modeled the title character on his father, Seepersad, whose own father had come to Trinidad from India in the 1880s, part of the experiment in human engineering that had brought half a million East Indians to the Caribbean as indentured laborers in the decades after the British abolition of slavery. Seepersad Naipaul trained briefly as a pundit, married into a large and prosperous Brahmin family, floundered, and eventually discovered a vocation not only as a journalist but also as a writer of fiction, passing his own literary ambition on to his sons, Vidiadhar and the much younger Shiva. Yet though Seepersad may have been rendered homeless by his financial dependence on his wife's family, his oldest son has also made him stand as a type for all those to whom history has done the same thing. Mr. Biswas's childhood home is not only lost but destroyed, pulled down and replaced by the oil derricks of a subsequent, and more fortunate, owner. The world therefore carries "no witness to [his] early years" (B, 41). Yet what's lost isn't only a house but a village world of cows and marigolds that could have been transplanted, whole, from Uttar Pradesh. What's lost is the past, the ancestral world of those who have crossed the black water or survived the middle passage, the past that for Indians and Africans alike has been swallowed by the memory hole of Caribbean history, locked in what Derek Walcott calls the "grey vault" of the sea.[5]

It's crucial that the image of the boy in the vest remains untouched by a conscious self-pity, for in reading, one remembers that as a boy, Mr. Biswas himself had stood in front of such huts. And later he will note the "fragility" (B, 236) of his son, Anand, will see him "standing and staring" (B, 237) like that boy, and will know the failure of having been unable to give him more of a claim

on the world. Yet how, in this colonial society, could he have done
any more? After a fight with one of his brothers-in-law, Mr. Biswas
wanders out into the streets of the village and stops at an oyster
stall. And as he gulps the mollusks down, pepper sauce scalding his
lips, the drunken vendor tells him about watching a boy shoot tin
cans off a fence. "Look," the boy calls out, "I shoot work. I shoot
ambition. They dead" (B, 139). The oysterman begins to shout;
Mr. Biswas pays no attention and goes on eating. But the boy's
excited cry remains. The world is "too small," Mr. Biswas has earlier thought; the family he has married into is "too large" (B, 91).
For the Tulsis, ambition takes an entirely negative form: "Not to
be unmarried, not to be childless, not to be an undutiful daughter,
sister, wife, mother, widow" (B, 160). And for years their slipshod
yet heavy-handed way of maintaining their Hindu traditions almost
defeats his ambition to stand out, to create an individual self and
life. Yet ambition does not die; Mr. Biswas continues to believe
"that some nobler purpose awaited him, even in this limiting society" (B, 182). Nevertheless he soon stops reading *Self-Help*, Samuel
Smiles's mid-Victorian collection of exemplary tales; and he turns
instead to the Stoic philosophers, to the slave Epictetus and the
emperor Marcus Aurelius, for lessons in how to bear a world in
which individual aspiration seems to count for nothing.

   Yet it's clear that this sense of impotence involves something
more than ordinary poverty. Mr. Biswas knows that the traditional
mores of the Tulsis ensure that "his children would never starve."
But that knowledge is in itself dispiriting, for it means that "it didn't
matter if he were . . . alive or dead" (B, 304). The ruling power—
his mother-in-law—will take care of everything, and indeed Naipaul uses Mr. Biswas's family life to enact an ironic parable of colonial rule. When, as a young man, Mr. Biswas first begins to flirt
with Shama Tulsi, he is immediately annexed, made into a son-in-
law by an "old queen" (B, 104) who marries off her daughters
quickly, haphazardly, almost in a fit of absence of mind. With a
mixture of bluff and threats, Mrs. Tulsi even cajoles him into seeing
the arrangement as being to his advantage; in exchange for his freedom he will become identified with a powerful family. And when
Mr. Biswas finally achieves independence, he doesn't at first notice

the disrepair in which his new house's previous owner has left it: the rotten pillars on which it rests, the door that won't shut and the one that won't open.

But for Naipaul, colonialism's damage cuts much deeper than the simple rule of one people by another. At their initiation, Brahmin boys are told to go to Benares and study; they take a few ritual steps on the way and are then called back. Yet Ganesh Ramsumair in Naipaul's first novel, *The Mystic Masseur* (1957), keeps on walking and has to be physically restrained. "Stop behaving stupid," he's told, in English. "You think you really going to Benares? That is in India, you know, and this is Trinidad" (M, 21). The orthodox Hindu holds that the material world is *maya*, illusion, a distraction in the quest for spiritual truth. Naipaul suggests just the opposite. If Ganesh insists on literally tramping off to Benares, the novel emphasizes the equally literal fact that he can't. It is an illusion that this world is illusory, an illusion that one has access to something other than the realm of material fact. Yet that's precisely what Trinidad Hindus like the Tulsis refuse to recognize. The "old queen" knows very little about the old country; nevertheless, she continues to believe that only India can offer a sense of permanence and truth. Trinidad is but an interlude, "temporary and not quite real" (B, 147), and so nothing one does there quite matters; daughters are married off casually, and the sons wed Presbyterians. Even Mr. Biswas accepts the "derelict makeshift structure[s]" (B, 142) within which he lives, believing them a temporary accommodation only. But "the journey had been final," says Naipaul. "We who came after," he writes of his own generation in *An Area of Darkness* (1964), "could not deny Trinidad," (A, 31, 33), where the command to walk off to Benares seems just a bit absurd. In India, at least, one *could* do it, even if one usually didn't.

And yet these characters remain Hindu. They have lost caste in leaving the subcontinent to travel across the black water and must undergo a ritual purification to regain it. One of the central facts of their lives has been violated by their journey to the new world. Naipaul may play that scene of initiation for laughter, as indeed he does Mr. Biswas's relations with his in-laws, but in reading, one nevertheless knows that something has gone drastically wrong, knows that although these characters have the values of one land, they must live in another, estranged from their origins, in an ever more restless world of conflicting and interpenetrating cultures. They will never quite get over it.

II

That image of the white-vested boy in the clearing is one that matters not just to Mr. Biswas but to Naipaul himself, for he returns to it in a later novel, when in *The Mimic Men* Ralph Singh imagines a child crying "outside a hut at sunset, the fields growing dark" (MM, 75), crying tears of futility, for the "world is so big and unknown and time so limitless." Singh connects that vision to his dreams of "Central Asian horsemen, among whom I am one, riding below a sky threatening snow, to the very end of an empty world" (MM, 82). Such dreams provide a link to the past, offering a kind of solace for the voyage that has first brought his family from India to the Caribbean island of Isabella and has then taken him into political exile in an anonymous London suburb. For those horsemen have a reason for tramping through such emptiness; they are nomads, they are at home under this strange and lowering sky in a way that a lonely child can never be. And in remembering the people he thinks of as his "Aryan ancestors" (MM, 18), Singh tries to link his own journey to the past that the New World seems to have cut away, looking beyond the villages of the Gangetic plain to a time when his forebears had not yet become a settled people, when that wandering had seemed not futile but natural, not the mark of a "shipwreck" but simply a part of who one was. It is as if India itself were but a "temporary accommodation," its loss not to be lamented—and yet a loss whose magnitude is marked by the very desperation of Singh's ploy. He writes:

> It was my hope . . . to give expression to the restlessness, the deep disorder, which the great explorations, the overthrow in three continents of established social organizations, the unnatural bringing together of peoples who could

achieve fulfilment only within the security of their own societies and the landscapes hymned by their ancestors, it was
my hope to give partial expression to the restlessness which
this great upheaval has brought about. The empires of our
time were short-lived, but they have altered the world for
ever; their passing away is their least significant feature.

It is, he adds, a project that "fifty years hence, a great historian
might pursue" (MM, 32), but it isn't one that he can write about
directly, for he remains too much a victim of that restlessness to
describe it fully himself. Naipaul is more ambitious, and Singh's
words stand as the clearest definition the novelist has provided of
the way he conceives of his subject, his world. And as that walking
paradox, that seeming oxymoron, an East Indian West Indian, he
is himself the greatest embodiment of that "deep disorder," a writer
brilliant but not whole, whose entire career is a mark of imperialism's deforming power.

   Graham Greene has written that the writer's task is to "illustrate his private world in terms of the great public world we all
share."[6] For Naipaul that has meant finding a way to chart what
in *The Enigma of Arrival* he calls "the worlds I contained within
myself" (E, 147): his family's move from India to Trinidad; the
desire to write and his escape to England, where a literary career
seemed possible; the early critical success and the continued restlessness of his double exile; the wanderings recorded in the travel
books that by now outnumber his novels. Yet his interest lies less
in imperialism per se—in its formal structures, as in Paul Scott's
work, or in the process of conquest that Chinua Achebe describes—
than in the restlessness it has left behind. The original sin of empire
is implicit in everything he writes, but for him its "wound," in Mr.
Biswas's words, remains "too deep for anger or thoughts of retribution" (B, 483), and his analysis is symptomatic, not causal. His rhetoric stresses not how and why and at whose hands the people he
writes about were subjugated but the present-day experience of living within that "deep disorder." In consequence many readers have
seen his critique of the third world's "half-made" (EP, 216) societies as a form of blaming the victim, and in fact his sympathy is most

readily given to the victims of victims, like the Egyptian Greeks in "The Tramp at Piraeus." He refuses to excuse the mistakes of the present through an assignation of blame for the past, and shows instead how the attempt to redress that past can itself create a new injustice, such as the massacres that conclude *A Bend in the River.*

For those readers in the West who have maintained an Arnoldian belief in the possibility of a disinterested criticism, that refusal has had an important corollary. Just as Raymond in *A Bend in the River* is known as the Big Man's White Man, the African dictator's pet European intellectual, so Naipaul came in the 1970s to seem something like the White Man's Brown Man. He became the writer to whom many in Europe and North America looked for authoritative reports on the state of the third world, believing that because of what Irving Howe called the "steely perspective" of his attacks on that world—attacks by someone with *his* biography—they must necessarily carry the note of truth.[7] And the angrier the attacks grew, the more they were taken as a sign of his own impartiality. Yet if Howe's famous review of *A Bend in the River* amounted to something like a canonization, its judgment has been most often honored in the breach. For inevitably there has been a reaction, one marked by the assumption that Naipaul's "impartiality" is but a pose that conceals an allegiance to the West, to the metropolitan values of the land in which he has made his career: that his concentration on present disorder, the Conradian nihilism of his seeming refusal to believe in the efficacy of any political action or reform, carries a nostalgia for empire and a tacit apology for neocolonialism. And in retrospect one does indeed wonder how the rage and raw nerves of his travel books especially, how his admittedly meticulous account of his own hysteria, could ever have been taken for impartiality.[8]

Let me suggest two answers, the first having to do with Naipaul's extremely careful management of his own reputation and the second with the distinctive quality of his prose. In an essay on Conrad, he described what he terms "the myths of great writers" (EP, 227), and in his many interviews he has made his own myth into that of the writer as a displaced person, insisting that he is one who doesn't "have a side, doesn't have a country, doesn't have a community; one [who] is entirely an individual,"[9] a figure who has in consequence achieved a nearly Brahminical "ideal of non-attachment" (O, 16). Yet his most strenuous insistence on that detachment coincides with the years of his angriest books, with the decade that ran from *In a Free State* to *Among the Believers* (1981). Naipaul has always provided good copy; and those years made his position secure. But the anger and the claim of detachment are inseparable. If, as he suggests in *A Way in the World*, the comedy of his early books provided a way to control the "anxiety" (W, 98) of his colonial past, so too that detachment offered a way to separate himself from the bitter impatience with which he saw the failures of the decolonizing world. And in his most recent work he has distanced himself from that distance, has stopped insisting on his own detachment and has criticized the rhetorical excesses of his own younger self; *An Area of Darkness* was, he writes, the work of a "fearful traveller."[10]

I see no reason to doubt that statement's sincerity, still less its accuracy. Nevertheless it sounds uncannily like what a grand old man ought to say about his own early books.[11] Naipaul's work depends on an illusion of detachment, a fiction of objectivity. Perhaps the clearest example is *The Enigma of Arrival*'s wholly persuasive account of his solitary life; not once does he mention that he is married, that he shares the cottage with his wife. And the creation of that illusion depends above all on the deceptively simple and dispassionate style of his prose. "Mattresses and cushions were to be made, and possibly sold" (B, 420). So he writes in *A House for Mr. Biswas*, and in that comma lies all the heartbreak of the developing world. Yet its understated afterthought does make one laugh, and no one now writing can use the pace of an English sentence, its punctuation and pauses, to greater effect. Listen to the way the novel's precisely factual opening sentence adds insult to the injury of Mr. Biswas's death: "Ten weeks before he died, Mr Mohun Biswas, a journalist of Sikkim Street, St. James, Port of Spain, was sacked" (B, 7).

But a richer example of both that rhythm and that distance comes in the epilogue to *In a Free State:* "Perhaps that had been the only pure time, at the beginning, when the ancient artist, knowing no other land, had learned to look at his own and had seen it as complete" (F, 246). That evocation of a "pure time," now lost, is of course important, and I'll return to it below. Yet just as important is the fastidious purity of the sentence itself. It is periodic and yet direct, formal but not Latinate. Read aloud, its slow and stately progression of commas makes each word seem as if it has been dropped calmly and precisely into place. For though the sentence begins with the word "perhaps," Naipaul's measured tones—his "grimly perfect grammar," in Sara Suleri's inspired phrase—suggest above all his great confidence in his own judicious appraisal of the world.[12] Its Augustan rhythm embodies all the logic and clarity that the world he describes is without, and one hears in it something like the assurance of another colonial voice: "We hold these truths to be self-evident." Certainly it has that neoclassical reliance on abstractions—"pure," "beginning," "complete."

A prose so beautifully modulated carries something of the status of fact. It ensures that his work cannot simply be discounted, even as its claim of objectivity demands that one hold it to standards of truth that one doesn't apply to other writers—Dickens perhaps, or Nabokov, or even Rushdie. So the attacks on him have always had a special vehemence. Long ago George Lamming accused him of writing a "castrated satire" that ignored the Caribbean's non-Indian social groups; and his first travel books, *The Middle Passage* (1962) and *An Area of Darkness*, made him a figure of permanent controversy.[13] Over the years so much postcolonial writing has seemed a response to Naipaul that one is reminded of what Flannery O'Connor said of working in Faulkner's shadow: "Nobody likes to get caught on the tracks when the Dixie Flyer comes through."[14] Derek Walcott has written poems around the figure he calls V. S. Nightfall, and in fact it's Walcott who has most memorably voiced the charges against him: "You spit on your people, / your people applaud, / your former oppressors laurel you. / The thorns biting your forehead / are contempt / disguised as concern."[15] Yet such attacks have too often been cries of outrage and of betrayal, as in Selwyn Cudjoe's accusation that Naipaul's "lack of identification with the national struggles of Third World peoples" is a mark of his "neurotic indulgence."[16] If, as Jane Kramer has suggested, the conventional Anglo-American praise for Naipaul depends on his being "one of them,"[17] then the conventional attack on him is predicated on the belief that he's supposed to be "one of us." Both views, that is, depend on his not being white. Both see this as the most important thing about him; both views proceed, in an ultimately sterile debate, from Naipaul's refusal to conform to the role a nonwhite writer is expected to play.

Yet Naipaul himself shares the central assumption of his angriest critics. For both the vehemence of that criticism and his own sense of imperialism's deforming power grow out of a shared sense of the idea of a "people," the word Ralph Singh uses to describe the different social groups who have suffered "the unnatural bringing together" of empire. It is a concept at the heart of Naipaul's work, and one that's perhaps best understood in the terms proposed by the eighteenth-century theorist of national identity J. G. Herder. For Herder the character of any group is molded by its experience of a particular landscape and especially of a particular climate. Whoever lives in that climate will over many centuries come to be made in its image, even as its inhabitants will alter that landscape in turn; Europe was once a "dank forest," and only "the art and policy of man" make Egypt anything "more than the slime of the Nile."[18] That emphasis on human interaction with an environment does call into question any myth of an essential national or racial identity, and indeed Herder insists that man is everywhere one species. Yet the process of cultural change is for him so slow as to be virtually identical with such an essentialism. For Herder links his conception of culture to physical form. A migration from one region to another will alter that form but slowly; "the Negro in Europe . . . remains as he was."[19] But any sexual "intermixture with foreigners" will in a single generation effect a change that "the fair-complexioned climate could not produce in ages."[20]

In consequence "the ground of man's physical happiness everywhere consists in his living where it is his lot to live," in the security of the landscape hymned by his ancestors, the landscape in which his culture has been formed.[21] "Transplanted flowers," as Isaiah Berlin has written, "decay in unsympathetic climates; so do human beings."[22] Those who have been shaped by mountains will not blossom on the plains; an inland people cannot flourish by the sea. *"Too sudden, too precipitate transitions to an opposite hemisphere and climate are seldom salutary to a nation:* for Nature has not established her boundaries between remote lands in vain."[23] So in *Heart of Darkness* Conrad uses a Herderian rhetoric to describe the "black fellows" whom Marlow sees paddling a canoe near the start of the novel, men with a "wild vitality . . . as natural and true as the surf along their coast"; for unlike the Europeans, "they wanted no excuse for being there."[24] And Kurtz's fate is one that Herder might have predicted as well. Those Europeans who settle in the colonies often become "degenerated in body and mind" even as the imposition of European ways makes the indigenes decay in turn, changing "their manner of living without . . . giving them a European nature."[25] Animism may come naturally to Africans, and running a steamship may come naturally to Europeans, but mixing the two, as does Marlow's black helmsman, inevitably proves a disaster. For not only "physical happiness" but the "ideas of every indigenous nation are . . . confined to its own region," to the land in which one could indeed walk to Benares.[26]

"No words," Herder wrote, "can express the sorrow and despair of the bought or stolen Negro slave, when he leaves his native shore."[27] And his ideal, as Berlin has suggested, remains that of the "authentic" culture, its purity and "genuineness of expression" untouched by the world outside.[28] It is an ideal possible only so long as a group remains isolated, homogeneous, and small—an ideal with which Naipaul's characters live even as his work denies the possibility of its fulfillment. Herder's own anti-imperialism does, however, remain inextricable from what Anthony Appiah has called the "racialist" assumption that "heritable characteristics" such as the color of one's skin or the shape of one's nose point to something beyond themselves, that they are inseparable from a set of ideas and beliefs.[29] Herder argued that each of those ideas had, in its own land, an equal validity, and he wrote scathingly of the way colonialism judges "foreign peoples . . . in terms of customs unknown to them."[30] Nevertheless that racialism provided one of the grounding assumptions for the sense of racial hierarchy that was held to justify nineteenth-century imperialism. Yet Herder's

emphasis on the isolate society makes his work seem far closer to
the nativism that stands as empire's postcolonial counterpart: to the
systematic turning away from the West and its products and to the
consequent search, in Frantz Fanon's words, "for a national culture
which existed before the colonial era."[31] Nativism holds that the
recovery of the past will somehow allow one to regain the sense of
self-worth that colonialism has destroyed. It is a nostalgia for a time
of security, before the coming of imperialism's "deep disorder,"
before the restlessness of exile. So in the Hindu villages of rural
Trinidad, Naipaul's family continued to live as though they were
still in "eastern Uttar Pradesh" (A, 31). And though he himself
could not deny the reality of Trinidad's "multi-racial society," Naipaul writes that his own childhood remained marked by an ancestral
suspicion of outsiders. "They were what they were; we were what
we were . . . the moment any intercourse threatened, we scented
violation and withdrew" (A, 33).

This is the tension on which his work depends: between his
awareness of the human longing for and belief in an essential identity that separates the family, the clan, the people, from those who
lie outside, on the one hand, and his knowledge of the historical
processes that always undermine such identities, on the other. Look
once more at In a Free State's description of a "pure time." It comes
in an account of a visit to Egypt during which Naipaul makes the
tourist jog around the graves and temples of Karnak and Luxor,
drawn especially by the paintings on the walls of the tombs, by their
evocations of a world wholly known, a land whose every familiar
feature has been "exalted into design." In such an art, in such an
age, even the Nile itself "was only water, a blue-green chevron"
(F, 241), not yet the Nile but only the river, the center of the world
for a people who knew no other. At a rest house in the desert he
eats at a table with a pair of young Germans, watching boys in dirty
jibbahs beg for food and piastres from a party of Italians; later, back
at his hotel in this land to which so many empires have come, he
finds that "another, more remote empire was announcing itself,"
in the form of a troupe of Chinese acrobats (F, 246).

And it is in contemplating that mixture of peoples that he
reaches his great epiphany: "Perhaps that had been the only pure

time." Yet in traveling back to Cairo, past fields and trains and "dusty towns," Naipaul finds it "hard to believe that there had been such innocence," that any culture had ever been whole and inviolate; and his evocation of that Herderian ideal at once stresses its power and suggests that it has never been anywhere valid. It embodies a dream of fulfillment around which individual men and women could cluster, a community they could imagine, inventing a past to give some coherence to the present. But the very force with which it articulates that human longing grows from the fact that such purity has "always been a fabrication, a cause of yearning, something for the tomb." And so he leaves his readers, in the book's final image, with an existential vision of the placelessness that all his characters so acutely feel: a vision of defeated soldiers, lost in the desert, "trying to walk back home" (F, 246), to a pure time that has perhaps never existed and certainly doesn't now.

Where Rushdie will see an exhilarating sense of possibility in that "separation from origins and essences," Naipaul can find in it only a sense of violation, of estrangement from one's origins, and a consequent longing for an idealized home. Yet for both Naipaul and Herder that nativist yearning, however understandable, remains a fundamental mistake; in Berlin's words, it is "a crippling illusion as fatal as any for which it attempts to be the cure."[32] The past can offer no salvation. No Aryan horsemen ride beneath that darkening sky, and Naipaul reserves his fiercest attacks for those who try to "go back again to the beginning" (R, 6), who want to return to the security of the past in a way that, it seems, a part of him wishes he could himself. Hence we note the vehemence of his Islamic travel book *Among the Believers*, the scorn with which he views the fundamentalist longing for the time of the first caliphs. But nowhere is that return more impossible than in the Caribbean. To what past? To whose? Its aboriginal peoples have been long extinct. Most of its current inhabitants are descended from those brought together by slavery and indenture. Its languages took shape in the lands of the colonial masters, languages "native" neither to the region nor to those who must now speak them; indeed, as late as 1958 even C. L. R. James wrote, "The populations in the British West Indies have no native civilization at all."[33] And this is the sense in which one must understand Naipaul's use, in the epigraph of *The Middle Passage*, of James Anthony Froude's famously damning 1887 description of the Caribbean: "There are no people there in the true sense of the word, with a character and purpose of their own."[34]

Froude has always been reviled by Caribbean writers, and the Victorian writer's phrasing does indeed carry a knee-jerk, reflexive racism that suggests there are in the islands no individual men and women. But suppose we hear his words in Herder's sense? Not that there are no people in the Caribbean but that there is not *a* people, that there is not a Caribbean people as such. Just who are they? In 1960 Lamming defined the Caribbean in terms of what he called "the peasant sensibility . . . [a] common background of social history . . . [that] could hold Indians and Negroes together"—a definition in which history does the work of climate, eliding Marx with Herder to produce a sense of national identity.[35] That definition would seem to exclude not only the middle class but also many city-dwellers, both groups, admittedly, more prominent now than then. And Lamming excludes Naipaul in particular, for having, "with the diabolical help of Oxford University," wiped that peasant sensibility "out of his guts," as if his education had somehow canceled his claim to citizenship.[36] Yet Lamming's argument, however simplistic, does at least attempt to transcend racial divisions. James warned of the danger that "racial rivalry" posed to the unfulfilled dream of a Caribbean federation, arguing that although the "accentuation" of that rivalry was inevitable in a time of political awakening, it must nevertheless be resisted.[37] And Naipaul himself has both suffered from and shared in that accentuation—"They were what they were." Arnold Rampersad has written of the "campaign of humiliation and demoralization and threats of violence aimed at Indians that he would have encountered as a youth" in the 1940s.[38] Certainly Naipaul has always been hard on what he describes as the dream of "racial redemption" (EP, 70), the idea of a black power movement in a country that, like Trinidad, has a black majority; and perhaps his own suspicion of the idea that there is a Caribbean "people" stems from the fear that a majoritarian definition would make his own group ever more liable to marginalization and attack.

For Naipaul the different peoples that empire brought to the Caribbean have not become as one. They have failed to form a common culture, have collided without cohering. And he looks to Froude for the reason, quoting the earlier writer's suggestion that the islands have been valued not in and for themselves but "only for the wealth which they yielded."[39] They have been kept dependent, without "a character and a purpose of their own," as opposed to the one their subordinate position has defined for them: allowed no values except those taught by a colonial education on the one hand and those assigned to their bauxite and sugar and beaches on the other; discouraged even from growing the subsistence food crops that could have made them independent of metropolitan sources.[40] "What tone," Naipaul wonders, "shall the historian adopt" in writing of "this West Indian futility"? For he notes, "History is built around achievement and creation; and nothing was created in the West Indies" (MP, 29).[41] How can one unlock the past hidden beneath what Walcott describes as the ocean's "blank pages," recorded only in "colonnades of coral / [and] the gothic windows of sea-fans,"[42] a past in which "there is too much nothing"?[43] And Naipaul's novels stand as an attempt to represent that futility, to craft what he calls "a way of looking" (A, 227) that will allow us to see what we have not seen before: that boy standing in the bush, in a place without a character or a purpose of its own, a world with no reason for being there but one that nevertheless exists. His novels make us take account of a world the novel had never before noticed, make that boy into the subject of a literature that perhaps he could not read; and that description in itself provides a restoration of a shattered history.

Yet as the slippery meaning of that word "history" suggests, Naipaul's attempt to confront that problem of historiography is at best oblique; and Walcott offers a more enabling and perhaps more comprehensive model of the Antillean past. He takes the figure of Robinson Crusoe as an emblem for a Caribbean people who must "learn to shape . . . where nothing was / the language of a race," a race in which everyone is a castaway, cut off from their origins.[44] "I have Dutch, nigger, and English in me," Walcott wrote in "The Schooner *Flight*," "and either I'm nobody, or I'm a nation," a nation in which one must, however slowly, piece out a culture from the debris that history has washed ashore.[45] But Naipaul is too absorbed by disorder—too impatient, too committed to a sense of exile as an irreparable violation—to accept that sense of culture as process, the idea that there might become a Caribbean people, to accept that they are in fact constituted by Creolization, by that very process of becoming. And perhaps his denial that there is indeed such a people can hinder the creation of one, as can his attack on the idea of a Caribbean culture—his claim, which at the very least ignores his own work, that the Caribbean has produced nothing but steel bands and calypso. Is that such a small thing? In the short stories of *Miguel Street* (1959) he knows it's not. But then the music hadn't yet become a tourist attraction and so a mark of the islands' subordinate status.[46]

What happens to a society when all authority is imposed from outside, when it is without "standards of its own" (MP, 65), without a people in the Herderian sense? For Naipaul, Trinidad has "to a remarkable degree re-created the attitudes of the Spanish picaroon world" (MP, 79). The picaro lives "by his wits in a place where it is felt that all eminence is arrived at by crookedness" (MP, 78); his very dishonesty is applauded as a sign of his skill. It is for Naipaul "an ugly world, a jungle" (MP, 79), where success can be attained only by imposing oneself on others. Yet that same amorality has produced a sophisticated "tolerance for every human activity and affection for every demonstration of wit and style" (MP, 82). And this is the culture he described in *Miguel Street*, the first book he wrote (though the third published) and one in which colonialism's deep disorder wears always a comic mask: "A stranger could drive through Miguel Street and just say 'Slum!' because he could see no more. But we, who lived there, saw our street as a world, where everybody was quite different from everybody else. Man-man was mad; George was stupid; Big Foot was a bully; Hat was an adventurer; Popo was a philosopher; and Morgan was our comedian" (MS, 63).

A slum—but also a world of enormous possibility in which it seems that anything might someday happen. In *Finding the Center* (1984) Naipaul describes how he began to write that first book in

the freelancers' room of the BBC's Caribbean Service, passing its
opening pages around as he finished: simplifying and transforming
his once "disregarded" (FC, 10) memories of Port of Spain, adding
"one concrete detail to another" (FC, 14–5), establishing for the
narrative a sense of speed that matched the speed with which he
wrote it. It is a book marked above all by the writer's delight in
discovering his own world, not the one he lived in but the one he
could write about. And its unforced ease now feels a kind of miracle,
making it stand with Achebe's *Things Fall Apart* (1959) as a seemingly unmediated portrait of a world absolutely fresh and new.

Most of its stories take an anecdotal form. They begin by
introducing a character against the background of the street: "Everybody in Miguel Street said that Man-man was mad, and so they
left him alone." His "curious habits" (MS, 38) are quickly sketched:
in "Man-man," the way he runs for office in every election, spends
his days writing in chalk on the pavement, and speaks with an accent
like that of "a good-class Englishman" (MS, 39). Several times the
story seems to start over—"One day," "One morning," "Then one
day"—the last indicating the moment at which the piece moves
from a character sketch into narrative, with Man-man's claim that
"he had seen God after having a bath" (MS, 41). Eventually he asks
to be tied to a cross and stoned; but when the street takes him at
his word, he shouts, "I finish with this arseness." "The police took
away Man-man. The authorities kept him for observation. Then for
good" (MS, 44). And the story ends, its casual air an embodiment of
the picaroon society's moral laissez-faire.

For there's never a suggestion that Man-man's madness
means there's something *wrong* with him. It is simply who he is.
Naipaul writes that in composing *Miguel Street*, he decided to leave
out "the setting, the historical time, the racial and social complexities of the people concerned" (FC, 9), shaping his material in a way
that emphasizes the absence of a coherent culture, of a set of norms
against which behavior might be judged. By the end of the book
his characters are nearly all of them placeable, but in its opening
chapters especially they appear unmarked by social detail; it is as
if, as he writes in *A Way in the World*, their "history had been burnt
away" (W, 114). The collection's nameless adolescent narrator is,

admittedly, of Hindu origin, though that's much attenuated by the Port of Spain streets. But few of the other characters seem to belong to identifiable groups. Most of them go by nicknames: Bogart, Boyee, Big Foot, Popo. Others have either a first or a last name— George, Errol, Eddoes—but almost never both. Outsiders may have their skin color described ("a good looking brown man" [MS, 17]), but the color of those in "our circle" (MS, 25) remains unspecified. Nor is it immediately possible to tell the characters' ages. It takes several stories to realize that Boyee and Errol aren't yet adults and that they live with Hat—to whom their relation remains undefined until near the end of the book.

To read this urban pastoral, one must, then, learn to see what Naipaul has left out. *Miguel Street*'s charm—no, its originality—depends on a radical simplification of Trinidad's "racial and social complexities" and yet one that points to a larger truth about the confusion of a picaroon society. The street lives on rumor and half-information, on endless talk and fantastic stories about the world outside; it is a community marked by a delight in affectation, in the careful crafting of elaborate and stylish personae, a crafting that can nevertheless escalate into madness. On Miguel Street everyone stands out as an individual—but stands out against what? Not against any set of social norms but rather against both material want and that burning away of the past; it's a place in which the cultivation of style becomes a weapon with which to fight several forms of poverty. Yet the absence of those norms remains important. In his essay on Conrad, Naipaul suggested that "the great novelists wrote about highly organized societies. I had no such society" (EP, 213) and therefore no set of established conventions and expectations against which to plot the disorder of his world. The values his characters have brought from their homelands are meaningless in this new land; think of Ganesh trying to walk to Benares. In a "wounded civilization" one no longer has that kind of self-sufficiency.[47] And the picaroon society, being without standards— inhibitions, barriers—of its own, becomes a vacuum into which the detritus of other cultures can rush.

A character in *Miguel Street* adopts the manners of an American movie star and calls himself Bogart; the narrator of *In a Free*

State's "Tell Me Who to Kill" sees his life in terms of misremembered incidents from Hollywood movies. But of course British norms are more important. The cricket field, that well-documented form of colonial acculturation, plays an important role in Anand Biswas's education and is also a major topic of conversation on Miguel Street; or, as one character says after a great victory, "White people is God, you hear!" (MS, 155).[48] Yet for Naipaul even cricket seems minor in comparison with questions of language and literary form. At school Anand and his classmates use the ready-made phrases their teacher has supplied to write essays in which they "project a visit" to the beach, traveling with "laden hampers" in an "open car" to that "arc of golden sand"—essays in which they try to think themselves into the position of a middle-class English schoolboy (B, 356). And when Anand's father takes a correspondence course from the "Ideal School of Journalism," he is given exercises on "Guy Fawkes Night," "Some Village Superstitions," and "Summer—slap of fish on the fishmonger's slab." The only fish Mr. Biswas knows about "does come around every morning in a basket on the old fishwoman head" (B, 343). But he writes the article anyway and goes on to a Keatsian piece about autumn, in which Trinidadians happily chop wood for the coming winter.

It is as if the English language, now transplanted to Trinidad, were being asked to deny the island around it and do the equivalent of walking off to Benares instead. In *The Mystic Masseur* Ganesh announces that it "is high time we realize that we living in a British country and I think we shouldn't be ashamed to talk the people language good"; for even though he can write "correct English," he's embarrassed to speak it "except on very formal occasions" (M, 76). But when he persuades a friend to join him, all they can find to talk about is the weather: "It is hot today." "I see what you mean. It is *very* hot today" (M, 77). And so he drops the experiment. Ganesh's embarrassment implies that he still thinks of himself in the terms his colonial master has proposed, in which it seems absurd for Caliban to do anything but mutter and growl. But it also suggests the need for him to abandon the expectations of a borrowed culture and to replace them with standards of his own, standards that could either make him see himself as a legitimate user of that language or make him recognize the validity of what he calls his "dialect" (M, 76).

Yet the scene is also comic, and that comedy is itself problematic. For what makes it funny? What makes one laugh at this counterpoint of dialect with the master's tongue? Naipaul quotes Graham Greene's observation that comedy requires a "strong framework of social convention" (MP, 75) against which particular actions can be judged as absurd or incongruous; so the reader laughs to the degree that he or she has a sense of the standardness of standard English. And this, as the Caribbean critic Gordon Rohlehr has written, presents a problem. For Naipaul's conception of the Caribbean as a place in which "such a norm is absent" means that "while he laughs at his Creoles aping standards of pseudo whiteness, he can only do so by assuming those very norms himself."[49] Perhaps that's too harsh. Ganesh's aspirations may seem absurd and his use of standard English incongruous—indeed he himself sees it that way. But the opposition between these different forms of English is less stable than it appears, and if his British English seems impoverished, his Trinidadian tongue has an invigorating freshness, an admirable pith and vigor. Naipaul's essays ally his comic purpose with that of Evelyn Waugh, and as with the early Waugh, the seemingly disparaged has here an energy that won't let it be so easily dismissed. Nevertheless, Rohlehr's comments suggest the degree to which England provides an inescapable norm, even if it's one that can't be entirely accepted—a norm not only for these characters but also for Naipaul himself. Or as he puts it in the author's note to *The Mystic Masseur*, "Trinidad is a small island, no bigger than Lancashire, with a population somewhat smaller than Nottingham's."

III

For Mr. Biswas's need of a house is Naipaul's as well, one that has taken him in search of something more than physical shelter, in search of some entry into what Henry James called the million-windowed "house of fiction." The biblical cadences of James's famous metaphor suggest a vast and teeming building, from whose many mansions different novelists look out at "the spreading field, the human scene."[50] And in the years since *Miguel Street*, Naipaul has pierced new windows in that house, entering it through the very act of throwing up the sash on the "portion of the earth" that he, like Mr. Biswas, has claimed for himself. But how does one find that window of one's own? How can one escape from the world of laden hampers, from the conventions of what Naipaul's generation was taught to call the "mother country"? In an early essay he wrote that although "the English language was mine . . . [its] tradition was not" (O, 26). Yet Trinidad itself was then virtually without a literary tradition of its own; and in this, the Caribbean writer faced a more desperate situation than his counterparts in India or Africa, with their rich histories of written and oral literatures, literatures underpinned by their existence in some language other than English.

"The social comedies I write," Naipaul suggested in 1958, "can be fully appreciated only by someone who knows the region I write about." But for publication he had to "write for England," to depend on an English audience for whom the "very originality of [his] material" made it suspect; "it is easy for my books to be dismissed as farces" (O, 11). Breaching that regional barrier required some degree of reference to the norms of his English public; probably the best example is the incident I've referred to above: Ganesh's attempt to use standard English. Yet although Naipaul's invocation of that standard does stress Trinidad's absence of internal social norms, the very omnipresence of British values serves in turn to underline the consequences of colonialism. The need for those references becomes in itself a mark of the damage imperialism has wrought. For though one's initial reaction to Ganesh may be laughter, that laughter soon turns bitter in one's throat. The mimicry has made these people so much less than they are.

Mimicry. Mr. Biswas's experiences with the Ideal School of Journalism underline the degree to which the terms of a foreign literature have been imposed on his world from outside—but not only the terms of literature. In remembering his Caribbean childhood, *The Mimic Men*'s Ralph Singh suggests that all terms of reference and value seemed to come from outside the world he knew; and indeed that novel makes explicit the theory of colonial history that had been implicit in Naipaul's earlier work. One morning in school, during his teacher's evocation of Canada, Ralph thinks: "There, in Liege in a traffic jam, on the snow slopes of the Laurentians, was the true, pure world. We, here on our island, handling books printed in this world, and using its goods, had been abandoned and forgotten. We pretended to be real, to be learning, to be preparing ourselves for life, we mimic men of the New World, one unknown corner of it, with all its reminders of the corruption that came so quickly to the new" (MM, 146).

There, in Liege, was the "pure world"—not here, on the island of Isabella, the onetime sugar colony. It is the teacher's judgment, but his pupils share it. Mimic men: most often the phrase is taken as referring to the sort of imitation we see with Anand's school essays or with Ganesh Ramsumair in *The Mystic Masseur*, who eventually becomes a successful politician and changes his name to G. Ramsey Muir. It applies as well to people like Hari Kumar's father, Duleep, who knows that the English are amused by his accent, or to the upper-class Indians that Naipaul meets in *An Area of Darkness*, the box-wallahs whose manners seem a slavish copy of the Raj at its worst. The phrase refers to black skins, white masks; Macaulay's brown-skinned Englishmen, an Oreo cookie, a coconut. Or indeed a *chamcha*, the Urdu word for "spoon" and slang for "sycophant"; the name Rushdie gives to the main character of *The Satanic Verses*, an Indian-born professional mimic, a man of a thousand voices who in private life has remade himself as an Englishman—accent, bowler hat, member of the Garrick Club.

That kind of mimicry fills Naipaul with despair, for it provides not only a reminder of the violation of imperialism but an acceptance of it, of one's subordinate role and inferior culture, of the terms in which the imperial power has seen one. He cannot see that mimicry as a question of style: as a way, in Ashis Nandy's terms, of "domesticating the West . . . by reducing it to the level of the comic and trivial," a way both to acknowledge and to shuttle between the hybrid selves of the postcolonial condition.[51] Given Naipaul's longing for a "pure time," albeit one that he knows has never existed, he can treat it only as a mark of cultural fracture; and indeed hybridity itself often stands for him as a mark of degradation, as with the Hare Krishnas of "One Out of Many." Hybridity brands one as coming from a "wounded civilization," and he flinches from it as would his Brahmin ancestors from the shadow of an untouchable's hand.

For to Naipaul that mimicry is above all a sign of servitude. In *The Middle Passage* he quotes from Tacitus, from the *Agricola*'s account of a colonized Britain, where "in place of distaste for the Latin language came a passion to command it. . . . They spoke of such [things] as 'civilization,' when really they were only a feature of enslavement" (MP, 42). And seen in context, Naipaul's phrase carries a second and far more important meaning: not men who mimic but a mimic of a man, "pretend[ing] to be real." Always in Naipaul, those who seem whole are revealed as something less— broken, tattered, patched together, like that tramp at Piraeus. Jimmy Ahmed in *Guerillas* (1975) preaches a form of black power (for all that he is half-Chinese) but feels powerful himself only when he attracts the attention of whites, preferably whites from London. He sees his success solely in terms of his acceptance in the metropolis, for he has no standards of his own by which to judge himself, and the contempt with which he treats white people is an act of self-contempt as well. Salim in *A Bend in the River* becomes so absorbed by the science he learns from popular magazines that he looks to the West as the exclusive source of knowledge and becomes filled with a sense of how far he has to go to catch up. None of them are whole, sufficient unto themselves. They are instead dependent, at best half-made, an imitation of what a man should be; and so too are the societies from which they come. How could it be otherwise, in a world marked by the perpetual violation of one culture by another? The government of Ralph Singh's Isabella collapses under the weight of the few slogans he brings against it, for it had only been a shell in the first place.

But these characters' lives aren't passed in imitation of the West alone, and Naipaul's early fiction especially makes constant reference to the history of a forsaken India. Mr. Biswas gains his independence only after a family quarrel that turns his leaving the

Tulsi household into a form of Partition. And in *The Mystic Masseur* Naipaul writes that "the history of Ganesh is, in a way, the history of our times" (M, 18)—in a way, but in a way that's above all parodic, in which Ganesh's career stands as a New World burlesque of Gandhi's. Both undergo long years of preparation, and Ganesh writes a pamphlet called "Profitable Evacuation," which parallels Gandhi's writing on sanitation, to which Naipaul devoted half a chapter in *An Area of Darkness*. Both produce autobiographies, but where Gandhi calls his *The Story of My Experiments with Truth* (1925), Ganesh comes up with a volume called *The Years of Guilt*. Gandhi perfects *hartal*, the Indian form of the general strike; but when Ganesh starts his own political career, the best he can do is to master the art of walking out of meetings. In India, a Gandhi can become a world historical figure; but in Trinidad, one gets only Ganesh.

Nor does Naipaul exempt himself from that judgment. "To be a colonial," he writes, "is to be a little ridiculous and unlikely, especially in the eyes of someone from the metropolitan country" (O, 32)—or someone trying to look through those eyes, someone with a passion to command its language. How does one transform mimicry into individuality? How, that is, does one create a self? How does one move from dependency to development, when the tools of the latter are so often the chains of the former? The colonial writer sees the library shelves of the metropolis as a sign of his own irrelevance. So much has already been done! Yet he has no way to escape that sense of his own belatedness except by trying to fill a shelf, to pierce a window, of his own, embracing the very thing that oppresses him. Iris Murdoch glosses James's great metaphor in writing, "A novel must be a 'house fit for free characters to live in.'" The statement gains some point through the near-coincidence of Trinidad's independence with the first publication of *A House for Mr. Biswas*.[52] And in retrospect Anand Biswas discovers that his father's house has fostered that sense of freedom within him, that it has made his "memories coherent" and whole (B, 581). But for Anand the crucial moment has already come. One day he goes to the beach, where he almost drowns and has to be rescued. In school the next day he writes an essay in which he re-

fuses to use the phrases his teacher has supplied. His classmates
snicker at the admission that "he had not struggled with laden hampers into a car . . . but had walked to common Docksite." But his
instructor recognizes, and rewards, the originality of his simple de-
clarative sentences: "I opened my mouth to cry for help. Water
filled it" (B, 357).

And Mr. Biswas too will have a similar success, in trying to
compose a poem about his mother's death. It is for both of them
as if they had looked into their hearts and written. Such moments
in *A House for Mr. Biswas* are of course highly literary in nature;
like all realism, they gain their effects through persistent reference
to the models that the writer is in the process of discarding. But the
novel has some unrepudiated antecedents as well. Shortly before he
died Seepersad Naipaul wrote to his son, "I am beginning to feel
that I could have been a writer."[53] In 1976 Naipaul arranged for
the London publication of his father's stories, and in both his introduction to them and the autobiographical writing that has followed,
he has returned again and again to the importance his father's work
has had for him. In fact the opening pages of the novel that memori-
alizes his father are "cannibalized" from one of Seepersad's own
stories, "They Named Him Mohun."[54] And the tone of that novel
owes a great deal to Seepersad's longest tale, "The Adventures of
Gurudeva," especially in the dispiriting comedy that makes the cru-
elty of its world "just bearable."

Hearing his father read the successive drafts of "Gurudeva"
aloud was, Naipaul writes, "the greatest imaginative experience of
my childhood" (FC, 30), one more important than any of his reading, than even the Dickens to whose characters "I gave . . . the faces
and voices of people I knew." But Dickens remained important,
even though the young Naipaul had to turn his predecessor's "rain
and drizzle . . . into tropical downpours; the snow and fog I accepted
as conventions of books" (O, 24). And *A House for Mr. Biswas* is
indeed "Dickensian," and not only because it's long, funny, and
deals with poverty. For as V. S. Pritchett has argued, Dickens's
"strongest and fiercest sense" was that of isolation, and the distinguishing mark of his characters is their solitude. "They are people
caught living in a world of their own," talking not to each other

but to themselves, figures for whom the "pressure of society has created fits of twitching in mind and speech."[55] So Mr. Biswas is marked by the nervous tics and twitches of his periodic rages at the Tulsis; so he undergoes the psychic isolation of his madness at Green Vale. Perhaps that solitude made Dickens's characters accessible in a way that many of the other novelists the young Naipaul encountered were not. For a book to succeed with him it had to be capable of being adapted to Trinidad, at which point it "ceased to be specifically English" (O, 24). Any book that wasn't—whether because of its illustrations or because of a too-close attention to what Lionel Trilling calls "the buzz of [social] implication"—he rejected.[56] "*Wuthering Heights* worked; *Pride and Prejudice* didn't. Maupassant worked; Balzac didn't" (O, 24).

Naipaul's account of his own early reading brings us back to James's million windows, a metaphor whose biblical echoes make it above all a figure for the idea of a canon. And this too is part of Naipaul's myth—the Trinidadian Hindu who became a great British novelist, who built a house of his own. Yet as for Matthew Arnold, the concept of a canon was allied with that of the state, so in postcolonial criticism it has been increasingly identified with empire, and the question of Naipaul's relation to it has vexed some of his most sophisticated readers. For the universalist rhetoric of a colonial education, with its emphasis on a "great tradition" that always somehow turns out to be English, works by denying the value of a specifically colonial experience. Homi Bhabha has worried that the incorporation of *A House for Mr. Biswas* into such a tradition has come at the cost of ignoring that specificity.[57] Suleri finds that anxiety in Naipaul himself, suggesting that his own relation to the canon remains antagonistic. "The literary," she has written, "becomes an equal participant in the outrage of colonial history," and the arrival she sees in the enigmatic title of his 1987 novel is that of a figure like Naipaul himself on the literary scene.[58]

The Enigma of Arrival is the first book in which Naipaul imagines himself not as extraneous to England but as a part of it, and of England in the narrowest and most provincial sense. He is struck by the incongruity, a brown man in a country village—and yet as he moves across the downs, as he imagines himself in that landscape, he comes increasingly to feel at home. But the book also records the start of his career as a writer, and indeed the two processes are one and the same. When he first comes to Wiltshire he occupies a rented house on a great estate. It's only after he has built that line of books that he can allow himself to make a home—and literally so, knocking two laborer's cottages together into a new house of his own. What, however, does it mean for a writer whose very existence remains an implicit challenge to the colonial mind to locate himself in the landscape of Stonehenge? Doesn't his assimilation into it entail a loss of the power to criticize the structures of empire? Should he not instead accept his "minor" status? Ought not the postcolonial writer reject the canon rather than try to join it?

Yet such a criticism is perhaps too quick to identify not only the individual writer with those structures but the very idea of a literary canon as well. School reading lists are narrow, and in the colonies they were indeed used to provide a justification, in the realm of "culture," for the fact of British rule. But a curriculum shouldn't be mistaken for a canon, and in any case the assumption of marginalization carries dangers of its own. Mimicry may be servitude, but so is an insistence on one's own marginal status, and to resist the canon is above all to accept the permanence of that marginality. Put the question like this: does Naipaul's building himself a house on Salisbury Plain stand as a betrayal of Trinidad, or does it rather alter one's conception of the English countryside? He himself sees his presence there as a perpetual novelty, an alteration of its human community. But he extrapolates from that presence to a sense of a world marked by ceaseless activity and change, in which what looks permanent—his seemingly long-settled neighbors—is revealed as temporary and new. The countryside is always in flux, and as Naipaul's presence requires us to revise, however subtly, our sense of that landscape, so indeed his work demands that we similarly revise our sense of the tradition. As Suleri suggests, he destabilizes the canon by seeking to join it. It's worth remembering that the poet most commonly seen as the high priest of such structures had a fluid notion of them, writing in "Tradition and the Individual Talent" that each "really new" work of art alters all its predecessors.[59] It is worth remembering too that Gilles Deleuze and Felix Guattari's use of Kafka to exemplify minor literature is a deliberate oxymoron, for no writer in this century has, in another sense, been less minor.

In filling a shelf of his own, Naipaul has laid claim to his place in the world, has built himself a home. Or has he? "I wished," he writes in *A Way in the World*, "to belong to myself. I couldn't support the idea of being part of a group" (W, 18). One of the most extraordinary passages in his *ouevre* is an account, in *An Area of Darkness*, of the way he melts into an Indian street:

> And for the first time in my life I was one of the crowd. There was nothing in my appearance or dress to distinguish me from the crowd eternally hurrying into Churchgate Station. In Trinidad to be an Indian was to be distinctive. To be anything there was distinctive; difference was each man's attribute. To be an Indian in England was distinctive; in Egypt it was more so. Now in Bombay I entered a shop or a restaurant and awaited a special quality of response. And there was nothing. It was like being denied part of my reality. Again and again I was caught. I was faceless. I might sink without a trace into that Indian crowd. I had been made by Trinidad and England; recognition of my difference was necessary to me. I felt the need to impose myself, and didn't know how. (A, 45–46)

He becomes invisible. But it's not the invisibility of which Ralph Ellison writes, in which an individual cannot be seen because all that can be seen of him is the fact of his skin—the type of invisibility we saw with Hari Kumar. No, Naipaul's invisibility here stands as the antithesis of Ellison's. He has been made by Trinidad and England, where his individual identity is predicated on his racial difference from most of the people around him. In India, however, that individuality remains invisible precisely because that difference is not only unseen but nonexistent. Yet that identity of skin is also, in Naipaul's case, a lie. Like Hari Kumar, he's not an Indian, he only looks like one, and so he misses the "special quality of response" that has always marked his difference from other people. And indeed to lose that racial distinction is for Naipaul to lose his self, to watch his "reality . . . sink without a trace." But insofar as the self that India threatens grows from that distinctiveness, his very individuality depends on his membership in a racial group, on being the Indian he isn't—a group from which he remains separated by both his family's migration and the trajectory of his own life but one that nevertheless determines how he is, quite literally, seen.[60]

"It was a journey that ought not to have been made," he writes at the end of *An Area of Darkness.* "It had broken my life in two" (A, 279–80). So much of it shocked him. He knew enough to know that India's poverty was the least interesting, because it was the most obvious, thing about the country. Yet he was without what Rushdie calls the "city eyes" that have learned not to see;[61] and the book lingers almost lovingly over the excrement and the flies, with a kind of narrative delight in degradation. Thirty years later he would acknowledge that he had projected his own hysteria onto the country around him. He was hysterical because what India taught him was how little that mythic homeland could be a home for him, even as it did so much to determine his relation to the rest of the world. He had himself hymned a different landscape, and so India becomes both definitive and yet impossible, inescapable and yet irrelevant. And the implication is that there's no way fully to escape one's origins, as if the formation of the writer's identity, which depends on his difference from those around him, stands as but an extreme form of the process through which a child never quite separates himself from his family. Losing himself in the crowd may have accentuated Naipaul's own sense of homelessness, but it also suggests the degree to which the process of individuation, of creating a self, must remain always incomplete.

His work is filled with a longing for a time before consciousness, when the world was whole and undifferentiated, the Nile only water. It is in effect a longing for the world of childhood, and he has indeed described his own childhood in terms of such a pure time: the rural village, Hindi-speaking; a family so extended that all who weren't relatives were outsiders and were feared. Rampersad has written of the novelist's love for Trinidad, a love that until his most recent autobiographical writings he has been unable fully to admit.[62] Yet that love is there in his evocation of the "dazzling haze" of a Port of Spain morning (B, 307); it is there on every page of *Miguel Street* and *A House for Mr. Biswas* and even in the satire of *The Mystic Masseur*. It is a love for the homeland he had to abandon if he was to become the writer that both he and his father wanted him to be, if he was to create that self. At the end of *Miguel Street* the unnamed narrator leaves Trinidad for England, walking toward the airplane, "not looking back, looking only at my shadow before me, a dancing dwarf on the tarmac" (MS, 172). Is it too much to hear an echo of "The Waste Land," of its fear in a handful of dust, in that shadow before him? It seems as if his leaving and his isolation have together made him into that dancing grotesque, something less than a man; and even if he escapes colonial dependency he will not, somehow, escape absurdity.

So the creation of a self carries a great cost. It involves a separation from others, from the world of home, that can never be entirely complete; and its very incompletion inevitably makes one ask if it has been worthwhile. As the first sentence of *A Bend in the River* puts it: "The world is what it is; men who are nothing, who allow themselves to become nothing, have no place in it" (R, 3). Yet how can one avoid that fate? We have none of us fully had the making of ourselves. None of us belong to ourselves alone, and Naipaul's work, whose subject has always been "the worlds I contained within myself" (E, 147), turns on this paradox: the self is the same as the group. More, the self he has made depends on his membership in a group that others, that British imperialism, have defined as marginal and powerless. A. Sivanadnan has written of reading Naipaul with "a sense of self-betrayal," describing him as a writer who reminds his readers always of their own "subjugation."[63] Yet perhaps, as Suleri has argued, the time for such angry critiques has passed. Or at the very least such critiques must be prepared to admit that "Naipaul has already been there before them, and has been exquisitely angry at himself," at the way in which his very existence requires that self-betrayal.[64] Naipaul's work—his material and therefore, as a writer, his individuality— depends on the very forces that militate against the creation of that autonomous self: on a simultaneous acceptance and rejection of the terms in which the colonial master has seen him; on the devastating knowledge that he remains always "one of the crowd." Mimicry is inevitable in a world in which the work of individuation remains always unfinished. One may live under the illusion of being in a free state, but it is an illusion, and it leaves one in tatters, like that tramp at Piraeus. For there is finally no way to escape one's origins, one's "half-made" state, no way to become the sole author of the self. Texts are made of other texts. And so the frenzy and the fear, the raw nerves, the long line of books, the body of work built up as a stay against the pain of one's own dependency, desperately trying to write into being the self that one knows one can never fully achieve.

IV

As a young man, Mr. Biswas works in a relative's rum shop where, with the business closed for a funeral, he is one day left on his own. "The empty rooms, usually oppressive, now held unlimited prospects of freedom and vice; but Mr. Biswas could think of nothing vicious and satisfying. He smoked but that gave little pleasure. And gradually the rooms lost their thrill" (B, 63). It's the last sentence that carries Naipaul's distinctive dispiriting note; hear the way its concluding monosyllables drain its energy away. Experience in his world is never quite as rich as it seems it ought to be. One of his favorite words is "glamour," which he uses precisely, with reference to its original meaning. A modern, European-built city in Africa has a "colonial glamour" (F, 104). It casts a charm, but that charm is always illusory, a trick, a delusion. Nothing ever quite fulfills its promise, and that's especially true of the sexual life. "Intimacy," writes Ralph Singh, "the word holds the horror . . . it was violation and self-violation" (MM, 25). The desire for others destroys both their purity, their integrity, and one's own. It carries always the taint of violence, in *Guerillas* above all, a novel whose brutality makes one's skin crawl out of a fear of itself, a premonition of the corruption of all flesh. But that desire also challenges one's own dream of individual autonomy; it stands as a reminder of the insufficiency of the self. To Naipaul, "we violate no body so much as our own" (MM, 71); desire and intimacy are to him like that moment in which he melts into the Indian crowd, a moment hated and longed for at once. It is hated because longed for, because we have hoped that it might make us whole.

And that sense of violation seems especially to characterize relations between men and women of different races. "Nature has not established her boundaries . . . in vain," as Herder has written, and interracial liaisons in Naipaul's work invariably end as badly as they do in Kipling's. Halfway through *A Bend in the River* Naipaul's narrator, Salim, begins an affair with a European named Yvette. Salim belongs to an Indian merchant family long settled on the East African coast, but he has himself "fetched up in the centre of the continent," in the colonial city "at the bend in the great river" (R, 20). Yvette is the wife of Raymond, the Big Man's White Man, and she lives on what's called "The New Domain," a university city erected on the site of a "dead European suburb" (R, 102): "modern Africa . . . by-passing . . . bush and villages . . . [and] built in concrete and glass" (R, 100–101). She is the first woman for whom Salim hasn't had to pay, and their affair goes smoothly enough for as long as the country seems peaceful. But when the Big Man faces a threat to his power, they begin to quarrel; and one night Salim beats her.

Fanon writes that the black man sees whites as blessed, blessed by an assurance of their own place in the world, and that he therefore looks to the love of a white woman to gain that assurance himself, to convince himself that he is a man; at the same time his sexual desire carries a note of racial revenge.[65] But Fanon's words only begin to suggest the complexities of the sexual dynamic that Naipaul describes. Salim beats Yvette both because he thinks she has another lover, making him as one with her cuckold husband, and because her manner has started to remind him of "whores who thought they should pretend to be jealous" (R, 218–19), of the time when he had to pay for pleasure, of the time when he wasn't a man. And he ends by spitting between her legs. Yet his rage grows out of something other than that simple desire for revenge. He beats her because their intimacy has both fostered and then destroyed his illusions. Listening at her house, on the night of their first meeting, to a record by Joan Baez, Salim thinks, "You couldn't listen to sweet songs about injustice unless you expected justice and received it much of the time." He knows that in his daily life he can't afford to believe in justice, that in the city outside, one can take nothing for granted. But the sweet voice moves him just the same, and in that safe house on the New Domain, that place where whites and Indians have gathered in a room with "African mats on the floor and African hangings on the wall," it seems easy to believe in what the voice has to say, easy "to make those assumptions" (R, 128–29). Then he learns that the world of the New Domain isn't the safe place he thought—and that is when he beats her. He beats Yvette because her position in the world has proved as vulnerable as his own, because she remains prey to the same anxieties and insecurities that he does, because the "sweet songs" are illusions for her as well. He spits on her as a crowd in the novel attacks a policeman who stumbles.

Yet even as he beats her, Africa and Europe seem to coalesce. For Yvette's vulnerability undermines the absolute distinction Naipaul appears to make between "civilization" on the one hand and "bush" on the other. When he first arrives at the bend in the river, Salim finds a ruined monument inscribed with a Latin tag: *Miscerique probat populos et foedera jungi.* The ruins are those of a memorial the colonial steamship company erected to celebrate itself, and the words mean that the gods approve of the mixing of the continents and the peoples. The wreckage unnerves him—"the steamer monument had been knocked down," an attempt "to wipe out the memory of the intruder"—but the sentiment makes him hopeful (R, 26). Only the quotation is wrong, a mistake that prefigures his own later illusions about his affair with Yvette. For it's drawn from Book IV of the *Aeneid*, where the gods emphatically do not approve—and in consequence Dido perishes. When Salim learns the truth he both marvels at and is appalled by the way the imperial powers have manipulated the past in the service of their rule. It means that the city is based on a lie, the kind of lie that would later build the New

Domain—a misquotation that paradoxically confirms the opposition it attempts to deny.

Though is that opposition in fact so clear? The "bush villages" of *In a Free State*'s title story wouldn't be bush without the presence of the nearby capital city, where Africa has been reduced to "decor"—and vice versa (F, 103–4). They need each other; the Manichaean distinction between them makes them inseparable even as it insists on their separation. Naipaul rarely describes what one might call virgin or primeval bush. Nothing in his work corresponds to Conrad's account, in *Heart of Darkness*, of "going up that river . . . to the earliest beginnings of the world,"[66] and Naipaul uses the word "forest," not "bush," to refer to the "true, safe world" of a village living its traditional life (R, 9). "This isn't property," Nazruddin says in *A Bend in the River*. "This is just bush. This has always been bush" (R, 23). He's looking at some lots he has bought for development, and the word suggests the absence of an order he expected to find. For to Naipaul "bush" is less a place than an event. His politically controversial material has meant that too little attention has been paid to him as a maker, an artificer. A maker—and a destroyer—whose subject, as Peter Hughes has argued, is the way in which the world unmakes itself.[67] In *The Enigma of Arrival* Naipaul writes that even as a child in Trinidad, he had "the idea . . . that [he] had come into a world past its peak" (E, 23); later in that book he thinks of building a house as "creating a potential ruin" (E, 89). And bush is what grows upon the ruins. It is what comes back: the water hyacinths that clog the streams of *A Bend in the River*, the "doorless doorway" (F, 171) of a house, rubbish that hasn't been properly disposed of. Even in Wiltshire he uses that word, and not the expected "brush," to describe the undergrowth at the bottom of an abandoned garden.

But "bush" also stands for Naipaul as the natural but abhorred condition of humanity—disorderly, overgrown, and untended, unpruned by the careful shears of civilization. It is above all a state of mind: a mind that suffers always from what Ralph Singh calls a sense of "shipwreck"; a mind whose history has been burnt away. *The Mimic Men* was Naipaul's first attempt to reach beyond Trinidad to the larger world that empire has left behind, to conceptualize the assumptions that had governed his earlier work; it marks the emergence of the mature artist. But Naipaul has more often employed an African setting for that kind of generalization. *In a Free State* works by juxtaposing its title story to the two first-person monologues that precede it, "One Out of Many" and "Tell Me Who to Kill," each a chronicle of what can happen to a colonial in the metropolis if he doesn't have the luck and the talent of a Naipaul. "One Out of Many" is the more successful, the story of an Indian servant who in America learns to see himself as something other than a part of his employer's presence—to see himself as an individual. Yet in separating himself from his past, and indeed from his dependency, Santosh comes to believe that he has made himself nothing. For he cannot return to the safe world of India, to his recognized spot on the pavement. He has become a casualty of freedom, like the tramp in that volume's prologue, looking for some way to fill up the cracks in the self. And in the short novel that gives the book its title, Naipaul extends that sense of freedom's cost to less obvious casualties, to the expatriate whites at work in a newly independent African nation, the flotsam of a postimperial age. For to be in a free state is, in another sense, to be stateless. Naipaul's characters have no place of their own in the society in which they live. They are at once irresponsible and yet safe, and his account of that moral emptiness suggests the ways in which these relics of the other side of empire are also, in a sense, among the wretched of the earth. They too suffer from that sense of shipwreck, from what Georg Lukacs called the "transcendental homelessness" of a world without the possibility of wholeness.[68]

Yet that very act of generalization is in itself problematic. *A Bend in the River* uses the instability of Central African politics as the landscape against which to explore a world in which the past has been burnt away for everyone, in which humankind is everywhere homeless, so that the expatriate, estranged from the landscape his ancestors hymned, comes to stand as the representative figure of our time. And where *In a Free State* seems merely brilliant, its successor burns like a dark star. But does either book actually concern itself with Africa, as Africa, or do they both instead *use* it, use it as the means to a metaphor rather than treat it as an end in itself? Christopher L. Miller has described what he calls "Africanist discourse" as one that sees Africa neither as the West nor as its Oriental other but as "an empty slate . . . in the relationship between the self and others, the third is null."[69] And that assignation of nullity gives Africa a purely "paper reality,"[70] born of "European ideas and concerns,"[71] which makes it uniquely available as the site of whatever fantasy one cares to propose. Such a discourse even takes the darkness of African skin as the absence of light, a sign that there's something missing, an emptiness that is to be "written on by others," that can be filled with wonder or with horror, with anything but the specificities of actual African lives.[72]

What is most often written on that slate is the related discourse of primitivism: the return to one's origins, to the earliest state of the world, a return that allows the West simultaneously to escape from and yet to underscore its own modernity.[73] The paradigmatic text is of course *Heart of Darkness*, in which Africa becomes a metaphor for man's original state even as it also provides a metaphor for the darkness of the human heart. What Miller demonstrates is the degree to which such literary appropriations become entangled with the history of colonial exploitation. Africa's "emptiness"—Marlow, looking at a map, calls it a "blank space of delightful mystery"[74]—provides the excuse for a land grab. And Africa itself, as the critical commonplace now holds, becomes identified with evil; so in using the continent as a symbol for European depravity, Conrad's story participates, on the level of language, with the imperialism it appears to condemn.

From such a reading—the classic example is Chinua Achebe's 1977 article—grows the suspicion of metaphor that shapes much postcolonial criticism.[75] For metaphor proposes a similarity between two otherwise dissimilar things, remaking the foreign in terms of the familiar, as if figurative language itself were enrolled in the service of empire. In a decolonizing world one should, however, see a place on its own terms; a work set in Africa ought ideally to root itself in the particularities of African life and not simply treat the continent as a site in which to enact a drama about some supposedly universal human condition. Yet because the name itself has, in Miller's words, "no native source and so did not exist before its definition as an other in relation to Europe and Asia,"[76] Africanist discourse is inevitable to the degree that a writer conceives of his or her subject as "Africa" rather than as one or another of the continent's many cultures. To describe a writer as "Africanist" is therefore to do no more—but also no less—than to say that he or she does not write from within an Ibo or Xhosa or Kikuyu point of view. And perhaps the most that one can hope is that such a writer will construct his or her "paper reality" with a minimum of distortion. In fact Miller suggests that most Africanist writers are themselves conscious of that problem; well, that too is inevitable in a discourse predicated on the idea of unfathomable darkness. In Edgar Rice Burroughs it does not necessarily point to a saving self-consciousness about the limits of his own language. Nevertheless the finest Africanist writers do indeed brush that discourse against the grain, and for Miller, Conrad's insistence on the continent's incomprehensibility, on "alienation as meaning," serves finally to call the novelist's own rhetoric into question.[77]

And that is true of Naipaul as well. The title story of *In a Free State* said a great deal about the intertribal warfare that now determines the politics of Central Africa, and said it at a time when this was neither a commonplace of the newspapers nor the story— a bare decade after Independence—that the West most wanted to hear. But the book moves quickly past those politics and concentrates instead on the four-hundred-mile drive that two whites, Bobby and Linda, take across an unnamed country during a coup. They live in this country; they help determine its polices. Yet as they drive, and argue, they come constantly on things they do not understand; and Naipaul demonstrates over and over again what a woefully inadequate grasp they have of the world in which they reside. "Africa" overwhelms them, even as Africa itself appears to vanish in Naipaul's exploration of their rootlessness on the one hand and the bad faith and conscience of the postimperial West on the other. Meanwhile the country's people provide background, scenery, atmosphere—a rebellious servant, a face along the side of the road. Some are from the "king's" tribe, others the "president's," but only one of them has a name—"Peter"—and they aren't otherwise differentiated, are no more given voices or roles than they were in Conrad's work. Bobby and Linda could be anywhere.

But that is Naipaul's point. Like Bobby and Linda themselves, the novel may seem simply to drive through Africa, to treat it only as landscape. Yet that deliberate superficiality is a crucial element in Naipaul's creation of their peculiar "freedom." He limits himself to his characters' perceptions; he allows the novel to know only the sorts of things they do; he uses their simple terms— "Africans"—to suggest how little the world that colonialism has left behind has to do with that continent as such. For the "paper reality" that once covered "Africa" has found a postimperial counterpart in the anonymous universality of air-conditioning and international hotels. The newly built capital city remains "an English-Indian creation," imposed on the landscape rather than a part of it, a city where "Africa showed only in the semi-tropical suburban gardens, in the tourist shop displays. . . . Africa here was decor. . . . Everyone in it was far from home" (F, 103–4)—especially the men and women from the neighboring countryside.

The irony with which *In a Free State* provides both an example of Africanist discourse and a comment on it seems worthy of comparison with the Conrad of *The Secret Agent*. And Conrad lies behind *A Bend in the River* as well. Salim reaches the great curve of its title overland and from the east, rather than upriver and from the west. But it is recognizably the same place as the one to which Marlow journeys, Kisangani, the town that grew out of Kurtz's Inner Station. And not much has changed, despite the building of hotels and suburbs and marketplaces. Yet Conrad's Marlow only grudgingly admits his relation to his story's dominant metaphor. The Thames was *once* one of the dark places of earth, and it takes Africa to make him recognize the heart of darkness in himself. Salim doesn't have his predecessor's security, and from the start he knows that he is fully implicated in his narrative's central metaphor in a way that Marlow doesn't. So in watching people move from their forest villages to the river steamer, he sees a version of his own origins: "That was how, in our ancestral lands, we all began—the prayer mat on the sand, then the marble floor of a mosque; the rituals . . . of nomads" transformed into the ceremony of a court (R, 161). But Salim looks at those villagers always with a fascinated distaste, aware of what separates him from them and also of what doesn't, aware that he's not as far away from them as he would like. His protégé Ferdinand has gone from the forest to the polytechnic in the course of a single childhood. For Salim that historical process has been slower; his family has enjoyed centuries of prosperity on the East African coast, but a university education lies beyond the scope of their ambition. And when he travels inland he can't escape the sense that he's "going in the wrong direction" (R, 4), that he should turn around and head out, run for the refuge of a civilization whose locus he inevitably sees as London.

Hence his attraction to Yvette—and hence his disappointed violence. *A Bend in the River* describes a world in which different stages of history clash within the same person, a world in which Africa, India, and the West collide but do not cohere. And that collision is for Naipaul the source of history's tragedy. For one culture, one stage, always overwhelms the other; and the one that has been overwhelmed has no choice but to aspire to the fruits of the invader. It cannot pretend not to know. The ruins of the steamship memorial make Salim feel he lives "in a place where the future had come and gone" (R, 27), but he can never forget that it's been there. A culture may cling to an image of the years before things fell apart, when life was whole and the Nile only water. What it cannot do is go back to the time before contact, even though that's what is threatened in the understated apocalypse of the novel's conclusion. Yet the opposition between civilization and bush is never so absolute as it seems. The novel's Big Man—a national leader clearly modeled on Zaire's Mobutu—wants to build his "skyscrapers in the bush" (R, 136). But he also wants to celebrate the indigenous culture of the past—here, paradoxically, through a cult of the African Madonna. Yet he cannot take his people back to the past without using the machine gun, without the airfields that mean nowhere is safe, not even the forest villages he would supposedly preserve; so that in declaring his independence of the West he only increases his reliance on its products. "Whatever they say about going back to the beginning," Salim says at the end of the novel, "they'll be interested in the car" (R, 275).

The gods may not approve of the mingling of peoples; but it happens just the same. So bush and civilization fall into one, become metaphors for each other, not as something grudgingly admitted, some repressed primitive part of the self, but as a sign that "the world is what it is." And indeed Naipaul suggests, as with the beating of Yvette, that the instability of Central Africa now governs the life of the West as well. Salim does finally flee to London, yet though he admires the great cities of Europe, the care and the human concern that has planned them, he can no longer see Europe as a refuge. The Europe he has come to isn't the glamorous land of his imagination but rather "something shrunken and mean and forbidding" (R, 229). London too is a city in the bush—or rather the bush has come to London. For a refuge needs disorder as civilization needs bush, depends on its presence elsewhere, on the ability to draw a circle around the self and leave that confusion outside. London could provide a refuge only so long as it ruled an empire. Then it could keep the "restlessness, the deep disorder" that it had itself created, at arm's length. But now, as Salim's friend Nazruddin says, the world is everywhere in movement: "People have scraped the world clean, and now they want to run from the dreadful places where they've made their money and find some nice safe country" (R, 234). But the relative ease with which one can now reach the metropolis destroys that safety, removes some of the reasons for going there, and leaves Salim with a vision "of men lost in space and time, but dreadfully, pointlessly busy" (R, 241).

Even so, it's hard to escape thinking that for Salim, London seems shrunken and mean because it's now filled with "kiosks and choked grocery shops—run by people like" himself, people whom he doesn't like but whom he nevertheless wants to join (R, 230). Naipaul works his metaphors more subtly than Conrad, but still the novel does not—could not—quite manage to dodge its own Africanist rhetoric. Its fusion of civilization and bush sees Africa as providing a kind of norm for a world that is everywhere in flight from itself; Africa now offers the terms with which to understand

Europe, and not the other way around. In doing so, however, the novel also depends on ignoring the very real differences between them. After all, Salim *does* leave, and not because he's looking for more of the same. Yet that very fact suggests the possibility of a distinction between Salim's own rhetoric and the novel as a whole, as indeed does the mimic man's self-loathing with which he employs the very language that demeans him. And it's at this point that we need to turn to an account of the novel's narrative voice and of the slippery relation between Salim and his creator.

Certainly the character often seems to echo Naipaul's own point of view. The novel's second chapter contains an account of the history that has made Salim and of his family's ignorance of that history:

> When we had come [to Africa] no one could tell me. We were not that kind of people. We simply lived; we did what was expected of us, what we had seen the previous generation do. We never asked why; we never recorded. We felt in our bones that we were a very old people; but we seemed to have no means of gauging the passing of time. Neither my father nor my grandfather could put dates to their stories. Not because they had forgotten or were confused; the past was simply the past. (R, 11)

His people live as they have always lived because they have never known how to "assess" (R, 17) themselves; they don't have the "habit of looking" at their own lives, of "detaching [themselves] from a familiar scene" so that they can see it as a foreigner might. But Salim has learned to do that, by looking at postage stamps whose representations of "local scenes and local things" have given him an idea of what others might find interesting about his "region" (R, 15). He has learned to stand outside himself, and it has taught him that his own community, whose presence in Africa long antedates Europe's, "had ceased to count" (R, 17). And Naipaul has said similar things elsewhere, writing in *An Area of Darkness* of the need for "a way of looking" (A, 227)—a way that he says India lacks and that is for him inseparable from a sense of historical pro-

cess and change. Nevertheless, "It is well that Indians are unable
to look at their country directly, for the distress they would see
would drive them mad. And it is well that they have no sense of
history" (A, 212).

His argument is the same as Salim's, but his language isn't,
and that's precisely why *A Bend in the River* convinces as fiction.
When Salim repeats words and phrases, it's not because he has
made a conscious choice but because his limited education has given
him no others; the parallel structures that Naipaul himself employs
are beyond him. Salim is shrewd about other people. But he remains
throughout something of an ingenue, persistently naive about his
own situation and capable always of an open-mouthed wonder:
"Trade, goods! What a mystery!" (R, 88). When he speaks of the
"African terror of strange Africans" (R, 71), we recognize the language as that which an Indian merchant—who, despite his birthplace, has never seen himself as African—would use to describe all
blacks; the rhetoric is a part of his characterization. Yet take a moment, late in the novel, when he says, "Africa, going back to its old
ways with modern tools, was going to be a difficult place for some
time" (R, 201). "Modern tools," "difficult": is Salim conscious of
that euphemism, that understatement? Is he being ironic, or do we
see him ironically? I suspect the latter, and indeed one could easily
build a case for him as something like an unreliable narrator, and
not only because he beats Yvette. At key points, for example, Naipaul needs to supplement Salim's narrative: two old friends, Nazruddin and Indar, tell him their life stories and, in doing so, intro-
duce him into the knowledge of a larger world. And he's stunned
when, at the end of the novel, the economy is nationalized and his
business confiscated. He had thought he was protected, not seeing
that each man must make his own protection: his own home, his
own life. But even then he never acknowledges his own relationship
to the generalization of the novel's opening sentence—"men who
are nothing"—and seems instead to believe that escaping the bend
in the river has allowed him to escape that nothingness as well.

Yet something peculiar happens to—or rather because of—
Salim's naivete. Early in the novel he speaks of "the miraculous
peace of the colonial time, when men could, if they wished, pay

little attention to tribal boundaries" (R, 34). The phrase is unsettling, especially in reference to a region that includes the former Belgian Congo. Nevertheless Salim says it in all innocence, the innocence of a man concerned only with the conditions of trade; independence has made border crossings more difficult and has increased the need for bribes. The statement reveals his limitations; once again, it makes us see him ironically. But it does something else as well. It may indeed seem miraculous that anyone could consider the colonial time as one of peace, and yet in a peculiar sense it was. The modern tools remained under European control; the old ways—all of them—were discouraged. There was a kind of peace, in which trade could proceed, in a way that makes these words ironic about the very irony with which they ask us to see their speaker. It is as if the novel has two voices. The words Salim uses remain functions of his naivete, but they also come to have the force of ideas. "Ordinary," "Europeans," "lies," "look," "Africa," "people," even "simple" itself: these are simple words that seem immediately clear in their referents but that also carry the weight of the arguments developed at length in Naipaul's other work.

Such words come freighted with meanings that one is never quite certain Salim himself understands; certainly he doesn't understand the provocation they contain. Yet our awareness of the arguments to which they refer means that we cannot finally dismiss Salim himself as unreliable. "The world is what it is; men who are nothing, who allow themselves to become nothing, have no place in it." So sure of itself, that voice, and yet so idiosyncratic too, even as its bleak grandeur lays claim to a universality that seems to transcend all individuality. Even the stories told by Indar and Nazruddin seem in the end no more than a sophisticated echo of Salim's own voice, a voice to whose confident despair the novel offers no real alternative. *A Bend in the River* seems half case-study of hysteria and half objective statement of the way of the world. And one cannot choose between them, cannot decide how far to trust this narrator who seems to know so little and yet so much. For the radically unstable irony with which Naipaul blurs the conventional distinction between author and narrator is so perfectly controlled that there's no way to be sure his words can't be taken literally. The modern tools need not be machine guns—or not only machine guns. It is an art so sophisticated that it can dare to be naive. Contemptuous, confused, passive, naive, finicky, limited, panic-stricken, but not necessarily unreliable, so rational, so clear about the illusions of others, so capable of a grand vision of history—Salim may well be a stand-in for the author himself. But the question seems irrelevant. One can read Naipaul's travel books and assent to this, dissent from that, testing them against reality. The quirky objectivity of the novel involves us too completely for that. It is as if that voice knows in advance all the ways in which we might question its reliability, and admits them, nakedly; parades its neurosis and invites us to dismiss it, knowing we won't be able to. Nothing could be clearer and more accessible than Naipaul's prose. And nothing could be more difficult to grasp than this brilliant piece of ventriloquism, from which the author seems altogether absent even as his sensibility is etched in every line: the profoundly disturbing monologue of a man who is nothing, from whose claustrophobia the reader despairs of escaping, with a despair that matches the narrator's own.[78]

Far more than its explicit argument, far more than even its account of the Big Man's rule, the very form of *A Bend in the River* provides an embodiment of a world in which there seems finally no place for anyone. And the uncertainty with which it demands that we see Salim, the final illegibility of his character—that makes the novel terrifying, as if a gulf had opened beneath us and human meaning were impossible to hold. No other writer of our time has had Naipaul's ability to disturb his readers, to wound and to trouble them. But the ability I speak of is something more than the simple ability to outrage those readers, as *The Satanic Verses* has outraged so many Muslims or indeed as Naipaul has outraged so many of his critics. It is something different, perhaps something deeper, certainly something more personal. To read *A Bend in the River*, that long tone-poem of moral isolation, is to feel as if one's mind has been flayed, as if one's deepest anxieties lie quivering and exposed. For in his estrangement from the world, in the freedom that has made him nothing, Salim stands as the secret sharer of our thoughts and fears. Not of our capacity for crime, as in Conrad, but of our incapacity for making a self.

And the book's dominant note is finally that of anger. It is odd to say that, for the novel seems so quiet, its surface so apparently unruffled by the violence it describes. But yes, anger, an anger at one's inability to evade the forces that have made one, an anger that, as Suleri suggests, Naipaul has directed at himself above all and whose greatest mark is the emptiness at the heart of his greatest novel. And the book sounds a note of impatience too—again, an odd word. In *Finding the Center* Naipaul writes that from his father's stories he "arrived at the conviction—the conviction that is at the root of so much human anguish and passion, and corrupts so many lives—that there was justice in the world. The wish to be a writer was a development of that" (FC, 31–32). From that passion grows a permanent sense of fury, a hunger for justice *now*, a longing that gives him no tolerance for what Salim describes as "black men assuming the lies of white men" (R, 16), for a new injustice in response to the old one of empire. That impatience allies Naipaul with Fanon and with the Big Man's attempt to redress the pain of the past. He has that kind of rage, the rage that in other men and women brought independence into being, that made the postcolonial world; and like all great passions, that anger is itself capable of corruption and of an injustice of its own. But perhaps it is time to begin asking not what he is angry at, but what he is angry for.

The Novel in an Age of Ideology:
On the Form of *Midnight's Children*

I

Born into a rich Muslim family at midnight, August 15, 1947—the very instant of India's independence—Saleem Sinai grows up "handcuffed to history" (11), believing that the words with which Jawaharlal Nehru proclaimed the new nation's existence have been especially addressed to him.[1] He too wants to "build the noble mansion of free India, where all her children may dwell" (116); for hasn't Nehru himself suggested, in a commemorative letter to "Dear Baby Saleem," that the boy's life will be "the mirror" of the nation's (122)? So a childhood accident to the fictional Saleem leads in Salman Rushdie's *Midnight's Children* (1981) to the historical 1957 language riots that ended with the partition of the state of Bombay. What happens to him happens to his country; what happens to his country happens to him.

Rushdie presents the novel as Saleem's autobiography: one the character has written while working, at the age of thirty, in a Bombay pickle factory, written as a defense against the disintegration of his own body, written in despair at the way his "life has been transmuted into grotesquery by the irruption into it of history" (57). The book's title has come in popular parlance to refer to that generation born around the time of Independence—Rushdie's own generation and that of Rajiv Gandhi as well, a generation that has known only Indian and not colonial rule. Yet though Rushdie surely intends that large meaning, in the novel itself the phrase applies only to the particular group that Saleem comes to embody, the 1,001 children born in the first hour of India's independence, "seeds of a future which would genuinely differ from anything the world had seen" (193) and all of whom have magical powers:

> From Kerala, a boy who had the ability of stepping into mirrors and re-emerging through any reflective surface in the land . . . from Kashmir . . . a blue-eyed child of whose original sex I was never certain, since by immersing herself in water he (or she) could alter it as she (or he) pleased. Some of us called this child Narada, others Markandaya, depending on which old fairy story of sexual change we had heard . . . at Budge-Budge outside Calcutta a sharp-tongued girl whose words already had the power of inflicting physical wounds . . . a boy who could eat metal and a girl whose fingers were so green that she could grow prize aubergines in the Thar desert. (195)

The greatest gifts belong to those born the closest to midnight, and Saleem's gift is therefore the grandest of them all, that of telepathy, making his own mind into a sort of "All-India Radio" (164) that lets him tune into "the inner monologues of all the so-called teeming millions" (166). At first he uses his gift only for "voyeurism and petty cheating" in school (170). But soon, to "escape the intolerable pressures of eavesdropping on people [he] knew" (171), he starts to move further afield, entering now this mind, now that. One day he is a rich landlord; on another he starves. And on a third he discovers, "over twenty years before it became a national joke, that Morarji Desai 'took his own water' daily . . . I was inside him, tasting the warmth as he gurgled down a frothing glass of urine." As he penetrates the hearts and minds of others, Saleem comes to feel that he is "somehow creating a world. . . . I had entered into the illusion of the artist and thought of the multitudinous realities of the land as the raw unshaped material of my gift" (172). Within himself he encompasses the whole of that India to which history has handcuffed him, not an individual so much as the choral voice of national consciousness. And within that voice, Saleem discovers the separate tones of 581 other children with magical powers ("malnutrition, disease, and the misfortunes of everyday life" [193] having accounted for the rest of the 1,001) and decides to form them into a club, which he jokingly calls the MCC: not the Marylebone Cricket Club but the far more exclusive Midnight's Children's Conference.

For rather than simply listening, Saleem begins to broadcast, inviting those other children to join a nightly congregation in his mind. The Midnight's Children's Conference—the novel's central conceit—makes Saleem's autobiography an attempt to enact belief in another sort of narrative, in that of the India that the Mahatma Gandhi and Nehru conceived as a democratic, secular, and pluralist state, a dream that found its political voice in the Indian National Congress (INC). Congress claimed to represent all Indians, and it never abandoned that claim, even after the rise of Mohammed Ali Jinnah's Muslim League and the subsequent creation of Pakistan made Congress seem increasingly identified with Hinduism and even after Independence changed it from a resistance movement into a ruling party. And in evoking a similar congress, Rushdie attempts, with both the MCC and *Midnight's Children* itself, to provide a vision of the country he wants India to be: an attempt to imagine a unifying form for the subcontinent as a whole, from Kerala to Kashmir, from Bombay to the jungles of Bengal, a country that has indeed made a fresh start at the moment of independence, in which the differences between Hindu and Muslim and Sikh, Brahmin and beggar, are contained within a single structure.

Yet in describing that vision, that community, the adult Saleem, at work in the pickle factory where he preserves his past in vinegar and spice, sees himself as suffering from a peculiarly "Indian disease . . . [an] urge to encapsulate the whole of reality" (75). What makes it a disease—and one to which novelists as well as Indians are peculiarly liable—is the impossibility of shaping such disparate materials into a coherent narrative, not just those of his own autobiography but those of a partitioned and ever more fragmented India itself. "I hold it to be utterly wrong," the Mahatma said, "to divide man from man by reason of religion," for with questions of "religious usage and observances . . . a secular state has no concern."[2] But Jinnah believed it was a futile "dream that Hindus and Muslims [could] ever evolve a common nationality."[3] India's large Hindu majority meant it would always be a Hindu state, in which the rights of the Muslim minority would be trampled on, whatever the nation's constitution might say about secularism. And either argument can find ample support in India's subsequent history. The 1992 destruction of the mosque at Ayodhya by the Hindu fundamentalist Bharatiya Janata Party (BJP) makes Jinnah look right. Under both Indira and Rajiv Gandhi, Congress simultaneously encouraged sectarian Hinduism *and* granted special rights to Muslims as Muslims, all for the sake of short-term electoral gains; and that deadly contradiction has been the greatest cause of the rise of the BJP. But one can also argue that Jinnah himself did more than anyone else to unleash the force of communalism, the habit of thinking in terms of group identities and group rights.

Religion is, however, but the most important of the subcontinent's communal faultlines; and perhaps the centrality of caste, in daily life if not in India's constitution, makes such habits of thought inescapable. Even in the largely Hindu south, riots can flare between Tamil and Kannada speakers over water rights. And indeed Saleem's own family history is marked by a parodic version of that fragmentation. His maternal grandfather, a doctor, had wooed his wife through a hole in a "perforated sheet." She was in *purdah*, kept from the eyes of "strange men" (24); her father would let him see only that part of which she complained, which would appear in that opening while the sheet kept the rest of her body veiled. He came to know her not as a whole, but through one, and she always remained for him "a badly-fitting collage of her severally inspected parts . . . a partitioned woman . . . Glued together by his imagination" (26). So when Saleem starts to despair over the possible incoherence of his story, he insists that his own body has begun to fall apart, that it's become riven with cracks and fissures that no one but he can perceive; and his personal disintegration becomes a metonymy for that of the national collage as a whole, a country that looks whole on the map but that has, in the years since the novel's publication in particular, become increasingly divided from itself.

Within the novel the midnight's children themselves become the living expression of what Rushdie calls India's "national longing for form" (291). But modern India also has "five thousand years of history . . . [even though it] had never previously existed" (111), and its children, "however magical, are not immune to their parents." Even in the MCC the Marathi speakers loathe the Gujaratis, the fair are contemptuous of the dark, and the "Brahmins began to feel uneasy at permitting even their thoughts to touch the thoughts" (248) of what are now called the "scheduled castes." For another woman gave birth at the stroke of midnight on August 15, 1947, in the charity ward of the same nursing home where Saleem was born; but Vanita, a street musician's wife, hemorrhaged and died just three minutes after her son appeared. One child was born a rich Muslim, another a poor Hindu—and in the nursing home their name tags, and their fates, were switched. So the Saleem who receives Nehru's letter isn't the one to whom it's been addressed. Which of the children born at midnight is in fact the real Saleem? Which life will stand as the mirror of the nation's?

The street child grows up with the very common Hindu name of Shiva, the destroyer, and when he first appears on Saleem's mental screen, he's been running a gang whose only rule is "Everybody does what I say or I squeeze the shit outa them." He ridicules the rich boy's idea of the MCC as a "loose federation of equals, all points of view given free expression," and he proposes that the two of them run the club together—"Gangs gotta have gang bosses" (215). And though Saleem resists his double's temptation, it remains one to which his delight in "creating a world" makes him far from immune. "Who found the Children, anyway?" (222), he thinks. Who has received a letter from Nehru himself? For Shiva "there is only me-against-the-world!" (249), only self-interest in a life so impoverished that all other principles are luxuries. Self-interest finds him his first job, intimidating voters in the 1957 elections. And indeed it is Saleem's own self-interest that finally makes him exclude Shiva from "the increasingly fractious councils" (274) of the MCC. The communal tensions that "the national longing for form" has tried to contain lead finally to destruction, until it paradoxically begins to seem as if the only way to hold the country together is to embrace the very power that Shiva embodies. For in Rushdie's reading of Indian history, Mrs. Gandhi goes to war with Pakistan in 1971 only because it's an easy way to unify the country—or, rather, to consolidate her own power in a period when her Congress Party has degenerated into the slogan that Indira is India, India Indira.

For Mother Indira cannot endure the threat embodied in the pluralism of the MCC. History books may argue that Mrs. Gandhi declared the Emergency of 1975–77 because the economy had gone bad, because she feared a conspiracy against her, because she'd been caught in a bit of election fraud. But for Saleem, and for Rushdie, her declaration of that "continuous midnight which would not end for two long years" (404) had but one purpose: the destruction of the midnight's children. "Were we competitors for centrality?" (406), Saleem asks. Did she too see the country as raw material on which she could impose a form, and decide she couldn't stand the competition, that she would prefer to destroy the India that might be rather than risk losing her own power? With the Emergency comes "suspension-of-civil rights, and censorship-of-the-press, and armoured-units-on-special-alert, and arrest-of-subversive-elements" (404). With the Emergency comes the "birth-control campaign"—led by Mrs. Gandhi's son Sanjay—a euphemism for a program of eleven million sterilizations, most of them forced. And among Sanjay's victims is every survivor of the MCC.

Yet the midnight's children are not innocent of their own destruction, and Saleem in particular must pay for his own longing for centrality. Because of him "the children of midnight [are] denied the possibility of reproducing themselves." For under torture he gives Sanjay's storm troopers the information they need to track his confreres down, to put them under the knives of doctors so "truly extraordinary" that they can snip not only testicles and wombs but even "hope, too" along with the magical gifts of midnight. And "who," he asks, "escorted me to the chamber of my undoing?" (423). Major Shiva, the great hero of Mrs. Gandhi's war, has always worked for the only party with "really large sums to spend" (217).

II

That is the spine of the *Midnight's Children*. Yet in its most explicit form the conflict between Nehru's noble mansion and the communal strife that characterizes Indian political life fills only a few of the novel's pages. Instead Rushdie embodies both India's extraordinary diversity and the concomitant centrifugal force of its national form in the very structure of Saleem's narrative itself. For like the eponymous narrator of Rushdie's beloved *Tristram Shandy*, Saleem can't resist interrupting his story to observe himself in the process of telling it—questioning his own reliability, noting his doctor's visits, and wondering how the tale might go over with Padma, the illiterate factory worker, the Indian everywoman, who must and yet cannot be his audience. The novel seems itself a "badly-fitting collage," and in reading it, one even forgets the midnight's children for chapters at a time and follows instead, now enchanted, now appalled, Saleem's thousand and one digressions from the main narrative of his life: odes to chutney; Tai the Kashmiri boatman, who for years refused to wash; the pyromania of Saleem's sister, the Brass Monkey; a father who offers to have his daughter's teeth pulled and replaced with gold, as a dowry; the atrocities of the Bangladesh war; the ghostwomen of the Sundarbans; mango-kissing in the Indian film industry; smuggling in the Rann of Kutch; Bombay billboards, snake charmers, and bicycles.

Or the story of how Saleem's father, Ahmed, his mind "blurred by whiskey and djinn" (133), tried to make a fortune in Bombay land reclamation. But he doesn't bribe the right people, and so in opening his mail one morning, he finds himself shouting, "The bastards have shoved my balls in an ice-bucket!" His assets have been "frozen, like water," no longer liquid, not even "one anna to give alms to a beggar" (134). His wife, Amina, leads him toward the bedroom and tries to get him to relax. Once there, however, she finds: "Oh my goodness, janum, I thought you were just talking dirty, but it's true! So cold, Allah, so coooold, like little round cubes of ice!" (135). The family jewels have indeed been frozen. "Reality can have metaphorical content," Rushdie writes, but "that does not make it less real" (197). Yet such "metamorphosis is the contrary of metaphor," as Gilles Deleuze and Felix Guattari argued in their study of Kafka, and it's perhaps more accurate to say that Rushdie writes of a world without metaphor.[4] For he demands that we take such figures of speech as the "literal, by-the-hairs-of-my-mother's-head truth" (197), so that Saleem's own life, and his body as well, are in fact a mirror of the nation to which he's been "handcuffed by history." Psychological states become physical realities. When Amina has a love affair, she feels so clouded by guilt that a thick fog grows around her—"there were days when you could hardly see her head above her neck" (157).

That literalization of metaphor offers an initial point of comparison between Rushdie and the Western novelists to whom he was compared by the first reviewers of *Midnight's Children*. Rushdie may share a set of issues with Scott and Naipaul. But the style and the form of his fiction—and hence his treatment of those issues—link his work not to theirs so much as to that of a writer like Gunter Grass, in whose *The Tin Drum* little Oskar Matzerath willfully stunts his own growth at the age of three, or to Gabriel Garcia Marquez, in whose Macondo the streets run not only with blood but with blood that can round a corner, enter a house— "hugging the walls so as not to stain the rugs"—and pull up in the kitchen to announce a death.[5] Other names come to mind as well— Kundera, Pynchon, Calvino. And perhaps behind them all lies the Gogol of "The Nose" or "The Overcoat," whose characters are deformed into grotesquery by the tyranny of the bureaucracy within which they work, or Kafka's Gregor Samsa, whose insect body must above all be taken literally before it can be seen in terms of his social position or family relations.

Such fiction has been the most energetic and innovative and importunate of our age, an international style that is to us what the realism of George Eliot and Tolstoy was to the nineteenth century. Yet how should we make sense of it as a novelistic form? In "Art and Fortune," his 1948 investigation of the idea of the death of the novel, Lionel Trilling argued that the great nineteenth-century novels, "far more often than we remember, deal with developed ideas"—ideas about money, freedom, the position of women, the proper ordering of the state, the existence of God. Trilling suggests, however, that "the criticism which descends from [T. S.] Eliot puts explicit ideas in literature at a discount, which is one reason why it is exactly this criticism that is most certain of the death of the novel."[6] But Trilling himself is not so ready to place the novel in its tomb and instead makes three predictions about its future. First, there will be a renewal of interest in storytelling. Second, the novelist will be far less concerned with narrow questions of form, with the attempt to make the novel approach "the canons of poetical perfection."[7] And most interesting of all, he predicted: "The novel of the next decades will deal in a very explicit way with ideas. . . . Nowadays everyone is involved in ideas—or, to be more accurate, in ideology . . . [and its] conscious formulation. . . . Social class and the conflicts it produces may not be any longer a compelling subject to the novelist, but the organization of society into ideological groups presents a subject scarcely less absorbing."[8]

"Character isn't destiny any more," Alicja Cone says in Rushdie's *The Satanic Verses.* "Economics is destiny. Ideology is destiny. Bombs are destiny" (SV, 432). Character could be destiny only so long as the novel took the form of biography—*David Copperfield, Madame Bovary*—and found its material in the conflicts of social class, only so long as the novel remained the expression of one particular ideology, of the nineteenth century's emerging liberal individualism. But in the great fiction of the decades after World War II, the writer has felt called on to engage, and at times to repudiate, a world marked above all by ideological conflict and by the long nightmare of genocides and revolutions, fundamentalisms and wars, to which that conflict has led. And in consequence the novelist has, as Lucien Goldmann has written, attempted "to replace biography" with a formal structure grounded in the "ideas of community and collective reality" on which the politics of our century's mass societies have depended.[9]

Midnight's Children may seem to be the autobiography of Saleem Sinai. But even its title suggests the way it differs from the individual biography characteristic of nineteenth-century novels. If earlier writers sought protagonists who were, in Georg Lukacs's term, "typical" of their society, a novelist like Rushdie—or Grass or Kundera for that matter—chooses emblematic ones.[10] The difference lies in a foregrounding of the character's symbolic function. In reading Balzac, our appreciation of Rastignac's individual difficulties so dominates our awareness of his typicality as to make us forget it; indeed Rastignac most typifies his age precisely at the moment when we do forget it. It's essential to the novel's conception of society as a marketplace that we see him as a free agent; and the study of Balzac has, accordingly, emphasized the naturalization of that capitalist ideology in his work. For Balzac's fundamental ambivalence about the world he describes—his horrified fascination with capital and cash—is smoothly contained within a narrative of his characters' individual lives. It doesn't provide a structural feature of the text in itself but is rather mediated through the uneasy mix of loathing and desire those characters feel for what they call "the world." Yet such an emphasis turns political and social issues into what Homi Bhabha has described as a series of "individual and ethical problem[s]."[11] That has not seemed tenable in a period when the politics of a "collective reality" have made us ever more aware of ideology's supra-individual shaping force, and contemporary novelists are thus far more likely than their predecessors to expose their own ideological assumptions, to see the work as the site of a consciously articulated struggle between different cultural, political, or religious beliefs. So in Rushdie we never lose our awareness of the protagonist's emblematic value, for Saleem stands himself as the site of that struggle; he is always and explicitly as much the embodiment of the "polyglot frenzy . . . [and] the flooding multitudes" (166, 172) inside him as he is an individual.

Those multitudes call to mind Mikhail Bakhtin's conception of the "heteroglossia" of the novel form. Most literature has historically been "monoglot," like the pastorals in which "peasants . . . speak in the dignified accents of a stylized literary language."[12] The novel, however, works by juxtaposing the different levels of discourse within a given language, no one of which can fully capture that language's variety and resourcefulness. That gives Bakhtin's work a particular relevance to any "minor literature," but it's especially appropriate in working with an Anglophone Indian writer like Rushdie, in whose sentences Bombay street slang continuously flirts with Oxbridge English. But *Midnight's Children* enacts its heteroglossia on a thematic level as well as a stylistic one. No single member of the MCC can legitimately claim to represent India as a whole—not even Saleem, who writes, "The assassination of Mahatma Gandhi occurs, in these pages, on the wrong date" (164). In a congress of different voices no one person can be fully identified with the truth. For the linguistic pluralism of the heteroglot novel is an ideological one as well, discrediting the belief that truth is one and absolute, and holding that it is instead multiple, overlapping, conflicting. *A Bend in the River* can serve here as a kind of negative example: what makes it so frightening is the fact that Naipaul's monologic evenness of tone, the singularity of the novel's voice, allows us no escape from its narrator's despair.

For Bakhtin the novel becomes the place in which to ask questions without the need for answers—the site for what, using the ideological debates in Dostoevsky's work as his model, he describes as a "dialogic" encounter between different genres, systems of belief, types of language, and indeed whole cultures.[13] The novel maintains an ideological suspicion of ideological certainty, an acute awareness of ideology's deforming power, and therefore makes a corresponding assumption of what Kundera describes as "the wisdom of uncertainty"; and in this the novel remains, in the broadest sense of the word, a fundamentally liberal form.[14] Half a century later Trilling's predictions about the genre's future seem uncannily accurate. Certainly they fit such large loose baggy monsters of the postwar decades as *The Tin Drum* or *Midnight's Children*. And certainly those predictions point as well toward the cumbersome but accurate name that Linda Hutcheon has given such novels—"historiographic metafiction," a term that, she argues, characterizes the "postmodern" novel as a whole.[15] For Joyce's Stephen Dedalus, history was the nightmare from which he was trying to awake. But for the postmodern sensibility, history stands, in James Baldwin's words, as "the nightmare from which no one *can* awaken," a nightmare that has transformed us all into grotesquery.[16] The modernist can treat the history from which he hopes to escape as a source of allusion, a curio cabinet of fragments shored up against his ruin. But the postmodernist knows that escape will prove impossible, and so instead he subjects that past to a revisionary ransacking, simultaneously using and abusing the conventions within which he seems condemned to live, as *The Tin Drum* does those of the *kunstlerroman*.

Hutcheon derives her model for postmodernism from architecture, but in literary terms its great predecessors are the Joyce of *Ulysses*, Kafka, and Bertolt Brecht; indeed Brecht's account of his own intentions can stand as an account of the way the postmodernist alienates "the incidents portrayed . . . from the spectator . . . in order to make [him] adopt an attitude of inquiry and criticism."[17] The postmodern writer is suspicious of the grand narratives through which people have traditionally attempted to order their worlds; truth in his work can never be absolute but must always remain conditional, constructed—essentially fictive. Saleem describes his own project as "the chutnification of history" (442) but admits to the "inevitable distortions" (444) in any attempt to pickle time. Such a postmodernism is an essentially ironic form, based on parody, pastiche, and collage, and it works through a heteroglossia that breaks down the distinction between genres, modes of discourse, levels of literacy; a full reading of *The Satanic Verses* requires a knowledge not only of the Quran but also of the flashiest Hindi movies. Yet "how," as Rushdie asks throughout that novel, "how does newness come into the world?" (8). The danger for the postmodernist is that the world may seem to offer nothing truly new, only a history to be reconstructed or subverted, an endless exploration of a worn-out past. Pastiche becomes an end in itself; the artist does nothing more than reproduce for consumption our own cultural debris. This is the burden of Frederic Jameson's critique of postmodernism as "the cultural logic of late capitalism."[18] But at its best, that subversion can take on an instrumental quality. It performs—above all when the postmodern is also the postcolonial—what Anthony Appiah calls a "space-clearing gesture," a parodic mimicry from within which the new can emerge;[19] sweeps the table clear—glasses, plates, and silver cascading to the floor—so that it can be laid afresh. That expansive gesture provides in itself a response to a history from which the postcolonial can never fully escape. And so too does the stylistic flamboyance of postmodern fiction, which relies on what Frank Kermode calls a "gaiety of language as a means of projecting . . . humanity on a hostile environment."[20] In one of his essays Kundera asks, "What possibilities remain for man in a world where the external determinants have become so overpowering that internal impulses no longer carry weight[?]"[21] That, he says, is Kafka's question, and I would add that it is Rushdie's as well. Yet how should the writer structure our understanding of such a world, a world in which ideological conflict has indeed shaped—deformed—one's destiny? In his "Idea and Form in Literature," Lukacs draws a comparison between two horse races, one in Zola's *Nana* and the other from Tolstoy's *Anna Karenina*. In Zola, Lukacs argues, "everything that may be seen at horse races is described precisely, picturesquely, vividly," and yet the race seems far more an example of Zola's journalistic skill than an integral part of the novel itself; "[it] could easily be removed." In Tolstoy, however, the characters' lives begin "an entirely new phase as a result of the race . . . it is not merely a part of the scenery, but . . . a turning point in the development of the plot."[22] One account is purely descriptive, documentary. The other subordinates that description to narration. And for Lukacs, the difference between them points to an essential difference in the writers' comprehension of the worlds they describe. The fact that Zola cannot assimilate the horse race to the novel's overall narration suggests that he lacks a coherent interpretation of that world, an interpretation that would allow him fully to master the totality of the experiences with which his work is concerned. He remains at their mercy, overwhelmed by the intransigence of the world's details. But Tolstoy's world does have that coherence, one embodied in a narrative in which everything he describes has its place and, because of that place, is profoundly meaningful.

The writer who would confront the nightmare of history

must choose between these two approaches. The first is documentary. It holds that the human mind cannot encompass such pain, that the only response to it is a simple recording of names, places, and facts, as in Claude Lanzmann's Holocaust film *Shoah*. There should be no poems after Auschwitz, Theodor Adorno said, because poetry aestheticizes in a way that makes it appear as if "the unimaginable ordeal . . . had some ulterior purpose. It is transfigured and stripped of some of its horror, and with that, injustice is clearly done to the victims."[23] Instead, there must be silence—or testimony, a list of facts to make us remember what happened, where, and to whom.[24] Against Adorno's view one might place Naipaul's attack on what he calls "the documentary heresy."[25] Naipaul argues that a simple record of the facts of pain and degradation is never enough. For such a record, he suggests, seems to acquiesce in that degradation by acknowledging one's powerlessness before it, one's inability to do anything with those facts except note them. The writer must instead accept his "interpretive function" and through that interpretation give us some way to comprehend experience.[26] The writer must choose Tolstoy over Zola and turn nightmare into narrative. For "the refusal of narrative," as Hayden White puts it, "indicates an absence or refusal of meaning itself."[27]

So in "The Prague Orgy" (1985), Philip Roth evokes a now-vanished Jewish ghetto built out of stories, out of "all the telling and listening to be done, their infinite interest in their own existence, the fascination with their alarming plight . . . the construction of narrative out of the exertions of survival. . . . In Prague, stories aren't simply stories; it's what they have instead of life. Here they have become their stories, in lieu of being permitted to be anything else. Storytelling is the form their resistance has taken against the coercion of the powers-that-be."[28] Narrative gives one the ability to resist that coercion, a way to survive one's experience by comprehending it, by crafting an interpretation that will make it meaningful. Saleem's own fantastical fear of disintegration grows from his worry that he won't be adequate to that Indian disease, the "urge to encapsulate the whole of reality," that he will prove unable to give his life a meaning by constructing a narrative whose every part is integrally related to the whole. For to shape the chronology of

one's own life into a story is to resist becoming a statistic; hence
the urgency of his plea that however fantastic the MCC may sound,
we take it literally and not think of it as merely "the bizarre creation
of a rambling, diseased mind" (197).

Roth's account of narrative as a form of resistance stresses
the oral, performative nature of storytelling, what he describes as
its "wizardly" tricks and "thousand acoustical fluctuations of
tempo, tone, inflection, and pitch."[29] And the revival of storytelling
that Trilling foresaw has been accompanied by a marked renewal
of interest in such performances, in the traditional forms of oral
literature. It's an interest often combined with the most radical
probing of the nature of fiction; think of Calvino, collector of *Italian
Folktales* and author of *If on a winter's night a traveller.* The folktale,
the fantasy, the improvisation of Sterne, the *conte philosophique,* the
picaresque structure of Cervantes and Rabelais—these are what
Kundera describes as the "cemetery" of opportunities ignored by
nineteenth-century realism and its modernist successors.[30] And paradoxically it is by turning toward that past that the novel has found
a new life after the dead end of late modernism. Such forms seem
especially appropriate in a period when fiction has moved away
from biography, in which character is no longer destiny; for neither
Candide nor the heroes and villains of folktales are depicted in
terms of their individual psychology, as is a character like Anna
Karenina. Instead they function as emblems of our collective life,
traditionally serving, as Bruno Bettelheim has shown, to literalize
the psychological truth of a child's fears and fantasies about his
position in the family.[31]

The postmodern writer transforms that psychic emblem
into a political one; so Grass draws on the archetypal figures of fairy
tales in his exploration of German history. "Our crucial problem,"
as Garcia Marquez said in his Nobel Prize lecture, "has been a lack
of conventional means to render our lives believable," implying that
only what is itself unbelievable can do justice to the extra-ordinary
reality of Latin America's violent history.[32] And indeed the reliance
on fantasy that seems inherent in the use of folk motifs makes such
novels oddly mimetic—a realism not of presentation but of assess-
ment[33]—of those countries in which, as Rushdie writes, the truth

is always in danger of becoming "what it is instructed to be" (315). But Rushdie explains his own use of fantasy in somewhat different terms, calling it an "attempt honestly to describe reality as it is experienced by religious people, for whom God is no symbol but an everyday fact." In such a description the rationality of realism can seem "like a judgement upon, an invalidation of, the religious faith of the characters," and one therefore needs a form in which "the miraculous and the mundane . . . co-exist" (IH, 376). Most Westerners, Rushdie writes, find that a reliance on fantasy "is exceptional. For me it seems to be normative." That belief in the everyday presence of the miraculous has shaped a set of narrative conventions that holds that fiction should be essentially "untrue . . . a lie," not bound by probability but full of wonders instead. "And the belief was that by telling stories in that . . . marvellous way," in which horses and carpets are *expected* to fly, "you could actually tell a kind of truth which you couldn't tell in other ways," as Rushdie does with Ahmed Sinai's little cubes of ice or indeed the very existence of the midnight's children themselves.[34]

Rushdie's own interest in writing was sparked by an early experience of reading *The Arabian Nights,* to whose Scheherazade Saleem, in his desperation, compares himself, suggesting that his life—the nation's life—depends, like hers, on his storyteller's skills.[35] And in *Haroun and the Sea of Story* (1990) Rushdie has drawn on a Hindu equivalent, the *Katha Sarit Sagara,* the "Ocean of the Streams of Story," an eleventh-century compilation, many of whose tales survive in the repertoire of India's village storytellers.[36] He is suspicious, in ways I'll describe below, of the uses that India's politicians have made of what he calls its "folkloristic straitjacket" (SV, 52). But *Midnight's Children* nevertheless employs a full share of what Saleem's "myth-ridden nation" (197) has to offer, casting its ideological battles in terms of the stark and unambiguous characterization of fairy tales. Mrs. Gandhi becomes "The Widow," evil stepmother to a nation, and as their sobriquets suggest, such characters as Parvati-the-witch and Shiva-of-the-Knees are no more the rounded figures familiar from nineteenth-century realism than are Rapunzel and Rumpelstiltskin. And Saleem's own enormous and eternally dripping nose provides an echo of Bombay's favorite

Hindu deity, the elephant-headed Ganesh, who broke off a tusk to take down the poet Vyasa's dictation of the *Mahabharata*.

In fact Saleem's snot plays much the same role in *Midnight's Children* as excrement does in the Rabelais whom Bakhtin has so memorably described. In *Rabelais and His World*, Bakhtin extended his analysis of heteroglossia into a consideration of social forms and especially of the medieval carnival. The carnival is counterhegemonic, it is antitotalitarian, it is exempt from the "norms of decency and etiquette," firmly against the coercion of the powers-that-be.[37] And Saleem's overflowing nose is the mark of what Bakhtin calls the "grotesque body" in which carnival receives its fullest form: a body at once degrading and yet regenerative in the way that it remains "unfinished, outgrows itself, transgresses its own limits."[38] Saleem's grandfather Aadam Aziz is told that there are dynasties waiting in his own large nose, waiting there "like snot" (15)—like as not? For noses, as everybody knows, are traditionally linked with the phallus. Saleem eventually not only loses his telepathic powers but becomes sexually impotent as well. Yet that's precisely when his pencil begins to drip its words upon the page. For the novel is carnival's literary heir: the place, the *piazza*, where all rules are broken, all genres mixed, and our most precious beliefs have their backsides bared; a place in which, as the Brechtian poet Baal proclaims in *The Satanic Verses*, "the demotic force[s] its way into lines of classical purity and images of love [are] constantly degraded by the intrusion of elements of farce" (SV, 370). With his claim that his life is a mirror of the nation's, Saleem even stands as a kind of carnival king, both crowned and mocked because of it.

And in some ways the particular ideas, or rather the particular political systems, with which that carnivalized style contends do not much matter. For the novel as a genre has an ideology—it *is* an ideology—of its own, one that lives by attacking the tendency of ideology itself to abandon "the wisdom of uncertainty" in the pursuit of a totalizing system. The gaiety of the carnivalized novel provides what Bakhtin describes as a consecration of "inventive freedom," a liberation from clichés that offers "the chance to have a new outlook on the world, to realize the relative nature of all that exists, and to enter a completely new order of things"—a space in which to breathe.[39] Yet in the history of the novel the carnivalesque has waxed and waned. It seems almost entirely absent in the fiction of the immediate postwar period, in the grim little "monoglot" novels that stressed the essential absurdity of the "human condition."[40] The triumph of "historiographic metafiction" lies in wedding that sense of the absurd to the festively antinomian world of carnival, through a reliance on folk motifs and fantasy, through the linguistic energy and improvisatory nature of its own performance.

For Rushdie has taken more than the belief that fantasy is normative from the wondrous narratives he knew as a child. After his sterilization, after the end of the MCC, Saleem returns to the Bombay of his birth in the company of Picture Singh, the champion snake charmer of the Delhi magicians' ghetto. For the great man has learned that a nightclub snake-handler called "The Maharaja of Cooch Naheen" has laid claim to his title as the "Most Charming Man in the World," and he is determined to challenge the upstart.

> How long, in that sunless cavern, did they struggle? Months, years, centuries? I cannot say: I watched, mesmerized, as they strove to outdo one another, charming every kind of snake imaginable, asking for rare varieties to be sent from the Bombay snake-farm . . . and the Maharaja matched Picture Singh snake for snake, succeeding even in charming constrictors, which only Pictureji had previously managed to do. In that infernal Club the two virtuosi goaded snakes into impossible feats, making them tie themselves in knots, or bows, or persuading them to drink water from wineglasses, and to jump through fiery hoops. . . . And at last it became clear that the younger man was tiring first; his snakes ceased to dance in time to his flute; and finally, through a piece of sleight-of-hand so fast that I did not see what happened, Picture Singh managed to knot a king cobra around the Maharaja's neck.
>
> What Picture said: "Give me best, captain, or I'll tell it to bite." (438)

Yet Picture Singh hardly seems an essential part of the narrative. He first appears four-fifths of the way through the novel, and one has to ask what role this incident plays in *Midnight's Children* as a whole. Rushdie has often noted his interest in the eclectic *form* within which India's traditional oral storytellers work, his fascination with the fact that it is "not at all linear . . . the story does not go from the beginning to the end but . . . in great loops and circles back on itself, repeats earlier things, digresses." It seems "chaos" but of course it isn't; this type of storytelling, which in a largely illiterate nation still commands an enormous audience, is thousands of years old and "has adopted this shape for very good reasons." For the storyteller's digressions themselves serve to hold the audience. "The novelist doesn't see the moment at which people shut the book and get bored," but the storyteller always does—"people get up and walk away or they throw eggs or whatever."[41] Scheherazade places story within story, piles digression upon digression to keep from ever getting to the end of *The Arabian Nights*, for she has discovered that the constant novelty of this "gymnastic, convoluted, complicated form" is in itself the very reason that the king keeps listening, delaying her execution by one night more.[42] And so too Saleem constantly interrupts his narrative, comments on it, introduces new characters, and throws up new marvels, all to keep us reading on, eager to see what will happen next.

For in the intricate art of Picture Singh, in the art with which Rushdie himself has placed this virtuoso account precisely here, at the low point of his hero's fortunes, one finds a kind of anecdotal antidote to the despair of Saleem's situation. "What I tried to do," Rushdie has written, "was to set up a tension in the text, a paradoxical opposition between the form and content of the narrative. The story of Saleem does indeed lead him to despair. But the story is told in a manner designed to echo, as closely as my abilities allowed, the Indian talent for non-stop self-regeneration. This is why the narrative constantly throws up new stories, why it 'teems.' The form [is] multitudinous, hinting at the infinite possibilities of the country" (IH, 16). And indeed the seeming formlessness of its form, an imitation of the storyteller's oral art, has as much to do with the book's evocation of the national life as does its account of the MCC. That form makes *Midnight's Children* into a catalog of India's possibilities and, in doing so, provides an "optimistic counterweight to Saleem's personal tragedy." The novel ends with an image of destruction, in which all India tramples Saleem underfoot, "reducing [him] to specks of voiceless dust . . . sucked into the annihilating whirlpool of the multitudes" (446). But in reading, one barely notices that grim conclusion and remembers instead the carnivalesque capacity for "non-stop self-regeneration" with which Rushdie has endowed his narrator's voice, a proclamation of the imagination's ability to reshape from within the lives on which brute force is imposed from without.

III

The exuberance of Rushdie's style makes his chronicle of Saleem's growing despair more entertaining, more bearable and more hopeful, than it would otherwise be. His conceit about Saleem's disintegration provides an alternative to that disintegration itself, a gesture of imaginative freedom in an otherwise intractable world. That "gaiety" is most obviously a response to Pakistan's 1971 invasion of its own East Wing (now Bangladesh) and to the incipient totalitarianism of the Emergency. But the playfulness of the novel's form also stands as an attempt to engage the ideologically defined discourses of both colonialism and its nationalist counterparts. Timothy Brennan has described Rushdie as the very type of the "cosmopolitan" writer, those who because of either social class or emigration (both in Rushdie's case) are in "perpetual flight from a fixed national or ideological identity."[43] Cosmopolitan writers are at once anti-imperialist and yet suspicious of "radical decolonisation theory."[44] Instead they engage in what Brennan describes as the demythification of third world nation-building, in a way that's sometimes held to confirm Western prejudices, showing that a new nation "can act as abominably as the British did."[45] In consequence, Brennan suggests, many third world critics feel that such a writer isn't firmly on their side against a West that will use such work as an excuse for one form or another of neocolonialism; though as

Tariq Ali points out, *Midnight's Children* "says nothing that Indians or Pakistanis do not say to each other in private."[46]

Disagreements should be kept in the family, not aired in public—that is, in English. The charge of cosmopolitanism is one that Rushdie himself poses in *Shame* (1983), through a peremptory, italicized voice that dialogically interrupts and challenges his own narrative:

> *Outsider! Trespasser! You have no right to this subject!* . . . I know: nobody ever arrested me. Nor are they ever likely to. *Poacher! Pirate! We reject your authority. We know you, with your foreign language wrapped around you like a flag: speaking about us in your forked tongue, what can you tell but lies?* I reply with more questions: Is history to be considered the property of the participants solely? In what courts are such claims staked, what boundary commissions map out the territories? (S, 23)

"Nobody ever arrested me"—this is sad irony in the aftermath of the *fatwa*. To be cosmopolitan is, on this reading, to be inauthentic. Yet Rushdie's work as a whole can perhaps best be seen as an attempt to contest the terms on which such judgments get made. In *The Satanic Verses* he provisionally identifies the movie star Gibreel Farishta with the "good"—good because he constantly reaffirms his Indian origins, because he wishes to "remain . . . *continuous*— that is joined to and arising from his past . . . his is still a self which . . . we may describe as 'true.'" And Rushdie opposes Gibreel to Saladin Chamcha, "a creature of *selected* discontinuities" and one who therefore seems "false"—and not only in his capacity for evil (SV, 427). For Saladin's Anglophiliac mimicry of British norms has indeed made him a *chamcha*, the subcontinent's equivalent of an Oreo cookie—a "Toadji" (SV, 58). Yet Rushdie no sooner establishes those identities than he undermines them: Gibreel has lost his Islamic faith, and Saladin makes peace with the father he has spurned. Saladin shows himself capable of self-sacrifice; Gibreel reveals a corresponding evil. And in blurring the distinctions between them, Rushdie clears a space for the cosmopolitan by challenging, as Scott did with Hari Kumar, the very concept of cultural authenticity on which the assumption of Gibreel's "goodness" depends. *Midnight's Children* explores a complicated set of questions about cultural identity and allegiance, about the relations between India and England, colony and metropolis. Those questions are difficult in themselves, but they're made especially so by the fact that Rushdie rarely poses them in explicit terms. He locates them instead in the ground of the novel's language itself, in what he describes as "this Angrezi in which I am forced to write" (S, 34), and in doing so, he demonstrates that to be Anglicized isn't to stop being Indian. With the exception of an almost obligatory scene at the Jallianwallah Bagh, *Midnight's Children* doesn't appear to deal with British colonialism in any great detail. In terms of plot it seems almost irrelevant. And yet the colonial background proves inescapable. All Saleem's schooling is in English. His family and friends live in a small cluster of hilltop houses built by the British, and indeed the cut-rate terms on which they've bought those houses from the Englishman William Methwold stipulate that they're forbidden to throw anything away. At first they protest about the budgies and the "half-empty pots of Bovril" that the British have left behind, but soon they start drinking cocktails and "slip effortlessly into their imitation Oxford drawls" (98). For in Frantz Fanon's terms, Saleem's family stands as the very model of a native bourgeoisie, happy to "take over the posts that the foreigner has vacated."[47] Or as Saleem himself will later joke, "The businessmen of India . . . [are] turning white" (176).

Their English hilltop allows these mimic men to insulate themselves from India's "stream of chanting humanity" (186). At school, for example, Saleem's two worst subjects are Marathi and Gujarati, Bombay's chief indigenous languages; in fact Rushdie suggests that the boy's ignorance of them is what touches off the language riots of 1957. For neither Saleem nor the India he embodies can simply repudiate the British past, however much they both might want to. The novel hypothesizes that Saleem is a changeling, the biological son of the Hindu Vanita. But Saleem also claims that he is of mixed blood, that his actual father wasn't her street musician husband but was instead the Englishman Methwold. Just how he

knows this remains unclear—Vanita died in childbirth, and Methwold has gone back to Britain, out of reach of Saleem's telepathy.
His parentage remains conjectural, like that of Oskar Matzerath in
The Tin Drum. But Saleem's belief in his British blood shouldn't
be seen as the *chamcha's* desire to be accepted as English; in fact
Anglo-Indians have such a marginal social status that he's deeply
embarrassed. His British ancestry functions, rather, as a trope for
his hybrid cultural heritage, for the different forces that the novel
suggests have shaped modern India. Because the novel's most important attempt to engage the discourse of colonialism is also its
most obvious—one so obvious, so completely naturalized, that we
almost miss it. *Midnight's Children* is written in English.

Or is it? In *The Satanic Verses* Rushdie introduces a character
named Zeeny Vakil with this gloriously ramshackle sentence: "She
was an art critic whose book on the confining myth of authenticity,
that folkloristic straitjacket which she sought to replace by an ethic
of historically validated eclecticism, for was not the entire national
culture based on the principle of borrowing whatever clothes
seemed to fit, Aryan, Mughal, British, take-the-best-and-leave-the-
rest?—had created a predictable stink, especially because of its title." A maze of clauses, almost impossible to parse; a portmanteau
stuffed to bursting, with question marks and dashes serving as lug-
gage straps that barely hold it all together. That interjection about
the "folkloristic straitjacket," for example, is far more important
than what surrounds it, in a way that almost makes the sentence
feel as if it has wobbled out of control. A few lines later Zeeny
wonders why there should be "a good, right way of being a wog"
(SV, 52). Her question points most obviously toward Rushdie's
conception of the "national culture," in ways I'll describe below,
and yet his style itself seems to ask something similar. Why should
there be a "good, right way" of writing an English sentence? Where
Naipaul's language has a classic, almost eighteenth-century purity,
Rushdie's makes English prose an omnium-gatherum of whatever
seems to work, sprinkled with bits of Urdu, eclectic enough even
to accommodate cliché, unbound by any grammatical straitjacket.
The very structure of the sentence seems to open possibilities, to
recut the borrowed clothes of English until they've become those

of that new Indian language Angrezi. And while the sound of that
new name does onomatopoeically evoke the anger implicit in having to use a language marred by "the accumulated detritus of its
owner's unrepented past" (S, 34), it also transforms that bitterness
into laughter, the master's tongue appropriated for one's own sub-
versive purposes.

Gauri Viswanathan has shown how the disciplinary study of
English literature, both in India and in Britain itself, was a product
of the Raj's attempt to provide a rigorously moral but not explicitly
Christian education.[48] British literature came to be seen as the re-
pository of the wisdom and values that it had been England's unique
destiny to articulate, the values that Hari Kumar has been trained to
accept. And that literature was presented in the shape of a narrowly
defined Great Tradition, a tradition that even now determines the
curriculum of English education in India; Shakespeare and Milton
themselves were held to have a civilizing mission and in consequence became touched by the "officialism" that E. M. Forster says
makes "every human relation" suffer.[49] For post-Independence India, the English language and its literature stand as one of the struc-
turing institutions—like the army, the civil service, and the capital
in New Delhi—that the British left behind and that the current
nation-state can never quite discard. Even the revisionary impulse
of Rushdie's Angrezi depends on the existence of that inherited
tradition. What else is his evocation of the midnight's children but
a fantastic version of Rudyard Kipling's description of Kim's entry
into the Grand Trunk Road, with its "new people and new sights
at every stride—castes he knew and castes that were altogether out
of his experience"?[50] English is the language in which Nehru an-
nounced the new country's very existence, the tongue through
which India continues to present itself to the outside world. Yet
English remains the first language only of the Anglo-Indians and
of the tiny elite to which Saleem belongs—an elite who, even if
they are no longer what Gandhi called "foreigners in their own
land,"[51] still have, as Saleem's linguistic hilltop suggests, an attenuated relation to what he ironically if edgily describes as "the so-
called teeming millions."

There's no need to rehearse here the overall history of the

English language in India. What concerns us is its literary use. In the preface to *Kanthapura* (1937), one of the seminal novels of the Independence movement, Raja Rao wrote that although English had become the language of India's "intellectual make-up," it wasn't the tongue of its "emotional make-up." And he called on the Indian writer to create a distinctive dialect in which "the tempo of Indian life . . . [would be] infused into our English expression even as the tempo of American or Irish life has gone into the making of theirs."[52] But how could that Indian English develop when the cardinal rule of one's schooling was to deny that "emotional make-up" by writing and speaking an English as close to British norms as possible? Not to do so was to invite condescension and contempt. And most Westernized Indians tried to avoid the derision attached to "babu English," not by declaring their independence of British models, as did many African and Caribbean writers, but by demonstrating their mastery of the master's style. Yet in the end that Anglicization only underlined the fact that one was, in Bhabha's words, *"almost the same but not quite . . . almost the same but not white."* "What-ho, old Chumch," Gibreel says to Saladin; for in wanting to be a "chum," a *chamcha* is also a chump (SV, 3).

In practice, spoken Indian English soon became what in 1951 Nirad C. Chaudhuri described as a "mixed language," marked by a heteroglossia in which words, phrases, and even syntactic structures from Indian languages played a role in English conversation.[53] "There is a language for books," as Anita Desai has written, "and a language for conversation, and the two are not the same—so we were taught in school and so we believed."[54] Some allowance in the writing of fiction might be made for words—often italicized, to mark their foreignness—that denote food, clothing, or religious beliefs. And of course many such words, like "bungalow," have long since entered British English itself and are enshrined in *Hobson-Jobson*, the famous 1886 glossary of Anglo-Indian vocabulary. Some allowance was made as well for the dialogue of characters who don't know English, like R. K. Narayan's Tamil speakers, whose speech is marked by the sentence structure of their mother tongue. But those are the exceptions that prove the rule; Narayan's narrative prose remains largely monoglot, without the colloquial bite that makes spoken Indian English so distinctive. For Indians, Chaudhuri argued, were "not as yet permitted to write" that mixed language. "No Indo-English equivalent of the Indo Persian Urdu has as yet made its appearance as a written language."[55] That was not entirely true, for the first-person narration of G. V. Desani's *All About H. Hatterr* (1948) had indeed drawn on that spoken language. Insisting that "life is contrast," above all the contrast between the narrator's "rigmarole English" and the "higher English poetical works of the Bard," Desani created a difficult linguistic hybrid, and as in *Midnight's Children*, his narrator's mixed blood serves as a metaphor for the heterogeneity of his style.[56] For although Anglicization can indeed make one a *chamcha*, condemned by history to ape the West, Desani showed how a deliberate mimicry can use the essentially ironic difference in sameness that characterizes Anglicization to upset conventional expectations, to make that mimicry parodic, carnivalizing it, using it to guy the colonizer, as an impressionist does the politicians he caricatures. Rushdie has praised the novel's use of babu English—half parody, half revelation of its resourcefulness--as "the first great stroke of the decolonizing pen."[57] But it remained sui generis until his own invention of Angrezi, which, in Desai's words, "brought the spoken language off the street and onto the printed page, with such energy and electricity that . . . [India finally saw] the two tongues as one."[58]

"Proper London, bhai!" Gibreel calls out as he falls toward earth on the first page of *The Satanic Verses*. "Here we come! . . . Out of thin air, baby. *Dharrraaammm!* Wham, na? What an entrance, yaar. I swear: splat" (SV, 3). "Yaar"—the favorite interjection of the English-language fan magazines that serve Bombay's Hindi film industry. And perhaps Rushdie's stylistic roots can be found there as much as in Desani, for popular journalism has been far more willing than "literature" to acknowledge the hybridity of spoken Indian English. "Ek dum," his characters say when they want something done at once; "funtoosh," when they feel washed-up—and neither word is italicized. The illiterate Padma asks Saleem about the purpose of all his "writing-shiting" and tells him to "eat, na, food is spoiling" (25). And though earlier novelists had used Hindi words for food, Rushdie overfills the plate; neighbors arrive "bearing rasgullas and gulab jamans" (155), and when he's sick Saleem's ayah promises him "chocolate cake . . . laddoos, pistaki-lauz, meat samosas, kulfi. So thin you got, baba, the wind will blow you away" (234).

And always there is the All-India Radio of the streets—its filmi music, its channa-wallah's calls, its curses and epithets and endearments and interjections. Toward the end of *Midnight's Children* a "vendor of notions" who's found robbing the dead on a battlefield in Bangladesh makes Saleem an offer for his lapis lazuli–encrusted spittoon, the one family heirloom Saleem has left. "Ho sir! Absolute master thing! Is silver? Is precious stone? You give; I give radio, camera, almost working order, my sir! Is a damn good deals, my friend. For one spittoon only, is damn fine. Ho yes. Ho yes, my sir, life must go on; trade must go on, my sir, not true?" (360). The wheedling contempt with which the peddler views his victim would be memorable in any language—and so would the skill with which Rushdie tosses this portrait off, this character who exists but for a page. Yet the brilliance of that characterization lies in the way the peddler's phrasing departs from British norms: the lack of a pronoun with the verb "is," the placement of "only" and the plural "deals," above all the idea that the spittoon is an "absolute master thing!" One laughs, not because the syntax seems wrong but because its liberation from the rules of standard English creates a shameless energy that is at once monstrously inappropriate and yet absolutely right for a scene set on a field of corpses. It is like the knocking at the gate in *Macbeth*, a moment in which laughter makes us realize the extent of the horror before us.

The inventive impurity of Rushdie's heteroglot style provides a challenge to the idea of proper English, the King's English, and therefore to British colonialism. Though it stands itself as the belated consequence of Macaulay's "Minute on Indian Education," it nevertheless subverts the Minute's assumption that educated Indians should be British in everything but blood. Instead Rushdie's style bends and twists and transforms the language, refashioning it to fit the experience of contemporary Indian life, in a way that allows one to be something other than a *chamcha* in using it. Yet if the hybridity of Angrezi marks the postcolonial "separation" of

English from its "origins and essences," that same hybridity challenges any notion of the authentically Indian as well.[59] For Rushdie's account of Zeeny Vakil, one remembers, isn't a description of
the English language itself, even though it provides a model of how
to use it. No—it deals instead with a particular conception of India's "national culture."

Zeeny's rejection of "the confining myth of authenticity" in
favor of a "historically validated eclecticism" seems so closely allied
to the terms of Fanon's "On National Culture" as to suggest that
Rushdie has taken that essay as a model. Fanon's account turns on
what he describes as the desire of "native intellectuals to shrink
away from that Western culture in which they all risk being
swamped" and their consequent "search for a national culture
which existed before the colonial era."[60] This has been especially
true in Africa, where the novelist's task, in Chinua Achebe's words,
has been to help his or her people "regain belief" in themselves by
showing them that the past "was not one long night of savagery
from which the first Europeans . . . delivered them."[61] Yet because
colonialism exploited its subject peoples not as "Angolan [or] Nige-
rian" but simply as "the Negro . . . a Savage," Fanon argues that
in Africa the appeal to a precolonial culture is never conceived of
in national terms; indeed the nations themselves are colonial cre-
ations.[62] Instead the appeal becomes a racial one. The Francophone
concept of *négritude* stood as "the emotional if not the logical antithesis of the insult which the white man flung at humanity," for
it posited the existence of an essential—an essentialist—African
identity, whose mark could be seen throughout the Diaspora, in
Angola and Alabama alike.[63]

In India the appeal to an essential or authentic identity at
first appears to work in exactly the opposite way, for it's couched
not in terms of what is larger than the nation but in terms of what's
smaller, of one's religious or linguistic or caste affiliations. But
Fanon remains a reliable guide. In some ways India's national form
does seem a colonial construct, a creation of the British, like Kenya.
As late as the moment of Independence, the subcontinent contained, in addition to the territory under direct British rule, over
five hundred quasi-autonomous princely states, some of which

briefly tried to survive as independent nations on their own. We have made Italy, Cavour said, in placing that peninsula's crown on the head of the king of Sardinia; now we have to make the Italians. Or as Saleem's grandfather Aadam Aziz says to his wife on their honeymoon: "Forget about being a good Kashmiri girl. Start thinking about being a modern Indian woman" (35). Yet even if India were nothing more than a geographical expression, geography is still, as Herder reminds us, one of the main constituents of national identity. And Rushdie himself suggests that if India was invented by the British, it was nevertheless "a dream that everyone agreed to dream. And now I think there actually is a country called India"—and moreover one that's already five thousand years old.[64] For the British weren't the first to attempt India's unification.[65] Ashoka had done it before the birth of Christ, and the Mughal Emperor Akbar tried in the sixteenth century. Over the millennia, various religious movements had swept the whole subcontinent—Buddhism, the eighth-century Hindu revivalism of Shankara, the syncretic *bhakti* movements that tried to fuse Hinduism and Islam in the fifteenth century. The Indian National Congress made a nonsectarian appeal, and it succeeded—"not wholly or in full measure," as Nehru admitted, "but very substantially"—because the community it imagined coincided not only with the territory under British domination but also with earlier movements to which it could look for a model.[66]

Yet in spite of its "secular and egalitarian pronouncements," Congress found itself, as both a resistance movement and a ruling party, appealing to what Akeel Bilgrami describes as "a monolithic and majoritarian Hinduism" that sought to impose the myth of "a pan-Indian Brahminical ideology" on India's heterogeneous past.[67] Fanon's analysis suggests that such a nativist politics grows from the attempt to find an identity anterior to the national form that colonialism leaves behind. It is at best a reactive formation, limited by its failure to "take account of the . . . historical character" of human societies,[68] and it amounts as well to what Edward Said describes as an implicit acceptance of "the racial, religious, and political divisions" that imperialism imposes on its subject peoples.[69] For "why should there be a good, right way of being a wog," as Zeeny

Vakil asks, in rejecting "the confining myth of authenticity"? "That's Hindu fundamentalism" (SV, 52). Despite the increasingly sectarian identification of Mrs. Gandhi's Congress Party, her authoritarian populism never hesitated to divide and rule itself, offering concessions to minority groups in exchange for bloc votes. This didn't cost her party much with the Hindu bourgeoisie that had moved—metaphorically, at least—into the houses the British had left behind them. But it did cost her with a newly prosperous and self-consciously Hindu middle class, which has turned away from Congress and toward the BJP in what has become, in the years since the publication of *Midnight's Children*, a far greater challenge to Nehru's legacy than that posed by the separatists of Kashmir or Assam. The fundamentalism of the BJP sees India as a single entity, with an essentially *Hindu* unity that long antedates the national state. For the country itself is unchanging and eternal, it is *Bharat Matya*, Mother India, the land of the *Mahabharata* and the *Ramayana;* in fact the mosque at Ayodyha was destroyed because it was built on the site of Rama's alleged birthplace. The official secularism of the Indian constitution is but a foreign import, an attempt by British invaders to appease Muslim invaders. And so the nation must be redefined as an explicitly Hindu polity and the pollution of the outsiders' touch expunged. It is no accident that the BJP's constituency is largely upper-caste.

Rushdie's conception of the "national culture" uses the essential impurity of his own Angrezi to challenge not just the ideology of colonialism but that of such a "folkloristic straitjacket" as well. He depends instead on "an ethic of historically validated eclecticism" that rejects the myth of a pure and unadulterated *Bharat*.[70] His knowledge of what Fanon would call India's "historical character" tells him that the Aryan ancestors of the BJP were themselves invaders from the north, who imposed their rule and their Sanskrit tongue on the Dravidian South. Muslims have been in India for a thousand years, for longer than France has been France, and the glories of Rajput painting and architecture depend on Persian and Mughal models. The Bengali Renaissance of which the filmmaker Satyajit Ray was the last flower had its origins in an attempt, in the years before Macaulay, to demonstrate that the

West was not antithetical to Hinduism. And what about the fact that such a book as *Midnight's Children* can exist at all?

For Rushdie puts Angrezi—puts English—at the very heart of modern India's national identity. As Saleem well knows, his mastery of English does indeed detach him from the affiliations of region or language or religion through which most of India's people have historically defined their identities. It makes his position like that of Turgenev's aristocrats, acutely conscious of and somewhat guilty about the fact that they can never really know the peasantry who surround them, the people on whose labor they depend. Yet in doing so, that language, like the English blood of Kipling's Kim, paradoxically makes all India open to him; if, in the words of Kipling's Daniel Dravot, he has "grown to be English," he has also, and because of that, grown to be Indian.[71] He belongs nowhere— or anywhere, or everywhere in the imagined community of the independent nation-state. "O, my shoes are Japanese," Gibreel sings in *The Satanic Verses*, translating the words of a Hindi film song into English. "These trousers English, if you please. On my head, red Russian hat; my heart's Indian for all that" (SV, 5). He is no less Indian for all that because for Rushdie there is no sine qua non of Indianness. Saleem's biological parents are rich and poor, British and Hindu, but he grows up a Muslim. And he grows up an Indian—by choice, because the creation of Pakistan has given his family a choice, and they have consciously decided to think in terms of a national and not a communal identity. The very cosmopolitanism that might preclude Rushdie's solidarity with a mythical "people" is in itself a defense against the provincialism of sectarian politics. And so Saleem asserts his right to compare himself to Bombay's beloved god, "mammoth-trunked . . . garrulous" Ganesh (192). But his own great schnozz also recalls the important noses of Western literature, like Cyrano de Bergerac's or Tristram Shandy's, in a way that reveals the artificiality of any absolute distinction between India and the West. "We're all bad Indians" (SV, 52), Zeeny says, for to believe that there's such a thing as a "good, right way" of being Indian would force one to reject the very idea of the nation Rushdie has defined through the unfulfilled, but never abandoned, dream of the Midnight Children's Conference.

That India is as plural and impure as the Hindu pantheon itself, which finds room for Christ and Mohammed. It is a land of "non-stop self-regeneration," a collage of whatever clothes seem to fit—my metaphor is deliberately mixed—of hybrids like Urdu and the Sikhs and the Marxist Christians of Kerala. And the fundamentalist monoglot is the only one for whose beliefs its noble mansion does not have a room. The Angrezi of *Midnight's Children* is finally an attempt to imagine a sense of Indian national identity capacious enough to include someone like Saleem, or indeed like Rushdie himself. For neither British colonialism nor that "folkloristic straitjacket" has a place for such cultural conundrums, and his critique of the one is finally inseparable from his critique of the other. It stands as a subcontinental counterpart to Scott's anti-essentialist account of British national identity and provides a kind of rebuke to Naipaul's longing for an impossible "pure time."

Rushdie's work is in the end far more than a celebration of Indian diversity. His sense of the hubbub of voices within Saleem's mind not only coincides with what I've described as the ideology of the novel form but also becomes in *The Satanic Verses* a model for the construction of both the postcolonial and the postmodern self: a self that depends on the impurity of his own "mixed language." As Saleem contains that multitude within him, so too must those who, whether abroad or in the land of their birth, have to live in two cultures at once. The postcolonial self is no more singular than India itself. It is never pure, never what *The Satanic Verses* terms "one one one," but is instead always "two or three or fifteen" (SV, 102), always plural, not a *chamcha* but instead a hybrid. Indeed Rushdie suggests that such a self should actively choose the hand that history has dealt it: that it should reject Naipaul's wounded awareness of that lack of singularity for a ready acceptance of the fact that cultures are never inviolate, an acceptance that will allow one to learn the ways in which migrancy and mimicry can themselves become a creative force. "Perhaps we all are," he writes, "black and brown and white, leaking into one another . . . *like flavours when you cook*" (IH, 394). And out of that dialogue a new and

richer savor can emerge, one more sustaining than a continued—
and impossible—devotion to the landscape one's ancestors
hymned.

But Rushdie also pushes that conception of the self beyond
the postcolonial circumstances from which it grows to reject the
very idea that it can ever be anywhere whole. "O, the conflicting
selves jostling and joggling within these bags of skin," thinks the
professional mimic Saladin at the end of *The Satanic Verses*. "No
wonder we invent remote-control channel-hopping devices. If we
turned these instruments upon ourselves we'd discover more chan-
nels than a cable or satellite mogul ever dreamed of" (SV, 519).
D. H. Lawrence called on the novel to abandon its belief in "the
old stable ego of the character," and most modernist fiction has
indeed dealt with the process of that ego's disintegration—Lawrence's own, certainly, but also that of Faulkner and Woolf, and
indeed Naipaul as well.[72] But Rushdie suggests that we shake off
not just our customary belief in that stability but even the pain of
the loss of that belief, the pain of Mr. Biswas's ordeal at Green
Vale. The self becomes a pastiche, a collage of different styles, like
the "national culture" that Zeeny Vakil describes, a set of masks
improvised for different occasions. It is the point at which the postcolonial coalesces with the postmodern, a sense of the self as a series
of impersonations—of the final inauthenticity of the self in itself—
which corresponds to that provided in Philip Roth's *The Counterlife*.[73]

Yet the very fractures of the multiple self can be both a liberation and a source of strength. The Hindu faithful have traditionally believed that they lost caste in leaving India to travel over the
"black water." Because Rushdie's sense of the self has its roots in
his imagination of an India that isn't bound by such notions of purity, his own Indianness has therefore become a portable identity,
one that he could maintain through the years of English education
and the emigration that culminated in the writing of *Midnight's
Children*. And perhaps, one hopes, he has even been able to carry
it with him into that strange half-life of safe houses and security
guards in which he now lives.

IV

Midnight's Children ends with a glimpse of apocalypse, in which Saleem finally explodes under "the awful pressure of the crowd" (445) inside him, cracking and crumbling into his constituent specks of "voiceless dust . . . two three, four hundred million five hundred six" (446), one for each individual citizen of the nation he has embodied. India falls to pieces. For the MCC has failed to become anything other than a metaphor for the national life, failed to play what Saleem calls an "actively-literally" (232) role in the life of the state, and so India is trampled in the dust by the people who compose it. Within that house there are now a million mutinies, above all that led by Nehru's own daughter. Because of her the children of midnight will have no children themselves, not after the forced sterilizations of her "birth-control" campaign—except of course for Shiva, who has scattered his seed throughout the land. And it is Saleem himself who betrays those children to her, finally cooperating—against his will, under torture, yet cooperating just the same—with the Widow's identification of India with herself and herself alone. But Saleem also compares himself to the Widow, pits his version of India against hers. Perhaps, he says, they are competing for "centrality," for they both see "the multitudinous realities of the land" as raw material on which to impose a form. Saleem describes his task as that of "sniffing-out-the-truth" (299) about a land in which the powers-that-be have remade that truth in their own image, and yet that competition forces him to use the same means. India as Indira, or India as Saleem? For he too wants to make the truth about India into what he instructs it to be.

Or rather he wants to make it into what Rushdie tells it to be. Before concluding, I want briefly to explore my chief reservation about *Midnight's Children.* In a 1987 elegy for his brother Shiva, Naipaul argued: "There is a way currently in vogue of writing about degraded and corrupt countries . . . the way of fantasy and extravagance. It dodges all the issues. It is safe . . . empty, morally and intellectually; it makes writing . . . an aspect of the corruption of the countries out of which it emerges. I find . . . [an] insistence on rationality and the intellect more exhilarating."[74] Naipaul doesn't mention Rushdie, but it's hard to read these words without thinking of him as their target. And indeed one imagines a sense of rivalry between them, the English language's two most important writers of Indian descent. A comparison between them has been implicit throughout these last two chapters; and my conclusion will draw that comparison in more detail.[75] For Naipaul the nightmare of history is comprehensible; it can be explained through a rational analysis of historical processes, and hence the classical restraint of his style. Anything else, any move into fantasy, any assignment of a metaphorical content to reality, is "empty," an even greater abdication of the writer's interpretative function than what he calls "the documentary heresy." But though counterarguments can be easily made, I want to take Naipaul's charge seriously. For both the fantasy and the rhetorical extravagance of *Midnight's Children* can numb its readers to anything but its own saffron-and-green exhilaration. However entrancing—indeed, precisely because it is entrancing—Rushdie's style distances one from the horrors it describes, making his description of them not only bearable but even enjoyable; it keeps one from being disturbed by the things that happen to his characters, even by Saleem's treatment at the hands of the Widow.

Pushkin is said to have been surprised, in writing *Eugene Onegin*, to realize that his heroine Tatyana would turn one of her suitors down. But the contemporary novelist rarely endows his characters with that kind of freedom, and in reading, as Iris Murdoch has argued, we feel instead their "ruthless subjection . . . to the will of their author."[76] Rushdie would be incapable of Pushkin's surprise. His characters' fates seem cartoonishly overdetermined, and not simply because they're handcuffed to history's crude ironies. The whole narrative of *Midnight's Children* remains so firmly under the thumb of his self-regarding style that at times I find it hard to distinguish between the writer's fantasies on the one hand and the Widow's on the other, between the book and the totalitarian world it purports to attack. The bombs in the 1965 Indo-Pak War fall in such a way as to wipe out Saleem's whole family; it's symbolically useful at that point for Rushdie's narrator to become an orphan.

Rushdie's style precludes the close involvement with individual characters on which the novel of bourgeois liberalism depends, and that can indeed make his work seem an "aspect of the corruption of the [country] out of which it emerges." But in doing so, it remains homologous to an age dominated by what Goldmann calls the idea of "collective reality," in which individuals as such do not greatly matter, a homology that isn't an echo so much as a parody of the Widow's lust for centrality. As we acknowledge the absurdity of Saleem's claim to be India, so should we recognize that of Mrs. Gandhi's own as well. Late in the novel Saleem finds a brief refuge from history in the magicians' ghetto huddled in the shadow of the Jamma Masjid, Delhi's great Friday Mosque. And there he learns that for all their rope tricks and fire-eating, "the magicians were people whose hold on reality was absolute . . . they could bend it every which way in the service of their arts, but they never forgot what it was" (385). Those words can stand as Rushdie's own aesthetic principle: to bend Indian life this way or that, to make us believe in the illusions of telepathy or in metaphors that seem to come literally true—and yet always to remember what that reality is. The illusion becomes not an aspect of the country's corruption but a comment on it. For in reading, one no more forgets that reality than do either those Delhi magicians or their audiences, which happily attend to the smoke and the mirrors and so learn how easily one can be snared by fantasy, lured on by the promise of marvels. We even get to see how the trick has been done, and that does distinguish Saleem from the Widow, who would rather we didn't notice; he, at least, admits that his India is but one of the many millions of possible versions. And so we find that Rushdie has alienated us from the illusion even as he enthralls us, has made us think critically not only about Indian politics and identity but also about the terrible seductive force of Saleem's—of his own—desire to encapsulate the whole of reality.

We are on this interpretation *meant* to be bothered by the ways in which the novel doesn't disturb us.[77] That is supremely true of Grass's work, in which both Oskar's grotesque moral distance from the events he describes and the reader's own response to that distance serve to indict the Nazi abuse of language. With Rushdie I'm not so sure; *Midnight's Children* as a whole seems too full of an unironized nostalgia for Saleem's Bombay childhood to convince me that we're intended to read it with that kind of skepticism. And moreover the novelist himself points to that failure to disturb as a weakness in his own work, telling an interviewer that his books have so far contained "very little stuff at all about the deep emotions . . . one of the things I have failed to do, at the center of my work, is write about strong feeling, cathartic emotion, obsession."[78] Even in *The Satanic Verses* it's only when Rushdie abandons fantasy, in the concluding scenes between Saladin and his dying father, that the novel manages to summon that "strong feeling"; and Rushdie considers that ending "the best thing [he's] ever written."[79] The degree to which historiographic metafiction maintains a tyrannical relation to its own characters does indeed mark a limitation in the great novels of our age; we must learn to brush such works against the grain, to read them with the same kind of suspicion, the same attention to their implication in the corruptions of power, that we now direct toward the classic texts of nineteenth-century realism. Too much of the most innovative postwar fiction has depended on "fantasy and extravagance" for me fully to share Naipaul's categorical condemnation. But neither can I wholly discount it, and in the end I remain troubled that a book about the nightmare of history cannot make me care about the individual characters to whom that history happens.

Yet that fantasy, that flamboyance, offers so much that I'm willing to accept such a fault as the price of the ticket: a way to deal with politics on a large scale, rather than in terms of individual ethical dilemmas; a method to present the ways in which the "external determinants" of ideology have transmuted us into grotesquery; a way to cope with events that the mind refuses to comprehend in terms of the rational explanations that realism presumes and for which it therefore seeks a more primitive, often mythic answer. And *Midnight's Children* could not do any of those things so vividly if it did not allow itself the freedom to find the metaphorical content of reality and render it a literal one. Any account of the Indian novel in English must recognize that Rushdie has given it a new start, a new and bolder life. No one else has done so much to remake English into an Indian language; no one else has so fully used that language to probe the nature of national identity or to define a model for the postcolonial self. No other writer in English has so energetically and joyously peopled the immigrants' London or the great city of Bombay; and no one since Dickens has offered as engaging a gallery of self-dramatizing rogues and charlatans and madmen. Rushdie's work, moreover, contains so powerful a sense of possibility as to render it a force for change, in a way that makes Naipaul's insistence that "the world is what it is" seem quietist. For Naipaul the nightmare of contemporary history is comprehensible, and yet his insistence on rationality can leave one with a sense of despair, locked into a nightmare from which there seems no escape. Rushdie's reliance on the fantastic may dodge some issues, but it may also help keep the imagination alive in an otherwise intractable world.

Midnight's Children stands as an attempt to preserve the spirit of India's secular and democratic independence—a process that Saleem describes as the "chutnification of history." For as its final conceit, the novel suggests that each of its chapters is a particular flavor of pickle, a jar in which Saleem has managed to preserve not just "fruit, vegetables, fish, vinegar, spices," but also "memories, dreams, ideas"—special recipes all ready to enter "mass-production [and] be unleashed upon the amnesiac nation" (443), helping it recall the majesty of the mansion that Nehru had left it. Sometimes, Saleem admits, he hasn't gotten the recipes quite right—there's an "overly harsh taste," for example, "from those jars containing memories of my father." And the process of pickling can lead, like the magicians' tricks, to some "inevitable distortions," for the flavors of history are altered and intensified by the spices and vinegars that preserve them—a metaphoric concentration of tamarind or lime or indeed of India itself. Yet in the process, something quite unpalatable—an unripe mango, a massacre in Bangladesh—will be transformed, made bearable, even enjoyable, in a way that grants us a bit of sustenance out of which hope and action may grow. Saleem acknowledges that even so, some pickles may remain "too strong for some palates, their smell may be overpowering, tears may rise to eyes." Yet he hopes that each jar will nevertheless contain "the authentic taste of truth." For they are all of them, "despite everything, acts of love" (444).

"Burn the Books and Trust the Book": *The Satanic Verses*, February 1989

The briefest of the dreams from which the Bombay film actor Gibreel Farishta suffers over the course of *The Satanic Verses* concerns a house in Kensington in which a "bearded and turbaned Imam" in exile plans the overthrow of his country's wine-drinking Empress (205).[1] To the Imam such blasphemy "is enough to condemn her for all time without hope of redemption." He himself drinks only water, "whose purity . . . communicates itself to the drinker" (209). And he is similarly determined to remain "in complete ignorance" of London, that "Sodom in which he had been obliged to wait; ignorant, and therefore unsullied, unaltered, pure" (206–7). The Imam relies on an "American filtration machine" (209) to purify his water, on the radio his disciples use to broadcast the words I've taken for my title. Nevertheless he stands resolute against the idea of historical process that such technology implies, seeing it as the "greatest of the lies—progress, science, rights—against which . . . [he] has set his face. History is a deviation from the Path, knowledge is a delusion, because the sum of knowledge was complete on the day Al-Lah finished his revelation to Mahound" (210).

But this vision of a Khomeini-like absolutism isn't the only place in which Salman Rushdie's novel seems to prefigure the Islamic world's response to it. In the Jahilia chapters that lie at the heart of what has now gone beyond a controversy, the poet Baal defines the writer's job: " 'To name the unnamable, to point at frauds, to take sides, start arguments, shape the world and stop it from going to sleep.' And if rivers of blood flow from the cuts his verses inflict, then they will nourish him" (97). Rushdie's work has always insisted on what in *Midnight's Children* he called the "metaphorical content" of reality. Yet surely he couldn't have expected, or wanted, the wounds his own satire inflicts to come so grotesquely alive. Nourishment? Riots, bombs, bounties, rumors of death squads—they make Baal's thought too grim for me to enjoy the irony, in a way that reminds me that metaphors aren't finally real.

Or are they? Because that literalization seems to me what the quarrel is about. Is the book blasphemous, as so many Muslims have charged? The prophet that Rushdie calls Mahound has no use for Baal's satires; he compares writers to whores and has Baal beheaded. When I first heard the news of the February 12th riots in Islamabad, which seem to have sparked Khomeini's call for Rushdie's death, I was both moved and troubled by the fact that people had died in a protest about a book. I couldn't imagine anyone here taking any single book so seriously, and I recalled the comparison Philip Roth once made between the American writer, for whom "everything goes and nothing matters," and the Eastern European writer, for whom "nothing goes and everything matters."[2] Now I am not so sure. I believe there is such a thing as blasphemy. But I also believe that its definition lies so much in the beholder's eye that the punishment for it belongs to God alone and not to any man who claims to act for Him. As I write that sentence I'm struck by how Western, and how secular, such a thought is. And by the belief that the freedom to have such thoughts matters profoundly even if nothing else does.

It will be years—if ever—before we can separate *The Satanic Verses* from the storm around it. I was disappointed in the book at first. Its vision of good and evil seemed too cartoonish for what turned out to be a story of personal betrayal; as I read I kept thinking that a Jamesian psychological realism would have yielded a far more complex sense of evil, in particular, than Rushdie's reliance on fantasy was capable of. More tellingly, the book's thousand and one digressions made it seem not so much a loose and baggy as a bulbous monster: a structural mess, a book of brilliant pages— including those in which a group of prostitutes assume the names of Mahound's wives for business purposes, much as strip joints claim to feature "college girls"—but not a whole. The main line of Rushdie's narrative deals with the fractured personal identities of the immigrants' London, that "city visible but unseen" (241) by most whites, where teenagers may call their parents' homeland "Bungleditch" (259) and yet settle into arranged marriages. But what relation did the Jahilia scenes, did the whole of Gibreel's dreams, have to that narrative? I didn't see much of one at first, but the events of the last ten days have made me think hard about that question. Looking back over the novel, I'm now struck more by its thematic consistency than by its heterogeneous structure; one could say, in fact, that that heterogeneity is itself the chief element in that consistency. *The Satanic Verses* is a thematic whole, and that whole does indeed offer a radically different vision of the world than that held by any Imam.

At issue are the two chapters in which Gibreel dreams about the birth of a monotheistic religion in the desert city of Jahilia, chapters that so heavily parody Islamic history and tradition as to puzzle most Western readers. The name "Jahilia," for example— to Muslims it means "darkness" or "ignorance" and is used with particular reference to pre-Islamic times. Here, however, the darkness doesn't vanish when Mahound proclaims the Word of the One God. Such sharp anticlerical satire has long been familiar in the West but remains foreign to the Islamic world. Too bad. The joke on "Jahilia" isn't one that most Westerners will have the background to get, but the fact that Rushdie uses it anyway suggests that in some ways his ideal audience, however much the novel wounds them, might be precisely those British Muslims who burned his book in Bradford.

Muslims have found any number of other insults and blasphemies in these chapters. But the most important charge against Rushdie is that he suggests the Quran is not the uncreated Word of God, as dictated by the angel through the mouth of the prophet Mohammed, but was instead written by man. In Rushdie's novel the character Salman the Persian, who serves as Mahound's amanuensis—and a figure of that name was one of the actual Mohammed's earliest followers—grows suspicious of the way the revelations Mahound claims to receive from Gibreel accord too neatly with what the Prophet has already decided he wants to do. And so Salman begins to test Mahound, to change the dictation in subtle ways: "If Mahound recited a verse in which God was described as *all-hearing, all-knowing,* I would write, *all-knowing, all-wise.* Here's the point: Mahound did not notice the alterations. So there I was, actually writing the Book, or rewriting, anyway, polluting the word of God with my own profane language. But good heavens, if my poor words could not be distinguished from the Revelation by God's own Messenger, then what did that mean?" (367). Salman hopes that Al-Lah, if there is an Al-Lah and if the Book is really His, will not allow Mahound to preach a mistaken Word, hopes that the Prophet will catch the error and so confirm his faith. But Mahound doesn't notice, and the substitutions remain, implying that the Word is not the only one, that the text of the Quran is not only human but corrupt. Or, as Salman says, "It's his Word against mine" (368).

"Why do I fear Mahound?" the polytheistic merchant Abu Simbel asks himself in the first Jahilia chapter. "For that: one one one, his terrifying singularity. Whereas I am always divided, always two or three or fifteen. I can even see his point of view" (102). The one one one truth sees any concept of pluralism, of conflicting and overlapping truths, of Salman's words rather than the Word, as an assault on its authority. It's of no use to say that Rushdie presents these scenes, which in themselves enact the conflict over *The Satanic Verses,* in the form of Gibreel Farishta's dreams, the dreams of a character who's going mad. For Islam's central belief that the Quran is not just divinely inspired but is itself Divine seems to demand a belief in the absolute integrity of words. It posits a virtual identity of words, belief, and action in a way that denies the Western distinction between the metaphoric and the literal, between character and author. If you accept that distinction, then you are already on the way to seeing Salman the Persian's point—already on the way to a belief in free speech.

But polytheists aren't the only ones who are "always two or three or fifteen." So are immigrants, who unlike the Imam can never remain in "complete ignorance" of their new countries, who are never "unsullied, unaltered, pure." Their identity can never be fixed or singular but is instead fluid, plural, however much they cling to tradition or however much they try to shed it. But what's lost in shedding one life, one identity, to take up another? And how much of one's old identity remains? "A man who sets out to make himself up," Rushdie writes early in the novel, "is taking on the Creator's role, according to one way of seeing things; he's unnatural, a blasphemer, an abomination of abominations. From another angle, you could see pathos in him, heroism in his struggle, in his willingness to risk: not all mutants survive" (49). The Muslim Gibreel Farishta has built a career out of playing Hindu gods in the "theologicals" cranked out by the Bombay film industry. Yet he rejects that multiplicity in his own life, wants only to remain "*continuous*—that is joined to and arising from his past." But the strain of maintaining that continuity, that oneness, proves too much. He dreams at night of the archangel whose name he bears, and his dreams keep leaking into and overwhelming his "waking self" (427). The novel's other main character, the "unnatural" Salahuddin Chamchawalla, has chosen a different sort of singular identity, doing his best to shed his Indianness and remake himself as an Englishman. When, for example, he's offered *masala dosa* for breakfast instead of "packet cereal," he complains about having "to eat this filthy foreign food" (258). In coming to Britain he's even shortened his name, to Saladin Chamcha. (That's another of Rushdie's linguistic jokes, since *chamcha* means "spoon" in Urdu and is slang for "sycophant"—"Toadji" (58) as the Bombay art critic Zeeny Vakil calls him.) But while he aspires to singularity, Saladin earns his living as a mimic, whose thousand voices have made him much in demand for radio voice-overs—though sometimes, when he's with Indian friends, his perfect Oxbridge accent slips.

Rushdie takes as his epigraph this passage from Daniel Defoe's *The History of the Devil* (1726): "Satan, being thus confined to a vagabond, wandering, unsettled condition, is without any certain abode; for though he has, in consequence of his angelic nature, a kind of empire in the liquid waste or air, yet this is certainly part of his punishment, that he is . . . without any fixed place, or space, allowed him to rest the soul of his foot upon." After surviving his own miraculous fall from an exploding airplane at the start of the novel, Saladin finds himself briefly sprouting horns and growing hooves, until he looks so goatish that his British wife refuses to take him back into his house. The Devil is a wanderer, one without any fixed place or certain abode: stateless, fallen, no longer purely of one place or another, no longer purely one thing or another—an immigrant. And for the immigrant that Rushdie imagines, the Imam's purity of belief is impossible. He must live instead in the world of Salman the Persian, in which the conflicting demands and truths of different cultures must be weighed against each other. Devil? Yes, a "foreign devil"; yes, in the sense that immigrants are often demonized by their new countries. Rushdie writes that he has given his prophet the name "Mahound," the "demon-tag the farangis hung around his neck," because "to turn insults into strengths, whigs, tories, Blacks all chose to wear with pride the names they were given in scorn" (93). So too with Saladin, who through the literalized metaphor of those horns and hooves comes to learn both that he cannot so easily shed his past and that there are more ways than one of being British. He learns, for example, to accept the Indianness he has checked at the door of his beloved Garrick Club—and does so because the only people willing to accept his goatish self are the residents of that "city visible but unseen," the Asian East Enders he has always shunned.

   Rushdie's character Zeeny Vakil has written a book attacking India's "confining myth of authenticity, that folkloristic straitjacket which she sought to replace by an ethic of historically validated eclecticism, for was not the entire national culture based on the principle of borrowing whatever clothes seemed to fit, Aryan, Mughal, British, take-the-best-and-leave-the-rest?" (52). In *The Satanic Verses* those words stand most obviously as a reproof to Zeeny's friend Saladin, who has sought a different but no less confining "myth of authenticity." But they also describe the eclectic pluralism of Rushdie's vision of Indian identity in *Midnight's Children* and can serve as well for the bazaar of his style as a whole, in which British English gets fused with bits of Hindi, with Bombay film slang, with what used to be despised as "babu English." Such prose seems much closer to the inventive energy with which Indians actually speak the language than does the limpid English of an older writer like R. K. Narayan. And perhaps that style can offer a new and liberating model of postcolonial identity. For it suggests we learn to see that identity as a consciously created pastiche of "whatever clothes [seem] to fit," and in doing so it calls into question V. S. Naipaul's concept of the colonial as an essentially unthinking and impotent mimic man, condemned by history to ape the West. But Zeeny's words can also apply to *The Satanic Verse*'s vision of what Britain and being British should be, for both native and immigrant. *There Ain't No Black in the Union Jack*—so says the title of the sociologist Paul Gilroy's study of race in England. One of the challenges this novel offers is that it asks us to imagine the ways in which there might be. The sad irony, as Rushdie has noted, is that Muslim protests over his novel will "confirm, in the Western mind, all the worst stereotypes of the Muslim world" and so make that act of imagination a more difficult one for whites and nonwhites alike.[3]

In *The Sense of an Ending*, Frank Kermode suggests that there is this difference between myth and fiction: "Myth . . . presupposes total and adequate explanations of things as they are and were. . . . Fictions are for finding things out. . . . Myths are the agents of stability, fictions the agents of change. Myths call for absolute, fictions for conditional assent."[4] Milan Kundera has written that the novel was born on the day Don Quixote looked out on the world and, finding he could no longer recognize it, began to conceive of that world as a question—not the answers of myth, of any totalizing system of belief.[5] What Salman Rushdie has done in *The Satanic Verses* is set fiction against a particularly powerful, absolute, and peremptory myth—a myth that has governed a part of his own life. He has done it as a way of examining a conflict between two mutually exclusive ways of imagining the world: between purity and pluralism, monologue and dialogue, orthodox answers and skeptical questions—the very conflict that *The Satanic Verses* itself has provoked. In Gibreel's dreams, in Jahilia, the conflict takes a religious form; in London, that of examining what, in an interview, Rushdie has called the "discomfort . . . [of having] a plural identity . . . made up of bits and fragments from here, there."[6] One wonders at the obliquity of this, in a writer whose earlier work has been about as subtle as a skyrocket. But it is the same issue throughout, and in

fact the different ways in which Rushdie puts that issue serve in the
end to underline the novel's essential unity, to emphasize its identity of theme and form.

Salman the Persian's rejection of the Word for words—of
the Book for books—has a lesson for us. For it is in his world, and
not the Imam's, that Saladin, that we all, must now learn to live.
Nothing, paradoxically, demonstrates this better than British Muslims' "discomfort" with their own inevitably plural identities, a discomfort that *The Satanic Verses* has made so many of them feel.
Within the novel, the implicit conflict of values that Rushdie poses
between Salman and the Imam is an unequal one. The battle outside will not be so easy.

Notes towards a Redefinition of Englishness

I

"You are here to kneel where prayer has been valid"—so the speaker commands himself in T. S. Eliot's "Little Gidding." And by kneeling where other knees have worn a path before you, you lift yourself out of the historic present and into a union with eternity. The prayer and the posture remain constant, and that constancy allows one to achieve an "intersection" with a place that is "England and nowhere. Never and always"—a place that seems both particular and universal at once, somehow more than itself.[1] But to what does the speaker pray? The church at Little Gidding, in Northamptonshire, was in the seventeenth century a place of Anglican retreat and was associated with the Royalist cause; the site of a religious community that Charles I is said to have visited after his defeat at Naseby, a community broken up by the Puritans at the end of the Civil War. The poem posits a union, now lost, between a sacred order and the state, and so when Eliot writes that "in a secluded chapel / History is now and England," the very name of the nation itself seems to become a kind of sacred text.[2] So let us consider "Little Gidding" as a national rather than a religious poem. The rhetoric is much the same in any case, for as Benedict Anderson has argued, the modern nation-state is often described in the mistily exalted terms once reserved for "the great sacral cultures," like Christendom or the Ummah Islam.[3] Little Gidding is for Eliot a place where one has an acute consciousness of English history.

And by locating one's self in relation to it, by kneeling where prayer has been valid before and will be valid tomorrow, one cements the past not just to the present but to the future as well. In this model England "is continuous," as George Orwell wrote in attempting to define the national character. "It stretches into the future and the past, there is something in it that persists . . . [that has] the power to change out of recognition and yet remain the same."[4] But what defines that continuity—what defines the Englishness of the English? The answer, Orwell suggests, is a suspicion of outsiders, a devotion to hobbies, a love of flowers. He frets at relying on such "trivialities" but finds it hard to get beyond them.[5] Englishness remains "somehow bound up with solid breakfasts and gloomy Sundays," which he takes as "*characteristic* fragments of the English scene."[6] But that seems maddeningly circular, as if Englishness could be described only in terms of what's already defined as English, as if that island were not merely insular but entirely self-referential. And though Orwell does move on to other, seemingly more substantive features of the national life, such as its strain of working-class anarchism, he returns again and again to the idea that a nation is a kind of organism, possessed of a continuous life that develops and changes and yet remains the same. Indeed that very consciousness of continuity comes itself to seem the determining feature of the national character. For "in whatever shape England emerges from the war," it both should and will go on being recognizably English.[7]

But has it? Writing during the crisis years of the Blitz, Eliot could strike a bluntly peremptory note—"kneel." For Philip Larkin in the 1970s that confident posture was less easily maintained. "Grey day for the Show, but cars jam the narrow lanes. / . . . Bead stalls, balloon men, a Bank; a beer marquee that / Half screens a canvas Gents"—wrestling, animal judging, exhibits of "blanch leeks like church candles," scones, pony races.[8] "Show Saturday" is one of Larkin's last major poems, an evocation of "the ended husk / Of summer" in the English countryside, an entry into a world of peaceful accustomed pleasures, a world that seems to vanish at the very moment it becomes most fully realized. Horse boxes begin to move, the car park thins, "they're loading jumps on a truck." And the fair-goers themselves turn:

> Back now to private addresses . . .
> Back now, all of them, to their local lives . . .
> To winter coming, as the dismantled Show
> Itself dies back into the area of work.
> Let it stay hidden there like strength, below
> Sale-bills and swindling; something people do,
> Not noticing how time's rolling smithy-smoke
> Shadows much greater gestures; something they share
> That breaks ancestrally each year into
> Regenerate union. Let it always be there.[9]

The key word is "regenerate." Standing at the head of the last line, it figures as both adjective and verb, for the fair both embodies the renewal of a communal life and is itself the way in which that life seems perpetually reborn. Indeed for Larkin the temporary community that the fair creates exists precisely because of its continuity with the past, with the other Show Saturdays that have ancestrally punctuated the seasons. "Let it always be there"—less a command than a wish, and a fear that "time's rolling smithy-smoke" may not allow that union to endure.

Larkin saw his work as an attempt to restore a "native" tradition in English poetry, one that drew on Thomas Hardy and the Georgian nature poets, a tradition that had seemed superseded by the international modernism of Eliot. The show may briefly take people out of their local lives, but in doing so, it both creates and confirms a local identity—the exact opposite of the universalizing abstractions that characterize "Little Gidding." And its plea for continuity crucially depends on the place where Larkin locates that continuity—on what, in particular, he wants always to be there. For the countryside figures as the site for an essentialized conception of an enduring England and, as such, has been used to sell everything from beer to the Campaign for Nuclear Disarmament. And perhaps "Show Saturday" itself can stand as a kind of understated advertise-

ment for the heritage industry. Certainly that's true of one of Larkin's less successful poems, the 1972 "Going, Going," in which
the country seems all high-rises and parking lots, the "first slum of
Europe"—except, of course, "for the tourist parts."[10]

But just what parts are those? Stately homes, the Tower,
cathedrals, all that of course—the fantasy cult of the home counties.
Yet visitors now find the kitchens and servants' quarters among the
most interesting parts of great houses, and in the late 1980s new
museums of local and people's history were opening every two
weeks. For the concept of "heritage," as the historian Raphael Samuel writes, has been "broadened . . . to take in the terraced street
. . . and even the city slum. . . . Family history societies . . . encourage
people to celebrate humble origins."[11] Certainly "Show Saturday"
fits that democratized model of English heritage. Its images, though
rural, aren't limited by class; it balances "men with hunters, dog-
breeding wool-defined women" with allotment gardens and "business calendars hung up in kitchens." Nevertheless, there remains
something troubling about the poem, for the "preservation mania,"
in Samuel's words, tends to aestheticize whatever it touches. "Man-
gles no longer serve as symbols of toil when they are treated as *objet
d'art*," and the past as a whole stands in danger of becoming a version of pastoral.[12] And of course Larkin's poem relies on its reader's
knowledge of pastoral, of the tradition that Raymond Williams out-
lined in *The Country and the City*, in which a rural perfection is
located in the immediately vanished past.[13] But it goes that tradition
one better, for "Show Saturday" says "No, not yet, not gone yet,"
holding out the precarious hope that the fair's "regenerate union"
means that it will never even need to be revived but will somehow
naturally endure.

Toward the end of his career Larkin often used such images
of continuity as a stay against his own mortality. Yet in other poems
he chafes at the constraints of such a continuity, like the habits that
"harden into all we've got" in "Dockery and Son," defining the
self in negative terms: "No son, no wife, / No house or land." To
such a poet, "Life is first boredom, then fear. / Whether or not we
use it, it goes, / And leaves what something hidden from us chose, /
And age, and then the only end of age."[14] Larkin's subject, as he

said of his friend Barbara Pym, is the experience of not having, the observation of absence—of God, of family, and of any ability whatsoever to change "what something hidden from us chose." The choices have all been made before, somewhere back in the past. For Larkin everything important has already happened, and so one suffers from a sense of one's own belatedness, capable only of waiting for a death that seems itself without meaning. And it is precisely that sense of living in an aftermath that made him the national poet of a postimperial England.[15]

In 1977, in the middle of Britain's decade as Europe's sick joke, Larkin served as chair of the Booker Prize judges. The winner that year was Scott's *Staying On*, the story of an army couple, in which, as Larkin wrote, the "unsuccessful history" they trail behind them serves to link "the end by death of a marriage . . . to the end by history of an empire."[16] But that note of lament sounds even more clearly in a book that Larkin singled out as a runner-up: Pym's *Quartet in Autumn*. The novel follows the lives of four unmarried middle-class people in their sixties. They work together in an office, two men and two women, though Pym never says just what sort of work they do. At the women's retirement party, in fact, "the (acting) deputy assistant director" tries to make it a point in their favor that "nobody knows exactly, or has ever known exactly, what it is that they do," and in consequence nobody can possibly be "found to replace them."[17] Their jobs will be phased out, their whole lives superfluous. But several moments in *Quartet in Autumn* provide an intriguing suggestion about the condition of England and about the main character Letty's increasingly attenuated relation to it, in a way that complicates one's sense of the novel's elegiac tone.

"KILL ASIAN SHIT"—so runs the novel's report of a bit of typical graffiti in the Underground.[18] And when Letty's landlady sells her house, she has a most surprising tidbit to impart about the new landlord. "Mr Olatunde," she tells her assembled tenants, "comes from Nigeria." The news is not particularly welcome, though one of the tenants does try to take comfort in the fact that although Mr. Olatunde is undoubtedly black, "until very recently Nigeria *was* British. It was pink on the map." But Letty feels that "the way things were going, nothing was pink on the map anymore"; and for a moment it seems as if England's loss of its empire is itself responsible for her own unhappiness.[19] It is as if they are somehow equivalent: Letty, aging and tired, so unimportant that she won't even be replaced when she retires; and England, worn out as well, irrelevant on the world stage. And Letty seems for a moment to believe that if the map were still pink, none of this would be true. England would still be powerful, and she wouldn't have to worry about the uncertainties her new landlord presents, her fears of "noise and exuberance, all those characteristics exemplified by the black girl in the office which were so different from her own."[20]

But the connection between Letty's unhappiness and England's dwindling power is subtler than it might at first appear. Pym certainly suggests that Letty has to live in a world for which she wasn't made. Both she and her country have to live out the consequences of choices made long ago. They are each governed by a set of conventions that have "harden[ed] into all [they've] got," even though those conventions no longer fully apply. Yet it's not simply that life, history, has passed them by but rather that Letty and the things she represents, the days when the map was pink, are becoming increasingly irrelevant to England itself. For Pym suggests that England has begun to take on a new form, albeit one that Letty can neither fully recognize nor fully accept. Mr. Olatunde comes from Nigeria; he is also a Christian, and his faith is far more vigorous and warm—far more vital—than that of Pym's white characters, with their almost academic interest in ritual. But Letty resists that warmth and retreats instead into her own quiet Anglicanism, a "grey, formal, respectable thing of measured observances and mild general undemanding kindness to all."[21] And she refuses the Olatundes' dinner invitation, not out of racism per se but out of her fear of the new, of surrendering the narrow canons of behavior through which her identity has been defined. Of course most people Letty's age do feel out of touch with their society. Pym's triumph lies in the way she draws the connection between that individual feeling and a kind of national out-of-touchness, her sense of an England out of touch with its own contemporary reality.

II

When Eliot kneels in the church at Little Gidding, he does something more than assert the continuity of the present with the past. He also locates himself, an expatriate American, a naturalized British citizen, in relation to English history, as indeed his earlier "East Coker" had found its title in the village from which his family had left for the New World. It lets him see himself as a part of that history, allows him to enter into an imaginative communion with the past and therefore with the present as well, an act through which he can imagine himself as English. Forty years later another immigrant writer would do the same thing with a different part of the English landscape. In *The Enigma of Arrival*, Naipaul writes that Salisbury "was almost the first English town I had got to know, the first I had been given some idea of, from the reproduction of the Constable painting in my third-standard reader" (E, 7). Now, as an adult, he has come to live in that landscape. Salisbury is the market town for the country life he describes in that book, and one of his regular walks takes him to a spot from which he can look out on Stonehenge. At first he sees his presence there as an "oddity . . . part of something like an upheaval, a change in the course of the history of the country" (E, 15). For what relation, he wonders, can a Trinidad Hindu have to those Druidical stones, that cathedral Close, to the wide disused droveways—that Hardyesque word, unknown in his "tropical island" (E, 7)—of ancient paths to market. People like him have not been there before. And he contrasts himself to his neighbor Jack, who seems "genuine, rooted." At work in his garden, Jack fits smoothly into the landscape, "a remnant of the past (the undoing of which my own presence portended)." It even seems appropriate that Jack lives in the midst of decay, his cottage surrounded by "junk" (E, 15). For "there would have been no room" for Naipaul (E, 52) if he had come to Wiltshire before a time of decay, in a time when the past—the great houses, the empire that supported them—had not yet been superseded.

Then Naipaul learns that he's wrong about Jack, that Jack too is a newcomer. In consequence "much that had looked traditional, natural, emanations of the landscape, things that country people did . . . now turned out not to have been traditional or instinctive after all" (E, 47). They are simply Jack's way of doing things, a matter of individual style. Naipaul learns, in fact, that "change [is] constant" (32), even at the edge of Salisbury plain: change, and not decay, for "decay implied an ideal, a perfection in the past" in which he no longer believes. "Wasn't the place now, for me, at its peak?" (E, 210). And so he learns to see this landscape not as fixed and permanent but as marked instead by ceaseless change, and to see himself as but one more newcomer. Life on these chalk hills comes to seem defined by discontinuity, as if the only permanence lies in flux; and in reading, one remembers that the continuity Naipaul's predecessor Eliot had asserted was in fact a broken one. All things alter. People die, move house, put up fences; agriculture is mechanized, gardens are cleared and grow over. Jack dies; Naipaul remains. And that very understanding of the constancy of change allows Naipaul to place himself within a history that had once seemed to have no room for him: to recognize himself at last as a part of the English landscape rather than alien to it, and to locate himself in the line of English nature writers that includes Cobbett and Hardy and Clare.

In both my introduction and my chapter on Scott I described how British imperialism helped create a particular sense of English national identity. As any reader of Orwell's "Shooting an Elephant" will remember, the imagined community of the British Empire required that its members act in predictable and even automatic ways. The imperialist must always perform his own Englishness, must demonstrate that he has the qualities the English are supposed to have, and so "he becomes a sort of hollow posing dummy, the conventionalized figure of a sahib. . . . He wears a mask, and his face grows to fit it."[22] That makes Englishness into what Naipaul calls a "creation of fantasy" (A, 209), and indeed he writes that "at the height of their power the British gave the impression of a people at play, a people playing at being English of a certain class" (A, 211). But the fantasy was a double one. E. M. Forster writes that his characters enjoyed amateur theatricals, in which they could stop playing the *sahib* and "dress up as the middle-class English people they actually were."[23] For along with the stiff upper lip, the Raj's fantasy of Englishness stressed the compensatory coziness of a country as unlike the empire as possible—an England all chintz and cottages and weathered Cotswold stone that seems to have been there always. It was the dream of "Home," the green and pleasant land, that district officers and their wives nourished around the globe and then attempted to create when they retired to Cheltenham or Tunbridge Wells.

It is, in fact, the same dream that one sees in the shops of the late twentieth-century clothiers and perfumers and marmalade manufacturers who have invented traditional identities for themselves. Naipaul suggests in *An Area of Darkness* that imperialism made "Englishness" less a matter of geographical origin than a canon of taste and a code of behavior; and in consequence the writer shifted his or her attention "from human behavior to the Englishness of behavior, Englishness held up for approval or dissection" (A, 209). The writer no longer maintains the concern with the condition of England that had so animated the Victorians but develops instead a fascination with the English condition—a condition, an identity, that seems at once fully and yet narrowly defined. Indeed the terms of that behavior still control the image of England—what Larkin called the "tourist parts"—and not only for foreigners. Seemingly anything that can pass itself off as authentically English can now be sold to the English themselves, for that fascination with the English condition has, of course, only increased as the empire recedes into the past. Not all postimperial British literature has sounded a note of lament. But it has been marked by a sense of things ending, of the inescapability of a past that has "harden[ed] into all [they've] got," a national narrative of diminished expectations that includes not only Larkin and Pym but also a writer of very different politics like Margaret Drabble, a narrative in which the most original voices have belonged to those unconcerned with the "Englishness of behavior," such as Doris Lessing and Harold Pinter.

Of course few people take that image literally, not even in the hegemonic south, though it may answer to the self-conception of those who welcomed Margaret Thatcher's patriotic drum. Most people—most writers especially—play with that identity, exploiting and subverting its conventions. Nevertheless they remain unable to step outside those conventions, outside the terms of a culture in which so much seems already determined; hence the continued fascination with the typical, with pointing out, as Orwell had, how very English is a particular bit of English life.[24] Yet that image excludes far more than it includes, for despite the democratization of heritage, it contains little room for the urban poor, for the working class, or indeed for the whole north of Britain. And what about those people whose very presence suggests the kinds of historic discontinuity and change that "Englishness" seems at such pains to deny? How can they assume an identity that seems to depend on the illusion of permanence? Or to put it another way, what about Pym's Mr. Olatunde?

In 1990 *The Observer* ran an account of a fight between gangs from different working-class areas of Bradford. "Me and my mates were just walking up here," one of the participants recalled, "and there were six or seven lads walking down . . . I got whacked from the side with a bar. They had lasses there and all and one of them took her shoes off and whacked me on the head with her stilettos." Mates, lads, lasses—working-class diction that could have come from the mouths of Lawrence's coal miners. But the speaker here is a Muslim, with family roots in South Asia, and he is describing a fight with a gang of white kids that started when the whites began chanting "Salman Rushdie is our leader."[25] The speaker himself was born in England, and when he speaks of his friends as "mates" he imagines his relation to them in a language that is continuous with the English past. But to his assailants he is a "Paki," and after the crisis over *The Satanic Verses*, some people took to using Rushdie's name as a taunt, an easy way of baiting those who some whites believe shouldn't be in England in the first place. In the wake of that crisis the term "British Muslim" came for the first time to stand for a recognizable identity; the words became linked in the public mind without the sense of oxymoron that would once have characterized them. And indeed that word "British" would at first seem the proper term for Mr. Olatunde: British, that is, a citizen of the United Kingdom of Great Britain and Northern Ireland. Yet a British identity is so frequently conflated with an English one as to make the terms in practice interchangeable, in a way that can seem unsatisfactory to both the National Front and immigrants alike. For as Paul Gilroy has argued, the different "national" or "ethnic" groups that have traditionally composed the United Kingdom—for example, the Scots—all have a homeland within that political structure.[26] What about the child of Pakistani immigrants whose only homeland is England? "My name is Karim Amir, and I am an Englishman born and bred, almost."[27]

That statement from Hanif Kureishi's *The Buddha of Suburbia* can stand as an example of what Charles Taylor calls "the politics of recognition," the demand by a subaltern group that their identity and presence be recognized as valid.[28] Yet Karim, like Scott's Hari Kumar, doesn't have the same relation to the English past as do the whites with whom he goes to school: a past in which people who look like them have defined themselves as a community in part by conquering people who look like him. What Kureishi calls for is, in consequence, an act of imagination on the part of "the white British," an act through which they can recognize that "being British isn't what it was," an act through which the community can be redefined, reimagined to include its new members.[29] In its most obvious sense, of course, what he demands is a change in the hearts and minds of whites—but not only whites, for both antiracists and their right-wing opponents have, as Gilroy suggests, historically equated race with culture in a way that makes both sides argue that people of color are historically alien to English life. In America, where Ellis Island is now as powerful a symbol as Concord or Gettysburg, taking the oath of citizenship is a ritual in which one becomes conscious of the millions who have taken it before. But something more seems necessary in a Britain that has never seen itself as a nation of immigrants: a country in which, as Orwell suggests, a sense of continuity with the past is in itself a crucial determinant of national identity, in which a person or practice or thing is seen as English to the degree that it's thought to have always been English already.

Yet as Defoe's "The True-Born Englishman" reminds us, Britain has in fact always had immigrants, even if it hasn't always wanted to recognize them. A century ago the Spitalfields courtyards and lanes, where Bangladeshi children now play, were occupied by Jewish clothiers; two hundred years before that, the same alleyways were the homes of Huguenot weavers. And Gilroy suggests that the best way to reimagine the national identity, to make it recognize the presence of the new, might be to concentrate on the role that blacks—and by extension, all the subject peoples of empire—have already played in English history. By way of example he cites Turner's 1840 painting "The Slave Ship" to show that "the imagery of race has a much longer lineage in English cultural life than the aura of postwar novelty allows us to see."[30] Gilroy reminds us, however, that Turner's canvas has historically been praised—most famously by John Ruskin—for its use of color and its depiction of water, praised for anything but its subject: slavers throwing the dead and dying overboard. Yet that subject is neither accidental nor alien to English life. With that hellish burnt-yellow sun separating the ship from the bulk of its jettisoned cargo, it is instead an integral part of Turner's conception of England's historical identity: the human price paid for its wealth, a price that English cultural history has on the whole striven to ignore. "We all live by robbing Asiatic coolies," Orwell wrote in 1942.[31] And what one now needs is an increased awareness of what that has meant, of the ways in which people of color are linked to what being English has historically been, an awareness that makes such people a part of the narrative of English life in a way that simple naturalization does not. But Gilroy adds that this awareness must be developed not only by the "white British" but by the new English as well. Because in its very brutality, Turner's picture presents a particular challenge for black Britons. It demands that they integrate the different aspects of their heritage in what he calls "the black Atlantic" in a way that allows them to recognize that their own history is not opposed to England's but is inseparable from it.[32]

III

In the 1950s Samuel Selvon and George Lamming built novels around the lives of West Indian immigrants in London, a tradition

that Naipaul himself drew on in *The Mimic Men*. Both Kureishi's
picaresque *The Buddha of Suburbia* and Timothy Mo's richly natu-
ralistic *Sour Sweet* (1982) offer accounts of growing up in a multiracial England, latter-day versions of the cultural conundrum I've examined in the person of Scott's Hari Kumar. Yet as Gilroy's work
might suggest, some of the most interesting British fiction of the
last two decades has involved the retrospective recognition that English history is far more complicated than its official image would
allow. That critical revisionism has put the national narrative in
flux and has motivated such novels as Graham Swift's *Waterland*
(1983) and Angela Carter's high-spirited *Wise Children* (1991). And
it also lies behind Mo's attempt to investigate the imperial past in
An Insular Possession (1986). At the start of that novel, set during
the First Opium War of 1839–42, the "empire" to which his characters refer has its capital in Peking, and the English think of themselves as traders. By the end of the book, however, the demands of
that trade have created both the city of Hong Kong and an imperial
consciousness in the English themselves. In a similar vein, the poet
David Dabydeen has, like Gilroy, drawn on "The Slave Ship" for a
fine long poem about the Middle Passage.[33] And in the multivoiced
narratives of *Higher Ground* (1989), *Cambridge* (1991), and *Crossing
the River* (1993), Caryl Phillips has peopled the black Atlantic from
the eighteenth century to the present: adopting now the voice of a
West African collaborator with English slavers, now that of a white
woman in love with a black man, now that of a literate slave, or the
voice of a black man imprisoned in the American South, but always
trying to push beyond the specificities of race to a larger sense of
dispossession and loss.

　　Yet as the example of *The Enigma of Arrival* would suggest,
there are other ways than writing about racism for the immigrant
writer to establish his or her relation to the English past. Naipaul's
locating himself in isolation against the Wiltshire downs does, however, seem characteristic of his desire to see himself and his work
as alone and unprecedented; as such it stands in marked contrast
to the way that in *The Satanic Verses* Rushdie peopled and gave voice
to the "city visible but unseen" (SV, 241) that is the immigrant's
London. As I suggested in my chapter on *Midnight's Children*, I

have in this book drawn a comparison between these two great writers. And now, before concluding, I want to extend that comparison
in order to suggest what their different models of the postcolonial
self have to say about the possibilities for immigrant life in England.
Both writers deal with characters whose lives, in Rushdie's words,
have been "handcuffed to history" and thereby "transformed into
grotesquery"; both are masters of a black and astringent comedy
that grows from the confrontation of one culture with another.
They see the same world. Yet the prose of the one is so sparely
rational and that of the other so prodigal as to suggest their radically
different visions of that world. And my chapters on them have suggested ways in which—as with their attitudes toward "purity"—
their work does indeed seem diametrically opposed.

It's tempting to see Naipaul's sensibility as a colonial one
and Rushdie's as postcolonial. The precise moment at which the
one spills into the other may be impossible to define, but the novelists' birth dates are suggestive. Born in 1932, some thirty years before Trinidadian independence, Naipaul writes out of what Sara
Suleri has described as a sense of his own incipient obsolescence,
recording "a perspective that knows its time is done even before it
has had the chance to be fully articulated."[34] In contrast Rushdie
was born in 1947, the very year of India's independence: into a
world in which the anticolonial struggle had in political terms already been won. That implies they're not so much opposed to one
another as illustrative of different stages in the chronicle of empire,
two aspects of a single historical process, in which colonial mimicry
eventually gives way to the postcolonial collage of the self. But the
biographical differences between them are both simpler and yet
more complex than that distinction would suggest. Trinidad is not
India. It is a small colony, the model of dependency, and during
Naipaul's childhood its Indian population was still largely rural,
guarding itself against the inevitable intrusions of the outer world.
Rushdie grew up in Bombay—subordinate to what he calls Proper
London, but a great city in its own right. He has the streetwise sass
that comes from a childhood in the subcontinent's most energeti-
cally cosmopolitan city, its gateway to the West, its film capital.
And there is a class difference as well. Naipaul's family may have

been Brahmins, but in Trinidad they clung to the lower edge of the middle class, just a generation away from cutting cane. He got to England only after winning a fiercely competitive scholarship. Rushdie, in contrast, grew up in a rich and Westernized family and was sent to an English public school before going on to Cambridge, as his father had before him. The one comes to England as a suppliant, the other almost as a matter of course.

Both writers take the migrant as the emblematic figure of our times; and for both, the postcolonial self is defined by what Homi Bhabha describes as its "separation from origins and essences."[35] Yet Naipaul, with his longing for a "pure time" that he knows has never existed, can only see that separation, and the mimicry that inevitably follows it, as a mark of cultural fracture. It is a sign that one comes from what he calls a "wounded civilization." And so his concept of postcolonial identity has all the bleak austerity of his prose, while Rushdie's has the inventive impurity, the sense of possibility, that so marks his own style. To Rushdie the self is never singular but always intrinsically plural, always "two or three or fifteen." For the migrant has chosen to translate one identity into another and, in doing so, has set "out to make himself up" in a way that forces his identity into fluidity, however much he clings to tradition or however much he tries to shed it. And if by force of circumstances one cannot be whole, then one should make that lack of wholeness a virtue and turn one's very fractures into strength. A self-conscious mimicry therefore becomes a way to shuttle between Bombay and London, between the hybrid selves of the postcolonial condition; it allows one to acknowledge that one lives between two worlds. So it is with Saladin Chamcha in *The Satanic Verses*, whose pursuit of Englishness is quite consciously chosen—this voice, rather than any of the many others he can perform. It is an act of will, a means toward the creation of a self; an act not all that different from Naipaul's own invention of himself, the Trinidad Hindu who became a great British novelist.

Rushdie's sense of the self's fluidity provides, perhaps, a model of the way we should all live; certainly its hopefulness seems preferable to Naipaul's sense of an always unfulfilled longing. Yet it is finally less capacious than it looks. For though it does encourage an acceptance of the discontinuities that seem every migrant's fate, it remains best suited for those most able to live with a sense of uncertainty and improvisation—for the gifted and the well-off, those for whom shuttling between London and Bombay is the literal and not the figurative truth.[36] Bharati Mukherjee puts it this way: "Either—following Naipaul—we are less than fully human, pathetic trained monkeys, mimic men; or we are miraculous translations, Lamarckian mutations, single lives that have acquired new characteristics."[37] And neither option offers much of a chance for ordinary people, for those who can't be trained so well as to make the tricks of the West their own or who can't withstand the transformations that Saladin must endure, growing goatish horns and hooves, before he'll accept the Indian side of his discontinuous self. We still need an enabling model of the self for the mass of immigrants as well, for the many who in their new countries still long for singularity and find being anything more an unbearable strain.

And perhaps Naipaul, however grim, comes closer than Rushdie to providing, not a model of the way things should be, but an account of the way they are. Because for all that the younger writer talks about the "discomfort . . . [of having] a plural identity," for all that his work engages with totalizing systems and the delusive quest for authenticity, he never seems quite able to take that quest seriously as a human longing.[38] It is as if the desire for purity comes already discredited by the narrative's own sophistication, as it does not in Naipaul; draw what connections you will to the seemingly unanticipated storm over *The Satanic Verses*. It's not my intention here to provide anything like a full reading of the crisis over that novel. But for my purposes the *fatwa* is a sideshow; the heart of the matter lies in the novel's public burning in Bradford and in the subsequent demands that the government make an official recognition of Muslim sensitivities. And Rushdie's own words still provide the best guide to the affair, for what the protests express is precisely that "discomfort with a plural identity."[39] Yet behind that discomfort lies a failure to imagine an England that includes both blacks and whites, a failure that grows from the belief that because blacks and Asians are relative newcomers to what has in the past seemed a

racially homogeneous society, their culture must inevitably remain
distinct from that of white England. That is what Enoch Powell
claimed in the 1960s and what Margaret Thatcher repeated in the
1980s; and that sentiment, albeit in different words and a different tone, has been echoed by the most articulate of Rushdie's British Muslim critics, Shabbir Akhtar of the Bradford Council of
Mosques.[40]

The Rushdie affair raises the issue of that troublingly ambiguous phrase "the multicultural society." The phrase is ambiguous
because it can mean either a society composed of many cultures,
or one that recognizes the varied cultural origins of its constituent
members but that stands as something other than the sum of its
parts. In either case, however, the multiculturalist believes in what
Leon Wieseltier has described as a "complex society of differently
simplified individuals, a multicultural society of monocultural people." Rather than the multicultural society, we should speak, as
Wieseltier suggests, of the "multicultural individual" who, like
Rushdie's migrants, is possessed of "two or three or fifteen" identities at once.[41] Yet the phrase itself has perhaps outlived its use-
fulness, for at the very least it implies that even if our individual
sources and influences are multiple, we can nevertheless tell where
one culture leaves off and another begins, that they remain separate
in essence. For separateness is always defined in relation to something, and insisting on it is itself a mark of its impossibility in a
world in which "we are all . . . leaking into one another . . . *like
flavours when you cook.*" But sometimes the flavors don't work. Pico
Iyer has described "the fundamental disconnections that the new
globalism obscures," the way in which "a world of differences [is]
made more difficult when everyone's living down the block."[42] In
the Rushdie affair the bitter arguments over pluralism that have
long characterized the United States came to the fore in Britain,
as indeed they have throughout the European Union. For diversity—real diversity, a diversity of beliefs instead of just cooking—
means conflict. And the mindless air of celebration that has characterized the rhetoric of multiculturalism has too often subverted its
own ends by masking the sheer difficulty of the demands that our
new world places upon us.

The writers with whom this book has dealt know full well the heartbreak of that world; and the whisper of possibility they offer is in no way an escape from its dangers. Scott writes in *The Day of the Scorpion* that India is where "the British came to the end of themselves as they were" (S, 3). One mark of that is the recognition that there is now such a thing as a British Muslim. But what has also come to an end as it was is English literature itself. Are Naipaul and Rushdie both British writers? They are if they want to be—and yet how limiting the question seems. My purpose here hasn't been to assimilate them to England but rather to suggest how England, and English, might assimilate itself to them. For one must recognize as well that throughout this past century, English literature, as traditionally and narrowly defined, has been but the superannuated uncle of literature in English and that for many younger writers, national identity now seems something not to embrace but to refuse. And not only for the young. In *A Way in the World* Naipaul moves beyond the home at which he has so enigmatically arrived and out into the world again, tracing the lives of others who contain his several worlds within them, finding in history a group of people who have made journeys that resemble his own. It is as if he remains isolated and yet somehow no longer alone; and in the process the question of just where one belongs seems to drop away, allowing him to recognize that for the type of colonial he has become, being perpetually between cultures offers not only pain but possibility.

Britain's illusory belief in its own historical homogeneity means that it will probably never become a fully multiracial society. Even if nonwhites can insert themselves into the continuity of English life, the terms of that life will change only in degree. Nevertheless their presence will have important consequences. After his transformation into a human goat, Rushdie's Saladin Chamcha finds himself in a hospital full of other foreign beasts: a manticore from Bombay, "businessmen from Nigeria who have grown sturdy tails . . . holiday makers from Senegal who . . . were turned into slippery snakes." And when Saladin asks what has happened, the manticore tells him that white British society has "the power of description, and we succumb to the pictures they construct" (SV, 168). But the map isn't pink anymore, and in describing themselves, in changing the face in England's mirror, such figures as Saladin may one day help loosen the coils of that island nation's seemingly endless past.

Introduction

1. Rudyard Kipling, "The Man Who Would Be King," in *The Portable Kipling*, ed. Irving Howe (New York: Viking Penguin, 1982), 38. Further references will be indicated by page numbers within parentheses.

2. This is the myth of Prester John and of many of Edgar Rice Burroughs's Tarzan novels. See Christopher L. Miller, *Blank Darkness: Africanist Discourse in French* (Chicago: University of Chicago Press, 1985), 58–59, and my own "Tact and Tarzan," *Transition*, issue 52, n.s., vol. 1, no. 2 (1991).

3. Rudyard Kipling, "The Ballad of East and West" (1889), in *Rudyard Kipling's Verse: Definitive Edition* (Garden City, N.Y.: Doubleday, 1945), 233. On Kipling's Freemasonry, see Angus Wilson, *The Strange Ride of Rudyard Kipling* (New York: Viking, 1978), 314–15.

4. Thomas Babington Macaulay, "Minute on Indian Education," in *Selected Writings* (Chicago: University of Chicago Press, 1972), 249.

5. Rudyard Kipling, "On the City Wall," in *"Soldiers Three" and "In Black and White"* (1888; reprint, Harmondsworth: Penguin, 1993), 154.

6. Rudyard Kipling, "The Ladies," in *Rudyard Kipling's Verse*, 441.

7. Paul Scott, *The Day of the Scorpion* (New York: William Morrow and Company, 1968), 269.

8. Homi Bhabha, "Of Mimicry and Man," in *The Location of Culture* (London: Routledge, 1994), 87.

9. Paul Scott, *A Division of the Spoils* (New York: William Morrow and Company, 1975), 105.

10. V. S. Naipaul, *In a Free State* (1971; reprint, Harmondsworth: Penguin, 1973), 246.

11. V. S. Naipaul, *The Mimic Men* (1967; reprint, Harmondsworth: Penguin, 1969), 32.

12. Homi Bhabha, "Signs Taken for Wonders: Questions of Ambivalence and Authority under a Tree outside Delhi, May 1817," in *The Location of Culture*, 120.

13. Salman Rushdie, *Midnight's Children* (New York: Knopf, 1981), 291.

14. Salman Rushdie, *The Satanic Verses* (New York: Viking, 1989), 52.

15. Ibid.

16. Examples would include M. M. Mahood, *The Colonial Encounter: A Reading of Six Novels* (Totowa, N.J.: Rowman and Littlefield, 1977), or Abdul R. JanMohamed, *Manichean Aesthetics: The Politics of Literature in Colonial Africa* (Amherst: University of Massachusetts Press, 1983).

17. Neil Lazarus, *Resistance in Postcolonial African Fiction* (New Haven: Yale University Press, 1990); Selwyn Cudjoe, *V. S. Naipaul: A Materialist Reading* (Amherst: University of Massachusetts Press, 1988).

18. Edward Said, *Culture and Imperialism* (New York: Knopf, 1993), passim. A good example is Jenny Sharpe's study of the rhetoric of rape in British fiction about India, *Allegories of Empire: The Figure of Woman in the Colonial Text* (Minneapolis: University of Minnesota Press, 1993).

19. Sara Suleri, *The Rhetoric of English India* (Chicago: University of Chicago Press, 1992), 5.

20. Sara Suleri, "The Geography of *A Passage to India*," in *E. M. Forster*, ed. Harold Bloom (New York: Chelsea House, 1987), 169.

21. Aijaz Ahmad, "The Politics of Literary Postcoloniality," *Race and Class* 36, 3 (1995): 9.

22. Linda Hutcheon, Introduction to "Colonialism and the Postcolonial Condition," *PMLA* 110, 1 (January 1995): 10.

23. Ella Shohat, "Notes on the 'Post-Colonial,'" *Social Text* 31–32 (1995): 107.

24. Ibid., 108, 107.

25. Anne McClintock, "The Angel of Progress: Pitfalls of the Term 'Post-Colonialism,'" *Social Text* 31–32 (1995): 88.

26. Naipaul, *The Mimic Men*, 32.

27. Gilles Deleuze and Felix Guattari, *Kafka: Toward a Minor Literature* (1975), trans. Dana Polan (Minneapolis: University of Minnesota Press, 1986), 16.

28. Scott, *Day of the Scorpion*, 3.

29. See Michael Valdez Moses, *The Novel and the Globalization of Culture* (New York: Oxford University Press, 1995), for a rich account of the way in which, over the past century, novels from around the world have come repeatedly to tell the same story: the way in which traditional society, whether in Thomas Hardy's Wessex or Chinua Achebe's Iboland, is overcome by the forces of modernity.

30. Benedict Anderson, *Imagined Communities: Reflections on the Origin and Spread of Nationalism* (London: Verso, 1983), 46–47.

31. George Orwell, "England, Your England," in *A Collection of Essays* (New York: Harcourt Brace Jovanovich, 1953), 254.

32. Ernest Renan, "What Is a Nation" (1882), trans. Martin Thom, in *Nation and Narration*, ed. Homi Bhabha (London: Routledge, 1990), 17.

33. James Joyce, *A Portrait of the Artist as a Young Man* (1916; reprint, Harmondsworth: Penguin, 1992), 205.

34. Renan, "What Is a Nation," 14.

35. Daniel Defoe, "The True-Born Englishman" (1701), in *The Novels and Miscellaneous Works of Daniel De Foe* (Oxford: Talboys, 1841), 20:19–20.

36. Renan, "What Is a Nation," 11.

37. See Bhabha, *Nation and Narration*, for a series of case studies, esp. John Barrell, "Sir Joshua Reynolds and the Englishness of English Art," and Francis Mulhern, "English Reading."

38. Linda Colley, *Britons* (New Haven; Yale University Press, 1992).

39. V. S. Naipaul, *An Area of Darkness* (1964; reprint, New York: Vintage, 1981), 206.

40. See Thomas Babington Macaulay, "Lord Clive," in *Critical and Historical Essays*, vol. 1 (London: Dent, 1907), 534.

41. E. M. Forster, *A Passage to India* (1924; reprint, New York: Harcourt Brace Jovanovich, 1984), 40.

42. Scott, *Day of the Scorpion*, 245.

43. Eric Hobsbawm, *Nations and Nationalism since 1780* (Cambridge: Cambridge University Press, 1990), 24.

44. See Naipaul, *Area of Darkness*, ch. 8, "Fantasy and Ruins."

45. V. S. Naipaul, *The Middle Passage* (1962; reprint, Harmondsworth: Penguin, 1969), 231.

46. Bhabha, "Of Mimicry and Man," 86, 89 (emphasis in the original).

47. The statistics and legal details in the next two paragraphs are taken from Dilip Hiro, *Black British, White British: A History of Race Relations in Britain* (1971; 3d ed., London: Grafton Books, 1991). See also Peter Fryer, *Staying Power: The History of Black People in Britain* (London: Pluto Press, 1984), and Jonathon Green, *Them: Voices from the Immigrant Community in Contemporary Britain* (London: Secker and Warburg, 1990).

48. Paul Gilroy, *There Ain't No Black in the Union Jack* (London: Hutchinson, 1987).

49. Hiro, *Black British, White British*, 260.

50. Enoch Powell, "Immigration," in *Freedom and Reality* (New Rochelle, N.Y.: Arlington House, 1969), 237.

51. Hanif Kureishi, *The Buddha of Suburbia* (New York: Viking Penguin, 1990), 3.

52. Rushdie, *The Satanic Verses*, 8. See also Homi Bhabha's "How Newness Enters the World: Postmodern Space, Postcolonial Times, and the Trials of Cultural Translation," in *The Location of Culture*, for a subtle description of "diasporic identity" (225) that draws not only on *The Satanic Verses* but also on Derek Walcott's sense of Caribbean history.

One

1. References to Scott's novels are incorporated in the text and are keyed to the four-volume 1978 edition of *The Raj Quartet* (New York: William Morrow and Company). I have used the following

abbreviations:

J *The Jewel in the Crown*
S *The Day of the Scorpion*
T *The Towers of Silence*
D *A Division of the Spoils*

Where two or more successive quotations are taken from the same source, the reference follows the last quotation. I have also made parenthetical references to Scott's volume of essays *On Writing and the Novel*, ed. Shelley C. Reece (New York: William Morrow and Company, 1987). This is abbreviated as "W".

2. Jenny Sharpe has identified a likely model for this painting in Val C. Prinsep's painting of the 1877 Delhi durbar, at which Victoria was declared empress of India. See Jenny Sharpe, *Allegories of Empire: The Figure of Woman in the Colonial Text* (Minneapolis: University of Minnesota Press, 1993). For a full account of that durbar, see Bernard S. Cohn's "Representing Authority in Victorian India," in *The Invention of Tradition*, ed. Eric Hobsbawn and Terence Ranger (Cambridge: Cambridge University Press, 1983).

3. Joseph Conrad, Preface to *The Nigger of the Narcissus*, ed. Robert Kimbrough (1897; reprint, New York: Norton, 1979), 145, 147.

4. T. S. Eliot, *The Complete Poems and Plays, 1909–1950* (New York: Harcourt, Brace and World, 1962), 129.

5. The quotation is from Emerson's essay "History," the opening section of his *Essays: First Series* (Boston: J. Munroe and Company, 1841).

6. Sara Suleri, "The Geography of *A Passage to India*," in *E. M. Forster*, ed. Harold Bloom (New York: Chelsea House, 1987), 169.

7. Sara Suleri, *The Rhetoric of English India* (Chicago: University of Chicago Press, 1992).

8. *The Garden of Fidelity: Being the Autobiography of Flora Annie Steele* (London: Macmillan, 1929), 226, quoted in Benita Parry, *Delusions and Discoveries: Studies on India in the British Imagination, 1880–1930* (Berkeley: University of California Press, 1972), 127.

9. Quoted in Percival Spear, *A History of India*, vol. 2 (Harmondsworth: Penguin Books, 1978), 191.

10. See Christopher Hitchens, "A Sense of Mission," *Grand Street* 4, 2 (Winter 1985).

11. See Francis G. Hutchins, *The Illusion of Permanence: British Imperialism in India* (Princeton: Princeton University Press, 1967), ix.

12. E. M. Forster, *A Passage to India* (1924; reprint, New York: Harcourt Brace Jovanovich, 1984), 40.

13. Edward Said, *Orientalism* (New York: Pantheon, 1978), 244.

14. Salman Rushdie, "Outside the Whale," in *Imaginary Homelands: Essays and Criticism, 1981–1991* (New York: Granta Books, in association with Viking, 1991), 90.

15. See, for example, Ashis Nandy, *The Intimate Enemy: Loss and Recovery of Self under Colonialism* (Delhi: Oxford University Press, 1983), for an account of the way imperialism brought "into prominence those parts of the British political culture which were least tender and humane" (32), in the process taking away "the wholeness of every white man who chose to be a part of the colonial machine" (71).

16. Joseph Conrad, *Heart of Darkness*, ed. Robert Kimbrough (1902; reprint, New York: Norton, 1971), 67.

17. Richard Rorty, *Contingency, Irony, and Solidarity* (Cambridge: Cambridge University Press, 1989), passim.

18. Hutchins, *Illusion of Permanence*.

19. V. S. Naipaul, *An Area of Darkness* (1964; reprint, New York: Vintage, 1981), 208.

20. See Suleri, *The Rhetoric of English India*, ch. 2–3.

21. But see Said's argument in *Culture and Imperialism* (New York: Knopf, 1993), in which he argues that imperialism does in fact structure the whole of nineteenth-century fiction, from *Mansfield Park* on. Much of the best recent scholarship on the nineteenth century attempts to define empire's often hidden importance; see especially Patrick Brantlinger, *Rule of Darkness: British Literature and Imperialism, 1830–1914* (Ithaca, N.Y.: Cornell University Press, 1988), for the fullest treatment of this issue. Nevertheless, empire's centrality often goes unacknowledged within the texts of such novels themselves. It remains largely offstage, like Sir Thomas Bertram's Antigua plantation in Aus-

ten's novel or the Australian penal colony in Dickens's *Great Expectations*; a partial exception are the sensation novels of Wilkie Collins and others, e.g., *The Moonstone*. It took Kipling to make imperialism the *explicit* subject and site of his work. The classic statement of this argument remains Orwell's; see his "Rudyard Kipling," in *A Collection of Essays* (New York: Harcourt Brace Jovanovich, 1953).

22. Hutchins, *Illusion of Permanence*, 5.

23. See Ronald Robinson and John Gallagher, with Alice Denny, *Africa and the Victorians: The Official Mind of Imperialism* (London: Macmillan, 1961), 10.

24. Orwell, "Rudyard Kipling," 121.

25. Rudyard Kipling, *Kim* (1901; reprint, Harmondsworth: Penguin Books, 1987), 49.

26. Ibid., 63.

27. Orwell, "Rudyard Kipling," 119–20, 131.

28. Forster, *Passage to India*, 126.

29. Ibid., 362.

30. P. N. Furbank, *E. M. Forster: A Life*, vol. 2 (London: Secker and Warburg, 1978), 106.

31. Quoted in R. J. Moore, *Paul Scott's Raj* (London: Heinemann, 1990), 177.

32. Ibid., 45, 176.

33. Ibid., 46.

34. Ibid., 177.

35. Ibid., 46.

36. Ibid., 177.

37. Ibid., 47.

38. Hilary Spurling, *Paul Scott: A Life of the Author of "The Raj Quartet"* (New York: Norton, 1991), 362.

39. Max Beloff, "The End of the Raj: Paul Scott's Novels as History," *Encounter* 272 (May 1976).

40. In Robinson and Gallagher, *Africa and the Victorians*. Exactly contemporary with Robinson and Gallagher—and oddly parallel, despite its radically different inflections—is Frantz Fanon's analysis of the bourgeois *comprador* classes in *The Wretched of the Earth*, whose first publication in French was also in 1961. See also *Imperialism: The*

Robinson and Gallagher Controversy, ed. Wm. Roger Louis (New York: New Viewpoints/Franklin Watts, 1976).

41. Spurling, *Paul Scott*, 371.

42. Anthony Burgess, "Letter from England," *Hudson Review* 19, 3 (Autumn 1966): 460.

43. Anthony Burgess, "The Greene and the Red: Politics in the Novels of Graham Greene," in *Urgent Copy* (New York: Norton, 1968), 15.

44. Kennedy Fraser, "Stones of His House," *New Yorker*, May 13, 1991, 104.

45. Spurling, *Paul Scott*, vii.

46. Hutchins, *Illusion of Permanence*, 112.

47. Francine Weinbaum, *Paul Scott: A Critical Study* (Austin: University of Texas Press, 1992), 103.

48. For examples of that ambivalent admiration, see Nirad C. Chaudhuri, *Autobiography of an Unknown Indian* (London: Macmillan, 1951) and Zareer Masani, *Indian Tales of the Raj* (Berkeley: University of California Press, 1987).

49. Spurling, *Paul Scott*, 94.

50. Chaudhuri, *Autobiography*.

51. Hutchins, *Illusion of Permanence*, 150.

52. Thomas Babington Macaulay, "Minute on Indian Education," in *Selected Writings*, ed. John Clive and Thomas Pinney (Chicago: University of Chicago Press, 1972), 249.

53. Homi Bhabha, "Of Mimicry and Man," in *The Location of Culture* (London: Routledge, 1994), 87 (emphasis in the original).

54. Ibid., 86, 89 (emphasis in the original).

55. *Chamcha*—Urdu for spoon, slang for sycophant—is the Anglicized family name of one of the two main characters in *The Satanic Verses*. V. S. Naipaul, *The Mimic Men* (1967). See my chapters on Rushdie and Naipaul respectively for an account of mimicry and hybridity as themes in their work.

56. Bhabha, "Of Mimicry and Man," 86.

57. Ibid.

58. Ashis Nandy, *The Intimate Enemy: Loss and Recovery of Self under Colonialism* (Delhi: Oxford University Press, 1983), 108.

59. Bhabha, "Of Mimicry and Man," 91.

60. "You behave as we behave, as we would behave. You think of yourself—others think of you—as a Negro? Utterly mistaken! You merely look like one." Frantz Fanon, *Black Skins, White Masks*, trans. Charles Lam Markmann (New York: Grove Press, 1967), 68.

61. Ibid., 63.

62. Forster, *Passage to India*, 7.

63. George Orwell, "Shooting an Elephant," in *A Collection of Essays*, 152.

64. Forster, *Passage to India*, 40.

65. Naipaul, *Area of Darkness*, 211.

66. Enoch Powell, "Immigration," in *Freedom and Reality*, ed. John Wood (New Rochelle, N.Y.: Arlington House, 1969), 219; Samuel Selvon, *The Lonely Londoners* (London: Alan Wingate, 1956); George Lamming, *In the Castle of My Skin* (London: Michael Joseph, 1953).

67. Fraser, "Stones of His House," 107.

68. "A man that is born falls into a dream like a man who falls into the sea. If he tries to climb out into the air as inexperienced people endeavour to do, he drowns—*nicht wahr?* . . . No! I tell you! The way is to the destructive element submit yourself, and with the exertions of your hands and feet in the water make the deep, deep sea keep you up." Joseph Conrad, *Lord Jim* (1900; reprint, Harmondsworth: Penguin Books, 1986), 200.

69. Rushdie, "Outside the Whale," 89.

70. See Sharpe, *Allegories of Empire*, for the fullest account of the way rape functions in colonial discourse.

71. Fanon, *Black Skins, White Masks*, 46; see also Ruth Prawer Jhabvala's novel *Heat and Dust* (New York: Harper and Row, 1975), in which an Englishwoman's affair with a nawab is indeed taken as a challenge to colonial rule.

72. The classic account—indeed the foundational account—of triangulated or mediated desire is Rene Girard's *Deceit, Desire, and the Novel*, trans. Yvonne Freccero (Baltimore: Johns Hopkins University Press, 1965). See also Eve Kosofsky Sedgwick, *Between Men: English Literature and Male Homosocial Desire* (New York: Columbia University Press, 1985), esp. ch. 8 and 9.

73. Suleri, *The Rhetoric of English India*, 16–17.

74. Ibid., 133.

75. Forster, *Passage to India*, 15.

76. To date, the fullest treatment of homosexuality and imperialism is in Christopher Lane's impressively researched *The Ruling Passion: British Colonial Allegory and the Paradox of Homosexual Desire* (Durham: Duke University Press, 1995). Lane argues that "sexual desire between men frequently ruptured Britain's imperial allegory by shattering national unity and impeding the entire defeat of subject groups" (4), and he pursues this argument through writers as various as Rider Haggard and Ronald Firbank; he does not, however, take it far enough into the twentieth century to deal with Scott. See also Allen D. Boyer, "Love, Sex, and History in *The Raj Quartet*," *Modern Language Quarterly* 46, 1 (1985), whose account of homosexuality in Scott's work antedates Spurling's discoveries.

77. Rudyard Kipling, "The Ballad of East and West" (1889), in *Rudyard Kipling's Verse: Definitive Edition* (Garden City, N.Y.: Doubleday, 1945), 233.

78. Leslie A. Fiedler, *Love and Death in the American Novel*, rev. ed. (New York: Stein and Day, 1966).

79. Sedgwick, *Between Men*, 2.

80. Suleri, *The Rhetoric of English India*, 133.

81. Sharpe makes a similar point, writing that Scott suggests "an innocent brown man accused of raping a white woman is himself metaphorically 'raped' " (1).

82. See Kenneth J. Dover, *Greek Homosexuality* (Cambridge: Harvard University Press, 1978); see also the Appendix to Richard Burton's translation of *The Arabian Nights: The Book of the Thousand Nights and a Night*, 12 vols. (London: H. S. Nicholls and Company, 1894).

83. Suleri, *The Rhetoric of English India*, 17.

84. Salman Rushdie, *The Satanic Verses* (New York: Viking, 1989), 168.

85. Eve Kosofsky Sedgwick, *Epistemology of the Closet* (Berkeley: University of California Press, 1990), 71.

86. Conrad, *Heart of Darkness*, 6–7.

87. Ibid., 36.

NOTES TO PAGES 57-62 187

88. Sedgwick, *Between Men*, 91. See also Chapter 10 in that book: "Up the Postern Stair: *Edwin Drood* and the Homophobia of Empire."

89. Ibid., 92.

90. In addition to Lane and Suleri, see Joseph Allan Boone, "Vacation Cruises; or, The Homoerotics of Orientalism," *PMLA* 110, 1 (January 1995).

Two

1. References to Naipaul's major works are incorporated in the text, keyed to the following abbreviations and editions:

M —*The Mystic Masseur.* 1957; reprint, Harmondsworth: Penguin Books, 1964.

MS —*Miguel Street.* 1959; reprint, Harmondsworth: Penguin Books, 1971.

B —*A House for Mr. Biswas.* 1961; reprint, New York: Vintage, 1983.

MP —*The Middle Passage: Impressions of Five Societies.* 1962; reprint, Harmondsworth: Penguin Books 1969.

A —*An Area of Darkness: An Experience of India.* 1964: reprint, New York: Vintage, 1981.

MM —*The Mimic Men.* 1967; reprint, Harmondsworth: Penguin Books, 1969.

F —*In a Free State.* 1971; reprint, Harmondsworth: Penguin Books, 1973.

O —*The Overcrowded Barracoon.* 1972; reprint, New York: Vintage, 1984.

R —*A Bend in the River.* New York: Knopf, 1979.

EP —*The Return of Eva Peron with the Killings in Trinidad.* New York: Knopf, 1980.

FC —*Finding the Center: Two Narratives.* New York: Knopf, 1984.

E —*The Enigma of Arrival.* New York: Knopf, 1987.

W —*A Way in the World.* New York: Knopf, 1994.

Where two or more successive quotations are taken from the same source, the reference follows the last quotation.

2. Bharati Mukherjee and Robert Boyers, "A Conversation with V. S. Naipaul," *Salmagundi* 54 (1981): 5.

3. *A Way in the World* appeared after my work on this chapter was essentially complete. Its importance in Naipaul's *oeuvre* lies in its recognition, however belated, that other West Indian intellectuals have made journeys that match his own: that he is not an isolated figure. As such, it provides a corrective to his earlier autobiographical work but does not significantly alter my sense of his novels. For the fullest accounts of *A Way in the World* to date, see Caryl Phillips, "The Way In," *New Republic*, June 13, 1994, and Philip Gourevitch, "Naipaul's World," *Commentary*, August 1994. Phillips comments usefully on the fusion of genre that characterizes Naipaul's late work—part fiction, part autobiography. In Gourevitch, see his observation that for Naipaul, "displacement, in space and in time, is the primal human experience" (30).

4. William Shakespeare, *King Lear*, III.iv, ln 109.

5. Derek Walcott, "The Sea Is History," in *Collected Poems, 1948–1984* (New York: Farrar, Straus, and Giroux, 1986), 364.

6. Graham Greene, "The Young Dickens," in *Collected Essays* (1969; reprint, Harmondsworth: Penguin Books, 1970), 83.

7. Irving Howe, "A Dark Vision," *New York Times Book Review*, May 13, 1979.

8. For the fullest dissection of Naipaul's "impartiality," see Rob Nixon, *London Calling: V. S. Naipaul, Postcolonial Mandarin* (New York: Oxford University Press, 1992).

9. Quoted from a 1971 interview in ibid., 23.

10. V. S. Naipaul, *India: A Million Mutinies Now* (New York: Viking, 1991), 491.

11. But see Fawzia Mustafa's argument that Naipaul has constructed his career in terms of an Aristotelian plot, "the resolution of which is a culmination of all that has preceded it, and which accords the hero initiation into an elect group." *V. S. Naipaul* (Cambridge: Cambridge University Press, 1995), 7.

12. Sara Suleri, *The Rhetoric of English India* (Chicago: University of Chicago Press, 1992), 149.

13. George Lamming, *The Pleasures of Exile* (1960; reprint, London: Allison and Busby, 1984), 225.

14. Quoted in a review of "Everything That Rises Must Converge" by Warren Coffey, *Commentary*, November 1965. Reprinted in *Critical Essays on Flannery O'Connor*, ed. Melvin J. Friedman and Beverly Lyon Clark (Boston: G. K. Hall, 1985), 38. See also Suleri's description of the "deeply internalized referential status . . . [the] submerged but vital presence" (*The Rhetoric of English India*, 216) that Naipaul has in postcolonial studies, especially for those made most uncomfortable by his work.

15. Derek Walcott, "At Last," in *Sea Grapes* (New York: Farrar, Straus, and Giroux, 1976), 77.

16. Selwyn Cudjoe, *V. S. Naipaul: A Materialist Reading* (Amherst: University of Massachusetts Press, 1988), 95.

17. Jane Kramer, "From the Third World," *New York Times Book Review*, April 13, 1980, 1.

18. Johann Gottfried von Herder, *Reflections on the Philosophy of the History of Mankind* (1784–91), trans. T. O. Churchill (1800), ed. Frank E. Manuel (Chicago: University of Chicago Press, 1968), 17.

19. Ibid., 24.

20. Ibid., 25.

21. Ibid., 39.

22. Isaiah Berlin, *Vico and Herder: Two Studies in the History of Ideas* (New York: Viking Press, 1976), 177.

23. Herder, *Reflections*, 29 (emphasis in the original).

24. Joseph Conrad, *Heart of Darkness*, ed. Robert Kimbrough (1902; reprint, New York: Norton, 1971), 13–14.

25. Herder, *Reflections*, 30–31.

26. Ibid., 41.

27. Ibid., 11.

28. Berlin, *Vico and Herder*, 173.

29. Kwame Anthony Appiah, *In My Father's House: Africa in the Philosophy of Culture* (New York: Oxford University Press, 1992), 37.

30. Quoted in Berlin, *Vico and Herder*, 160.

31. Frantz Fanon, *The Wretched of the Earth* (1961), trans. Constance Farrington (New York: Grove Press, 1968), 209.

32. Berlin, *Vico and Herder*, 180.

33. C. L. R. James, "On Federation," in *At the Rendezvous of Victory: Selected Writings* (London; Allison and Busby, 1984), 97.

34. James Anthony Froude, *The English in the West Indies* (1887; reprint, New York: Charles Scribner's Sons, 1897), 347.

35. Lamming, *Pleasures of Exile*, 225.

36. Ibid.

37. James, "On Federation," 87.

38. Arnold Rampersad, "V. S. Naipaul: Turning in the South," *Raritan* 10, 1 (Summer 1990): 45.

39. Froude, *The English in the West Indies*, 349.

40. See Eric Williams, *From Columbus to Castro: The History of the Caribbean* (London: Andre Deutsch, 1970), ch. 26.

41. Naipaul has been much attacked for this statement; but see James's similar statement, in his 1964 "A National Purpose for Caribbean Peoples": "We of the West Indies are a people who have not got much substantial history of our own at the present time" (143). The difference, perhaps, is that James spoke his words within the family, as it were, in an address to the West Indians Students' Association in Edinburgh.

42. Walcott, "The Sea Is History," 365.

43. Derek Walcott, "Air," in *Collected Poems*, 114.

44. Derek Walcott, "Crusoe's Journal," in *Collected Poems*, 94.

45. Derek Walcott, "The Schooner *Flight*," in *Collected Poems*, 346.

46. See Naipaul, *Middle Passage*, 75–76.

47. This is the subtitle of Naipaul's second Indian travel book: *India: A Wounded Civilization* (1977; reprint, New York: Vintage, 1978).

48. See C. L. R. James, *Beyond a Boundary* (1963; reprint, New York: Pantheon, 1983), and Ian Buruma, *Playing the Game* (New York: Farrar, Straus, and Giroux, 1991).

49. Gordon Rohlehr, "The Ironic Approach: The Novels of V. S. Naipaul" (1968), in *Critical Perspectives on V. S. Naipaul* (London: Heinemann, 1977), ed. Robert D. Hamner, 179–80.

50. Henry James, Preface to *The Portrait of a Lady*, in *Literary Criticism: French Writers, Other European Writers, The Prefaces to the New York Edition* (New York: Library of America, 1984), 1075.

51. Ashis Nandy, *The Intimate Enemy* (Delhi: Oxford University Press, 1983), 108.

52. Iris Murdoch, "The Sublime and the Beautiful Revisited," *Yale Review*, Winter 1960, 271.

53. Seepersad Naipaul, *The Adventures of Gurudeva and Other Stories*, with a foreword by V. S. Naipaul (London: Andre Deutsch, 1976), 10.

54. Ibid., 19.

55. V. S. Pritchett, *The Living Novel* (London: Chatto and Windus, 1946), 78.

56. Lionel Trilling, "Manners, Morals, and the Novel," in *The Liberal Imagination* (New York: Charles Scribner's Sons, 1950), 206.

57. See Homi Bhabha, "Representation and the Colonial Text: A Critical Exploration of Some Forms of Mimeticism," in *The Theory of Reading*, ed. Frank Gloversmith (Sussex: Harvester Press, 1984), 114–19.

58. Suleri, *The Rhetoric of English India*, 155.

59. T. S. Eliot, "Tradition and the Individual Talent" (1919), in *Selected Prose*, ed. Frank Kermode (New York: Harcourt Brace Jovanovich and Farrar, Straus, and Giroux, 1975), 38.

60. On Naipaul's existence as a racial body, see Suleri, *The Rhetoric of English India*, 162.

61. Salman Rushdie, *Midnight's Children* (New York: Knopf, 1981), 81.

62. Rampersad, "V. S. Naipaul," 47.

63. A. Sivanadnan, "The Enigma of the Colonized: Reflections on Naipaul's Arrival," *Race and Class* 32, 1 (1990): 33.

64. Suleri, *The Rhetoric of English India*, 158.

65. See Frantz Fanon, *Black Skins, White Masks*, trans. Charles Lam Markmann (New York: Grove Press, 1967), ch. 3.

66. Conrad, *Heart of Darknes*, 34.

67. Peter Hughes, *V. S. Naipaul* (London: Routledge, 1988), ch. 1. This remains the best book on Naipaul, the most comprehensive and balanced account of his sensibility.

68. Georg Lukacs, *The Theory of the Novel*, trans. Anna Bostock (1920; reprint, Cambridge: MIT Press, 1971), 41.

69. Christopher L. Miller, *Blank Darkness: Africanist Discourse in French* (Chicago: University of Chicago Press, 1985), 16.

70. Ibid., 61.

71. Ibid., 5.

72. Ibid., 16.

73. See Marianna Torgovnick, *Gone Primitive: Savage Intellects, Modern Lives* (Chicago: University of Chicago Press, 1990).

74. Conrad, *Heart of Darkness*, 8.

75. Chinua Achebe, "An Image of Africa: Racism in Conrad's *Heart of Darkness*," *Massachusetts Review* 18, 4 (Winter 1977). On colonialism and metaphor, see Eric Cheyfitz, *The Poetics of Imperialism: Translation and Colonization from "The Tempest" to "Tarzan"* (New York: Oxford University Press, 1991), along with "Tact and Tarzan," my review of Cheyfitz and Torgovnick in *Transition*, issue 52, n.s., vol. 1, no. 2 (1991).

76. Miller, *Blank Darkness*, 13.

77. Ibid., 182.

78. See Suleri, *The Rhetoric of English India*, for an account of the way Naipaul's "dazzling idiom . . . no longer needs to indicate the referents of its discourse . . . will never clearly identify the object of its indictment" (155).

Three

1. Page references to Rushdie's work will be included in the text. For *Midnight's Children* (New York: Knopf, 1981), this will simply be a page number in parentheses; for his other works, I will use the abbreviations below, followed by a page number. These editions have been used:

S —*Shame*. New York: Knopf, 1983.

SV —*The Satanic Verses*. New York: Viking, 1989.

IH —*Imaginary Homelands*. New York: Granta Books, in association with Viking, 1991.

Where two or more successive quotations are taken from the same source, the reference follows the last quotation.

2. Quoted in M. J. Akbar, *India: The Siege Within* (Harmondsworth: Penguin, 1985), 20.

3. Quoted in ibid.

4. Gilles Deleuze and Felix Guattari, *Kafka: Toward a Minor Literature* (1975), trans. Dana Polan (Minneapolis: University of Minnesota Press, 1986), 22.

5. Gabriel Garcia Marquez, *One Hundred Years of Solitude* (1967), trans. Gregory Rabassa (1970; paperback, New York: Avon Books, 1971), 130.

6. Lionel Trilling, "Art and Fortune," in *The Liberal Imagination* (New York: Charles Scribner's Sons, 1950), 259-60.

7. Ibid., 272.

8. Ibid., 273-75.

9. Lucien Goldmann, *Toward a Sociology of the Novel* (1964), trans. Alan Sheridan (London: Tavistock, 1975), 12-13.

10. Georg Lukacs, *The Historical Novel*, trans. Hannah Mitchell and Stanley Mitchell (Lincoln: University of Nebraska Press, 1962), passim.

11. In Frank Gloversmith, ed., *The Theory of Reading* (Sussex: Harvester Press, 1984), 105. I would here draw a comparison between Saleem and Naipaul's Mr. Biswas, who seems to me conceived as a "typical" character in Lukacs's sense, one whose representative status has been naturalized within the text. His dispossession can easily be read in terms of his colonized status, but Naipaul asks us to take it first as a function of his individual biography. That difference of course points to a difference between Rushdie's and Naipaul's conceptions of the novel form: Rushdie here uses it to articulate a sense of national identity, whereas Naipaul uses it to claim for his character the sense of individual dignity that colonialism would deny him. Both approaches seem to me valid, but Rushdie's does have the advantage of dealing with the full weight of what Bhabha would call the character's "historical and political significance."

12. Katerina Clark and Michael Holquist, *Mikhail Bakhtin* (Cambridge: Harvard University Press, 1984), 292.

13. Mikhail Bakhtin, *Problems of Dostoevsky's Poetics*, ed. and trans. Caryl Emerson (Minneapolis: University of Minnesota Press, 1984), passim.

14. Milan Kundera, *The Art of the Novel* (1986), trans. Linda Asher (New York: Grove Press, 1988), 7.

15. Linda Hutcheon, *A Poetics of Postmodernism* (New York: Routledge, 1988), passim.

16. James Baldwin, "Stranger in the Village," in *The Price of the Ticket: Collected Nonfiction, 1948–1985* (New York: St. Martin's/ Marek, 1985) 81.

17. Bertolt Brecht, *Brecht on Theatre: The Development of an Aesthetic*, ed. and trans. John Willet (New York: Hill and Wang, 1964), 136.

18. Frederic Jameson, *Postmodernism: or, The Cultural Logic of Late Capitalism* (Durham: Duke University Press, 1991).

19. Kwame Anthony Appiah, *In My Father's House: Africa in the Philosophy of Culture* (New York: Oxford University Press, 1992), 149.

20. Frank Kermode, *The Sense of an Ending: Studies in the Theory of Fiction* (Oxford: Oxford University Press, 1967), 156.

21. Kundera, *The Art of the Novel*, 26.

22. Georg Lukacs, "Idea and Form in Literature," in *Marxism and Human Liberation*, ed. E. San Juan Jr. (New York: Delta, 1973), 109–10.

23. Quoted in Irving Howe, "Writing and the Holocaust," *New Republic*, October 27, 1986, 28.

24. Such lists can of course be much more than a sign of our own inability to make sense of history. For they may themselves provide a comment on the way people become victims, treated as mere inessential details rather than as an integral part of a narrative; this is the impulse behind Maya Lin's Vietnam War Memorial in Washington, D.C.

25. V. S. Naipaul, "The Documentary Heresy," in *Critical Perspectives on V. S. Naipaul*, ed. Robert D. Hamner (London: Heinemann, 1979), 23.

26. V. S. Naipaul, "Conrad's Darkness," in *The Return of Eva Peron with the Killings in Trinidad* (New York: Knopf, 1980), 227.

27. Hayden White, "The Value of Narrativity in the Representation of Reality," in *On Narrative*, ed. W. J. T. Mitchell (Chicago: University of Chicago Press, 1981), 2.

28. Philip Roth, "The Prague Orgy," in *Zuckerman Bound* (New York: Farrar, Straus, and Giroux, 1985), 761–62.

29. Ibid., 762.

30. Kundera, *The Art of the Novel*, 15.

31. Bruno Bettelheim, *The Uses of Enchantment* (New York: Knopf, 1976). For an account of fairy tales that revises Bettelheim's Freudian version to consider anthropological and historical questions, see Marina Warner, *From the Beast to the Blonde: On Fairy Tales and Their Tellers* (New York: Farrar, Straus, and Giroux, 1995).

32. Gabriel Garcia Marquez, "The Solitude of Latin America," *Granta* 9 (1983): 58.

33. Ian Watt, *The Rise of the Novel: Studies in Defoe, Richardson, and Fielding* (London: Chatto and Windus, 1957).

34. Salman Rushdie, conversation with Gunter Grass, in "Fictions Are Lies That Tell the Truth," *Listener*, June 27, 1985, 15.

35. Rushdie's latest novel, *The Moor's Last Sigh*, appeared as I prepared this book for the press; there he makes the parallel with Scheherazade even more explicit, inventing a plot in which the novel's first-person narrator will be allowed to live only so long as he continues to write pages that amuse his captor.

36. The *Katha Sarit Sagara* is attributed to Somadeva Bhatta; the most readily available translation into English from Sanskrit is by C. H. Tawney (Delhi: Munshiram Manoharlal, 1968), 2 vols.

37. Mikhail Bakhtin, *Rabelais and His World* (1965), trans. Helen Iswolsky (Bloomington: Indiana University Press, 1984), 10.

38. Ibid., 26.

39. Ibid., 34.

40. *The Lord of the Flies, L'Etranger, 1984*, etc.

41. "Fictions are lies that tell the truth," 15.

42. Ibid.

43. Timothy Brennan, *Salman Rushdie and the Third World: Myths of the Nation* (London: Macmillan, 1989), 142.

44. Ibid., 30.

45. Ibid., 27.

46. Tariq Ali, "*Midnight's Children*," *New Left Review*, November-December 1982, 94.

47. Frantz Fanon, *The Wretched of the Earth* (1961), trans. Constance Farrington (New York: Grove Press, 1968), 158.

48. Gauri Viswanathan, *Masks of Conquest: Literary Study and*

British Rule in India (New York: Columbia University Press, 1989).

49. E. M. Forster, *A Passage to India* (1924; reprint, New York: Harcourt Brace Jovanovich, 1984), 235. For a detailed and perceptive discussion of these issues, see the essays collected in *The Lie of the Land: English Literary Studies in India*, ed. Rajeswari Sunder Rajan (Delhi: Oxford University Press, 1992).

50. Rudyard Kipling, *Kim* (1901; reprint, Harmondsworth: Penguin Books, 1987), 109. See also Richard Cronin, "The English Indian Novel: *Kim* and *Midnight's Children*," in *Imagining India* (New York: St. Martin's, 1989).

51. M. K. Gandhi, "Benares University Speech" (1916), in *The Gandhi Reader*, ed. Homer A. Jack (Bloomington: Indiana University Press, 1956), 131.

52. Raja Rao, Author's Foreword to *Kanthapura* (1937; reprint, New York: New Directions, 1967), vii.

53. Nirad C. Chaudhuri, *The Autobiography of an Unknown Indian* (1951; reprint, Bombay: Jaico, 1964), 492.

54. Anita Desai, "Indian Fiction Today," *Dedalus* 188, 4 (Fall 1989): 211.

55. Chaudhuri, *Autobiography*, 492.

56. G. V. Desani, *All about H. Hatterr* (1948; reprint, Harmondsworth: Penguin, 1972), passim.

57. Salman Rushdie, "The Empire Writes Back with a Vengeance," *The Times* (London), July 3, 1982, 8.

58. Desai, "Indian Fiction Today," 212.

59. Homi Bhabha, "Signs Taken for Wonders: Questions of Ambivalence and Authority under a Tree outside Delhi, May 1817," in *The Location of Culture* (London: Routledge, 1994), 120.

60. Fanon, *The Wretched of the Earth*, 209.

61. Chinua Achebe, "The Novelist as Teacher," in *Hopes and Impediments: Selected Essays* (New York: Anchor, 1989), 44–45.

62. Fanon, *The Wretched of the Earth*, 211.

63. Ibid., 212.

64. From an interview with Victoria Glendinning, "A Novelist in the Country of the Mind," *Sunday Times* (London), October 25, 1981, 38.

65. On British imperialism and Indian unification, see Francis G. Hutchins, *The Illusion of Permanence: British Imperialism in India* (Princeton: Princeton University Press, 1967), 141, 155–56.

66. Quoted in Akbar, *India*, 10.

67. Akeel Bilgrami, "Cry, the Beloved Subcontinent," *New Republic*, June 10, 1991, 31–34.

68. Fanon, *The Wretched of the Earth*, 216.

69. Edward Said, *Culture and Imperialism* (New York: Knopf, 1993), 227.

70. An important source for that conception—and, outside of Rushdie's own work, its most powerful articulation—can be found in the last chapter of Chaudhuri's *Autobiography:* "An Essay on the Course of Indian History."

71. See Cronin, *Imagining India*, 4–5.

72. From a letter to Edward Garnett, in *The Letters of D. H. Lawrence*, ed. Aldous Huxley (London: Heinemann, 1932), 198.

73. Philip Roth, *The Counterlife* (New York: Farrar, Straus, and Giroux, 1986).

74. V. S. Naipaul, "My Brother's Tragic Sense," *Spectator*, January 24, 1987, 22.

75. See my "Naipaul or Rushdie," *Southwest Review*, Summer 1991, for an extended treatment of that comparison.

76. Iris Murdoch, "The Sublime and the Beautiful Revisited," *Yale Review*, Winter 1960, 265.

77. Brennan mounts such an argument in his chapter on *Midnight's Children*—"The National Longing for Form"—arguing that Ruhside treats his own novel "as if it were a paradigm of the state lie" (98). My own version of that argument is also indebted to Brechtian notions of epic theater.

78. Gerald Marzorati, "Rushdie in Hiding: An Interview," *New York Times Magazine*, November 4, 1990, 85.

79. Quoted in James Fenton, "Keeping Up with Salman Rushdie," *New York Review of Books*, March 28, 1991, 32.

Appendix

1. This appendix originally appeared as a review essay in *Threepenny Review*, Summer 1989; my longer chapter on *Midnight's*

Children returns at greater length to some of the same issues—and uses some of the same quotations—that I first developed here. Despite that repetition, the essay still seems to me to be relevant and to have, in its sense of immediacy and crisis, a kind of documentary value. In reprinting it, I have added citations and have made minor changes in punctuation and style. References to *The Satanic Verses* (New York: Viking, 1989) will be indicated by page numbers within parentheses.

2. Hermione Lee, "The Art of Fiction LXXXIV: Philip Roth" (interview), *Paris Review* 26 (Fall 1984): 244.

3. Salman Rushdie, "Choice between Light and Dark," *Observer*, January 22, 1989.

4. Frank Kermode, *The Sense of an Ending: Studies in the Theory of Fiction* (Oxford: Oxford University Press, 1967), 39.

5. See "The Depreciated Legacy of Cervantes" in Milan Kundera, *The Art of the Novel* (1986), trans. Linda Asher (New York: Grove Press, 1988).

6. Quoted in Gerald Marzorati, "Salman Rushdie: Fiction's Embattled Infidel," *New York Times Magazine*, January 29, 1989, 100.

Conclusion

1. T. S. Eliot, "Little Gidding," in *The Complete Poems and Plays, 1909–1950*, 139.

2. Ibid., 144–45.

3. Benedict Anderson, *Imagined Communities: Reflections on the Origin and Spread of Nationalism* (London: Verso, 1983), 20.

4. George Orwell, "England, Your England," in *A Collection of Essays* (New York: Harcourt Brace Jovanovich, 1953), 254, 279.

5. Ibid., 254.

6. Ibid., 253.

7. Ibid., 279.

8. Philip Larkin, "Show Saturday" (1973), in *Collected Poems*, ed. Anthony Thwaite (London: Marvell Press, Faber and Faber, 1988), 199.

9. Ibid., 200–201.

10. Philip Larkin, "Going, Going" (1972), in ibid., 189–90.

11. Raphael Samuel et al., *Patriotism: The Making and Un-*

making of British National Identity, 3 vols. (London: Routledge, 1989), vol. 1, *History and Politics*, xlii, xlv.

12. Ibid., xliv, xlix.

13. Raymond Williams, *The Country and the City* (New York: Oxford University Press, 1973).

14. Philip Larkin, "Dockery and Son," in *Collected Poems*, 152–53.

15. Since his death and the publication of both his letters and Andrew Motion's biography, Larkin has come to be seen as the national poet in another sense—as the voice of a racist, sexist, and homophobic Thatcherite Britain. See Joseph Bristow, "The Obscenity of Philip Larkin," *Critical Inquiry* 21 (Autumn 1994), and the articles excerpted in "The Philip Larkin Controversy," *Contemporary Literary Criticism* 81 (1993).

16. Philip Larkin, "The Booker Prize 1977," in *Required Writing* (New York: Farrar, Straus, and Giroux, 1984), 97.

17. Barbara Pym, *Quartet in Autumn* (New York: Dutton, 1978), 101–2.

18. Ibid., 20.

19. Ibid., 57–58.

20. Ibid., 59.

21. Ibid., 66.

22. George Orwell, "Shooting an Elephant," in *A Collection of Essays*, 152.

23. E. M. Forster, *A Passage to India* (1924; reprint, New York: Harcourt Brace Jovanovich, 1984), 40.

24. See Martin Green, "Our Turn to Cliché," in *Transatlantic Patterns* (New York: Basic Books, 1977), for a perceptive analysis of the national habit of playing with quotation and convention.

25. *Observer*, February 11, 1990.

26. Paul Gilroy, "This Island Race," *New Statesman and Society*, February 2, 1990, 30–32.

27. Hanif Kureishi, *The Buddha of Suburbia* (New York: Viking, 1990), 3.

28. Charles Taylor, *Multiculturalism: Examining the Politics of Recognition*, ed. Amy Gutmann (1992; 2d ed., Princeton: Princeton University Press, 1994).

29. Hanif Kureishi, *My Beautiful Laundrette and The Rainbow Sign* (London: Faber and Faber, 1986), 38.

30. Gilroy, "This Island Race," 31.

31. George Orwell, "Rudyard Kipling," in *A Collection of Essays*, 120.

32. Paul Gilroy, *The Black Atlantic* (Cambridge: Harvard University Press, 1993).

33. David Dabydeen, *Turner: New and Selected Poems* (London: Cape Poetry, 1994).

34. Sara Suleri, *The Rhetoric of English India* (Chicago: University of Chicago Press, 1992), 150.

35. Homi Bhabha, "Signs Taken for Wonders: Questions of Ambivalence and Authority under a Tree outside Delhi, May 1817," in *The Location of Culture* (London: Routledge, 1994), 120.

36. "Most migrants tend to be poor and experience displacement not as cultural plenitude but as torment. . . . Postcoloniality is . . . like most things, a matter of class." See Aijaz Ahmad, "The Politics of Literary Postcoloniality," *Race and Class* 36, 3 (1995): 16, for a penetrating account of the tension between postcolonial theory and the postcolonial lives that theory tries to describe.

37. Bharati Mukherjee, "Prophet and Loss: Salman Rushdie's Migration of Souls," *VLS* 72 (March 1989): 12.

38. Quoted in Gerald Marzorati, "Salman Rushdie: Fiction's Embattled Infidel," *New York Times Magazine*, January 29, 1989, 100.

39. Ibid. For the richest journalistic account of the way that controversy has fed off issues in the British Asian community, see Clark Blaise and Bharati Mukherjee, "After the Fatwa," *Mother Jones*, April/May 1990.

40. See Shabbir Akhtar, *Be Careful with Muhammad! The Salman Rushdie Affair* (London: Bellew Pub., 1989).

41. Leon Wieseltier, "Against Identity," *New Republic*, November 28, 1994, 30.

42. Pico Iyer, "Strangers in a Small World," *Harper's*, September 1994, 14, 15.